NCAER

INDIA
POLICY FORUM
2012|13

VOLUME **9**

EDITED BY

Shekhar Shah
Barry Bosworth
Arvind Panagariya

NATIONAL COUNCIL OF APPLIED
ECONOMIC RESEARCH
New Delhi

BROOKINGS INSTITUTION
Washington, D.C.

⑤SAGE www.sagepublications.com
Los Angeles • London • New Delhi • Singapore • Washington DC

First published in 2013 by

 SAGE Publications India Pvt Ltd
B1/I-1 Mohan Cooperative Industrial Area
Mathura Road, New Delhi 110 044, India
www.sagepub.in

SAGE Publications Inc
2455 Teller Road
Thousand Oaks, California 91320, USA

SAGE Publications Ltd
1 Oliver's Yard, 55 City Road
London EC1Y 1SP, United Kingdom

SAGE Publications Asia-Pacific Pte Ltd
33 Pekin Street
#02-01 Far East Square
Singapore 048763

Library of Congress Serial Publication Data applied for

ISSN: 0973-4805
ISBN: 978-81-321-1316-4 (PB)

Published by Vivek Mehra for SAGE Publications India Pvt Ltd, typeset in 10.5/13 pt Times by RECTO Graphics, Delhi, and printed at Saurabh Printers Pvt Ltd.

INDIA POLICY FORUM
VOLUME 9 2012|13

INTRODUCTION

This *India Policy Forum 2012–13* comprises papers and highlights of the discussions at the ninth India Policy Forum (IPF) held in New Delhi on July 17–18, 2012. The IPF is a joint venture of the National Council of Applied Economic Research (NCAER) in New Delhi and the Brookings Institution in Washington, D.C. The IPF explores India's rapidly evolving—and sometimes tumultuous—economic transition and the underlying policy frameworks and reforms using policy-relevant, empirical research.

An international Research Panel of India-based and overseas scholars with an abiding interest in India supports this initiative through advice, active participation at the IPF, and the search for innovative papers that promise fresh insights. An international Advisory Panel of distinguished economists provides overall guidance. Members of the two IPF Panels are listed below.

Papers appear in this publication after detailed revisions based on discussants' comments at the IPF and the guidance provided by the Editors after the IPF. To allow readers to get a sense of the richness of the conversations that happen at the IPF, discussants' comments are also included here, as is a summary of the general discussion on each paper. The papers represent the views of the individual authors and do not imply any agreement by those attending the conference, those providing financial support, or the officers and staff of NCAER or Brookings.

As in every year, the IPF features an annual IPF Lecture. The 2012 IPF Lecture on "India: New Strategies for Economic Development" was given by Y. V. Reddy on July 17, 2012.

Starting in 2011, the IPF now concludes with a Policy Round Table. The 2012 IPF featured a discussion on "The Future of Economic Growth in India." Though no formal papers are presented, details of the Round Table participants are noted in the Editors' Summary.

ADVISORY PANEL

Shankar N. Acharya   *Indian Council for Research on International Economic Relations*

Isher J. Ahluwalia   *Indian Council for Research on International Economic Relations*

Montek S. Ahluwalia   *Indian Planning Commission*

Pranab Bardhan   *University of California, Berkeley*

Jagdish Bhagwati   *Columbia University*

Barry Bosworth   *The Brookings Institution*

Willem H. Buiter   *Citigroup*

PARTNERS

NCAER and Brookings gratefully acknowledge the generous financial support for IPF 2012 from the State Bank of India, HDFC Ltd, Reliance Industries Ltd, IDFC Ltd, SAGE Publications, and Citibank NA. The support reflects the deep commitment of these organizations and their leadership to rigorous policy research that helps promote informed policy debates and sound, evidence-based policy-making in India. Almost all these funders have been with the IPF since its inception, so their support also reflects their continuing confidence in the IPF to promote such research and open debate in India and elsewhere.

CORRESPONDENCE

Correspondence about papers in this Volume should be addressed directly to the authors (each paper contains the e-mail address of the corresponding author). All author affiliations are as of the IPF Conference in July 2012. Manuscripts are not accepted for review because this Volume is devoted exclusively to invited contributions. Feedback on the IPF Volume itself may be sent to: The Editor, India Policy Forum, NCAER, 11, Indraprastha Estate, New Delhi 110 002, or to ipf@ncaer.org.

NCAER TEAM

NCAER is primarily responsible for the planning, organization, publication, and fund-raising for the India Policy Forum. The Editors are deeply grateful to the following NCAER staff for their dedication and hard work on the IPF:

Geetu Makhija	*Team leader*
Jagbir Singh Punia	*Publication*
P. P. Joshi	*Hospitality & logistics*
Sangita Chaudhary	*Event coordination*
Shikha Vasudeva	*Event & media coordination*
Sudesh Bala	*Invitee coordination*
Sarita Sharma	*Event coordination*
Praveen Sachdeva	*Production & graphics*

Editors' Summary

The IPF, a long-standing partnership between NCAER in New Delhi and the Brookings Institution in Washington, D.C., held its ninth annual conference on July 17 and 18, 2012, in New Delhi. This issue of the IPF Journal contains the conference papers and the discussion around them at the conference. The first paper examines the priorities for primary education policy for India's 12th Five-year Plan (2012–17), appraising the effectiveness of past policy measures and future prospects. The second paper evaluates the first decade of India's Total Sanitation Campaign, and proposes several reforms going forward. The effects of demographic changes on the growth of the Indian economy form the subject of the third paper. The fourth paper focuses on the issue of groundwater depletion in India and the effectiveness of several conservation policies that have been tried. The final paper explores the impact of investments in information technology (IT) on the performance of the Indian manufacturing sector.

Priorities for Primary Education Policy for India's 12th Five-year Plan

Investments in education contribute to aggregate economic growth and enable citizens to participate more broadly in the growth process through improved productivity, employment, and wages. The past decade has seen substantial increases in Indian education expenditures with a consequent improvement in primary school access, infrastructure, pupil–teacher ratios (PTRs), teacher salaries, and student enrolment. Nevertheless, as pointed out by Karthik Muralidharan in his paper summarizing a decade of his own and other research in primary education policy, student learning levels and trajectories remain disturbingly low in India, with nationally representative studies showing that over 60 percent of Indian children aged 6–14 are unable to read at the second-grade level. Further, learning outcomes have shown no sign of improving over time, and may even be deteriorating. The poor performance of the education system in translating spending into outcomes threatens both aggregate productivity in the economy and also denies citizens the capabilities they need to fully participate in a modernizing economy.

A number of high-quality empirical studies on the causes and correlates of better learning outcomes in India based on large data sets and paying careful attention to the identification of causal relationships have become available in the past 10 years. Muralidharan notes that this research has yielded robust findings both on the interventions and inputs that do not appear to contribute meaningfully to improved education outcomes and on interventions that are highly effective. This research suggests that increasing inputs to primary education in a business-as-usual way is unlikely to improve student learning, unless accompanied by significant changes in pedagogy and/or improvements in school governance. The paper argues that the time is ripe for Indian education policy to shift its emphasis from simply providing more school inputs to improving education outcomes.

The most important components of Indian education spending in the past decade have been on improving government school facilities and infrastructure, improving teacher salaries and training, hiring more teachers to reduce PTRs, and raising expenditure on student benefits such as textbooks and midday meals. Analysis of both administrative and survey data shows considerable improvements in most input-based measures of schooling quality. But the research surveyed by Muralidharan finds very little impact of these improvements in school facilities on learning outcomes. This is not to suggest that school infrastructure does not matter for improving learning outcomes; it may be necessary, but is not sufficient to have a significant impact on improving learning levels and trajectories. Similarly, while there may be good social reasons for midday meal programs (including nutrition and child welfare), there is no evidence to suggest that they improve learning outcomes.

Even more striking is the fact that no credible study on education in India has found any significant positive relationship between teachers possessing formal teacher training credentials and their effectiveness at improving student learning. Similarly, there is no correlation between teacher salary and their effectiveness at improving student learning, and at best very modest positive effects of reducing PTRs on learning outcomes. Muralidharan argues that these very stark findings most likely reflect weaknesses in both pedagogy and governance, which he believes are critical barriers to translating increased spending into better outcomes.

These findings may appear quite discouraging, and could be interpreted as suggesting that improving learning outcomes—especially across millions of first-generation learners—is very difficult; so the best we can do is to provide the standard inputs associated with functioning schools and hope for positive effects in the long run. Fortunately, the news is not all bad, because Muralidharan also presents evidence from studies over the past decade that point to interventions that have been highly effective at improving learning outcomes, and are able to do so in much more cost-effective ways than the existing, status-quo patterns of spending.

A key determinant of how investments in schooling inputs translate into learning outcomes is the structure of pedagogy and classroom instruction. Getting aspects of instruction right is particularly challenging in a context such as India's where several millions of first-generation learners have joined a rapidly expanding national schooling system. In particular, standard curricula, text books, and teaching practices that may have been designed for a time when education was more limited may not fare as well under the new circumstances, since the default pedagogy is one of "completing" the textbook or the curriculum, which increasingly does not reflect the learning levels of children in the classroom who are considerably behind where the textbook expects them to be.

Evidence that the business-as-usual pedagogy can be improved is found in several randomized evaluations finding large positive impacts of supplemental remedial instruction in early grades that are targeted to the child's current level of learning. Four points are especially noteworthy. First, these positive results have been found consistently in programs run by multiple nonprofit organizations in several locations (including Uttar Pradesh, Bihar, Uttarakhand, Gujarat, Maharashtra, and Andhra Pradesh). Second, the estimated magnitudes of impact from these interventions (whose instructional time is typically only a small fraction of the duration of the scheduled school year) are considerable—often exceeding the learning gains from a full year of conventional schooling. Third, these interventions are typically delivered by modestly paid community teachers, who mostly do not have formal teacher training credentials. Finally, these supplemental remedial instruction programs are highly cost-effective and deliver significant learning gains at much lower costs than the large investments in the standard inputs mentioned above that have not been found to be effective.

Beyond pedagogy, another explanation for the low correlation between increases in spending on educational inputs and improved learning outcomes may be weak governance of the education system and limited effort on the part of teachers and administrators to improve student learning levels. The most striking symptom of weak governance is the high rate of teacher absenteeism in government-run schools. Teacher absence rates were over 25 percent across India in 2003. Seven years later, an all-India rural panel survey that covered the same villages as surveyed in 2003 found that teacher absence was still around 24 percent in rural India in 2010. The fiscal cost of teacher absenteeism has been estimated at around ₹7,500 crores a year, suggesting that governance challenges remain paramount in India's education system.

On the positive side there is evidence that even modest improvements in governance can yield significant returns. All-India panel data show that improving the monitoring and supervision of schools is strongly correlated with reductions in teacher absence. Estimates suggest that investing in improved governance by increasing the frequency of monitoring would yield an 8 to 10 times return on investment in reducing the fiscal cost of teacher absence and would be 10 to 12 times more cost-effective in reducing effective PTRs (the PTR after adjusting for teacher absence) than hiring more teachers.

The evidence also points to the importance of motivating teachers by rewarding good performance as a key lever in improving the performance of the education system. Rigorous evaluations of carefully designed systems of teacher performance pay show substantial improvements in student learning in response to even very modest amounts of performance-linked pay for teachers. Long-term evidence over five years in Andhra Pradesh shows that teacher performance pay was 15 to 20 times more effective at raising student learning than reductions in PTRs, the government's default policy position for improving education quality. More broadly, these results suggest that the performance of frontline government employees depends less on the *level* of pay and more on its *structure*. In particular, introducing small amounts of performance-linked pay is much more likely to improve public teacher performance than large amounts of across-the-board increases in pay, and is also much more cost-effective.

Muralidharan's paper proposes a number of bold ways of moving from this evidence to better policymaking. The evidence does not imply that India should stop improving school infrastructure or training teachers. Rather, it cautions that simply doing more of the business-as-usual expansions of education spending is unlikely to solve the crisis in learning outcomes. It also highlights the critical importance of judging cost-effectiveness in making education policy within an increasingly constrained fiscal environment. Muralidharan makes three policy recommendations based on this evidence.

First, he suggests making learning outcomes an explicit goal of primary education policy and investing in regular and independent high-quality measurement of learning outcomes. The Indian state has done a commendable job of getting what it measures: improving education indicators that are routinely measured (including school access, infrastructure, enrolment, and inclusiveness in enrolment). But it has fallen considerably short on the outcome indicators that are not measured (such as learning outcomes).

While independently measuring and administratively focusing on learning outcomes will not by itself lead to improvement, it will serve to focus the energies of the education system on the outcome that actually matters to millions of first-generation learners, which is functional literacy and numeracy, outcomes that the system is currently not delivering.

Second, Muralidharan suggests launching a national campaign of supplemental instruction targeted to the current level of learning of children rather than to the textbook, to be delivered by locally hired teaching assistants with the goal of reaching minimum, absolute standards of learning for all children. While gaps in enrolment between disadvantaged groups and the population averages have reduced, there are considerably larger gaps in learning levels that exist at the point of entry into the school system and continue to grow over time. Thus, the gains of the past decade made in terms of reducing inequities in primary school enrolment will be at considerable risk (because low learning levels are strongly correlated with the probability of dropping out) if urgent attention is not paid to the crisis in learning outcomes with a mission-like focus on delivering universal functional literacy and numeracy that allow children to read to learn. The evidence strongly supports scaling up supplemental instruction programs using locally hired short-term teaching assistants that are targeted to the level of learning of the child. The cost-effectiveness of this intervention also makes it easily scalable.

Third, Muralidharan argues for urgent attention to issues of teacher governance, including better monitoring and supervision, as well as teacher performance measurement and management. A basic principle of effective management is to have clear goals and to reward employees for contributing toward meeting those goals. The extent to which the status quo does not do this effectively is highlighted in the large positive impacts found from very modest improvements in the alignment of employee rewards with organizational goals. Implementing these ideas effectively in a public sector setting will take considerable effort, but the evidence highlights the potentially large returns to doing so.

The next 10 years will see the largest ever number of Indian children in the school system at any point in Indian history or in the future. It is critical that this demographic-dividend generation be equipped with the literacy, numeracy, and skills needed to participate fully in a rapidly modernizing world. In a fiscally constrained environment, it is also imperative to use evidence to implement cost-effective policies that maximise the social returns on any given level of public investment. The growing body of high-quality research on primary education in the past decade provides an opportunity to put this principle into practice.

To the credit of the IPF, this paper appears to have been very timely. In his chairman's concluding remarks at the IPF, Planning Commission Member in charge of education, Narendra Jadhav, called the paper a "game changer." Several of the paper's recommendations were incorporated into the final version of the 12th Five-year Plan's chapter on education, and again in the Government of India's *Economic Survey of India 2012–2013*. The key next steps and political and bureaucratic challenges will now lie in actually implementing these ideas and meeting the education goals of India's 12th Five-year Plan.

Policy Lessons from Implementing India's Total Sanitation Campaign

Open defecation is a major global sanitation problem, and it is substantially and importantly an Indian problem. About 60 percent of the approximately 1 billion people worldwide who defecate openly live in India. Although open defecation may seem remote in some parts of India's modern cities, 600 million people in India—over half of the population—defecate openly without access to a toilet or latrine. Widespread open defecation has major consequences for health and human capital in India. The paper by Dean Spears argues that ending widespread open defecation and pursuing feasible methods of safe excreta disposal must be a top policy priority for India.

The paper draws policy lessons from the first 10 years of latrine construction under India's Total Sanitation Campaign (TSC) during 2001–11. The TSC was a flagship program of the central government and represented a large effort to improve rural sanitation: over the approximately 10-year period it reported building one latrine per 10 rural people in India. The TSC was designed to improve upon perceived shortcomings of earlier programs: instead of emphasizing subsidies for building infrastructure, it included an ex post monetary incentive for local political leaders to eliminate open defecation and made use of village social structures to enforce compliance.

TSC was able to improve health and human capital among Indian children where it was implemented. The first 10 years of TSC, on average, prevented an infant death for a few thousand dollars each, a comparatively very low average cost. This initial success was in part due to the Clean Village Prize or Nirmal Gram Puraskar (NGP), the incentive for village governments to eliminate open defecation. But, sanitation coverage remained substantially incomplete under TSC. Spears finds that heterogeneity in the intensity and effectiveness of TSC implementation imply that the additional benefits of extending the TSC to the many Indian children who are still uncovered would probably substantially exceed the additional costs. Therefore, as the TSC becomes the Nirmal Bharat Abhiyan (NBA), India should not miss the opportunity to invest in the successful principles of total sanitation suggested by the TSC: quality data, effective monitoring, and motivational, ex post incentives.

Spears suggests the clear lessons for future policy from the TSC. First, improving sanitation—meaning safe excreta disposal—must be a top priority for India; and because open defecation has negative externalities, it is everybody's problem, and requires government action. Second, by promoting and incentivizing latrine use as the TSC did, publicly supported sanitation with an ex post incentive to motivate use can be a comparatively very inexpensive way to save babies' lives.

In addition, Spears argues that the village is the appropriate administrative level for rural sanitation interventions. Incentives to local leaders for achieving positive outcomes are useful and should be strengthened by both increasing the monetary incentive and devoting resources to ensure accurate evaluation and adjudication. Furthermore, achieving total sanitation coverage will require both safeguarding the quality of administrative data and investing in large datasets on health outcomes.

What is the path forward for rural sanitation policy in India? Adequately constructed and used pit latrines are well-known to be a safe method of excreta disposal. The data reviewed by Spears suggest that the TSC and the NGP incentive can motivate villages to construct and use such latrines.

However, coverage is still quite incomplete, and more of the same may not be enough. Increasing and publicizing the prize may be good first steps, but better monitoring of prize applicants will be crucial, especially if a larger prize makes submitting a false application more attractive. If it is true that sanitation must be implemented at the village level to be effective, policymakers in New Delhi and state capitals have no alternative but to focus on the details of what motivates local politics and policy. This may require developing alternative channels of information that bypass bureaucratic, financial, and political interests. Here, the difficult part of creating a useful administrative data system is not establishing a modern, online, computerized database; it is ensuring that the people collecting and entering the underlying data have an interest in meaningful and accurate information. The challenge is considerable, but given the substantial social costs of open defecation and the negative externalities that make latrines a social and government concern, meeting the challenge should be a top priority.

In the process of converting the TSC into the NBA, the government is planning to increase the subsidy to families to construct toilets. Spears argues that increasing the government's investment in sanitation promises important opportunities, but there will be risks as well—risks that more money will attract unwanted attention, and that the so-far successful incentives behind the TSC could be undermined. These risks can be minimized—and the promise of the NBA realized—by emphasizing the principles that contributed to TSC's success, the monitoring of outcomes and motivational, ex post rewards for latrine use at the village level. Before the TSC, India's Central Rural Sanitation Program (CRSP) emphasized subsidies for latrine construction rather than use, resulting in many latrines that were either never built or built but not used. Spears believes that if the NBA returns to these older CRSP principles, it will probably miss the opportunity to end open defecation in India. Instead, he argues for expanding the emphasis on sanitation outcomes and building on the TSC evidence.

Evidence from the Indian States on India's Demographic Dividend

India is in the midst of a major transition in its age structure. The country's working-age population as a share of the total population has risen substantially over the last three decades. This process is set to continue over the next 30 years or so, during which India will gain about 300 million workers. Has the increased share of working-age population delivered a growth dividend?

A demographic dividend accrues when workers are more productive and save more than dependants. Also, the process by which a working-age cohort increases in size can foster growth. Typically, the demographic transition begins with a sharp fall in mortality rates followed by a more gradual decline in the fertility rate. The number of potential workers increases and the number of young dependants declines. The accompanying health and social changes may act directly to induce a larger female labor supply and increase attention to primary education and well-being.

Shekhar Aiyar and Ashoka Mody examine the potential magnitude of the demographic dividend for India. Scholars have concluded that the economic miracles of East Asia were accompanied by—and partly fueled by—dramatic demographic shifts. China saw its population pyramid shift between the early 1980s and 2000, with the share of the working-age population swelling. India's demographic transition has come later than in East Asia and could confer considerable economic dividends over the next few decades.

The authors point out that the quantitative potential of India's demographic dividend has received little research attention. The most basic questions remain unanswered: What has been the size of India's demographic dividend to date? How much remains to be accrued? Their study is a first attempt at providing some answers.

Aiyar and Mody gather state-specific data on the age structure of the population from successive decadal rounds of the Indian Census. Those data show that Indian states have historically exhibited large differences in age structure, specifically in the level and growth rate of the working-age ratio. Grouping selected states into "leaders" (high-growth states, typically from the south and west of the country) and "laggards" (low-growth states, largely concentrated in the Hindi-speaking heartland) reveals some striking patterns. They argue that the divergence in economic performance between leaders and laggards is remarkably congruent with the divergence in demographic trends, especially since the 1980s. Per-capita income growth in the 1980s and 1990s in the leaders far outstripped growth in the laggards: 3.4 percent and 4.9 percent per annum versus 2.5 percent and 0.6 percent, respectively. Mirroring this, the working-age ratio for leader states rose steeply from 55.9 percent in 1981 to 62.1 percent in 2001, while for laggard states the ratio increased much more slowly, rising from 51.8 percent in 1971 to 53.4 percent in 2001. Thus, by 2001, the gap in the working-age ratio between leaders and laggards had widened to 8.7 percentage points.

A panel econometric framework with state-specific fixed effects is employed to identify the impact of the heterogeneous evolution of the age structure across states on economic growth. Both the initial working-age ratio and the growth rate of the ratio are found to be significant contributors to per-capita income growth. The result is robust to correction for inter-state migration (the concern being that the estimated relationship may reflect workers migrating across state borders in response to growth differentials rather than due to a demographic dividend). Moreover, the relationship is robust to numerous control variables drawn from the general growth literature and previous studies of convergence across the Indian states. Controls include proxies for education, health, gender bias, land, financial depth, as well as policy variables such as land and labor reforms. Perhaps surprisingly, Aiyar and Mody find little empirical evidence for complementarities between demographic variables and various facets of social development or the policy environment. It is possible that some of the social preconditions for a demographic transition may themselves generate the ability to benefit from it.

Applying the regression estimates to past data allows the authors to calculate the demographic dividend to date. To do this, they calculate the additional growth in annual per-capita income arising from changes in the age structure relative to a counterfactual in which the age structure remains fixed at the 1961 level.

They find that India's demographic dividend has already been substantial. In the two decades before the 2001 Census, changes in the age-structure of the population added between 1 percent and 1.5 percent per annum to per-capita income growth. Put another way, demographic change accounted for about 40 percent of the observed growth in per-capita income in these decades. This was the period when India began its economic liberalization. It was also the period when India's gross domestic product (GDP) broke free of its old "Hindu rate of growth." Unsurprisingly, this growth acceleration is often attributed exclusively to economic reforms. But the demographic evidence suggests that changes in the age structure of the population may have been an equally important, if much overlooked, part of the story. The Aiyar–Mody calculations also suggest that the states that led India's economic take-off were precisely those buoyed by the largest demographic dividend. Net of the demographic dividend, the gap in growth performance between the laggard states and leader states was much smaller.

Aiyar and Mody also apply their regression estimates to independent projections of India's future age structure to calculate the dividend going forward. These calculations suggest that the demographic dividend will peak over the next two decades, adding about 2 percentage points to annual per-capita income growth. Subsequently, as the working-age ratio stabilises from about 2030, the dividend will decline, while remaining positive. Finally, their analysis suggests that future demographic changes should promote income convergence. The states in the south and west of India have already under-gone the major part of their demographic transition, while the laggards have not. Since the bulk of the projected large increments to India's working-age ratio will come from laggard states, sustained growth acceleration in some of India's poorest states may now be feasible.

Role of Policy Reforms in Promoting Groundwater Conservation in India

India is the largest user of groundwater for irrigation in the world. Indian agri-culture is sustained by groundwater. According to the 2005–06 Agricultural Census of the country, 60.4 percent of the net irrigated area is irrigated using groundwater. Agriculture is the source of livelihood for the majority of the Indian population. In 2009–10, agriculture employed 52.9 percent of the working population. In addition, around 80 percent of the rural population relies on groundwater for meeting their drinking water needs. According to the Indian Council of Agricultural Research, groundwater irrigation has ensured food security in times of deficit.

In her paper Sheetal Sekhri argues that this pattern of development is not sustainable. Stocks of groundwater are rapidly depleting in India. According to the Central Groundwater Board, 15 percent of administrative blocks in India are over-exploited (more water is extracted than is replenished each year), and these blocks are growing at the rate of 5.5 percent per annum.

India's legal framework allows more or less unchecked open access to groundwater. Legally, any person who owns land can extract groundwater free of cost. In addition to this, most states provide huge electricity subsidies to the farm sector, further reducing the marginal cost of extraction. The central government's assured Minimum Support Price policy distorts the prices of food grains such as wheat and paddy, incentivizing growing paddy in areas not conducive for it. These factors compound the depletion problem.

Using data for 1980 to 2010 from monitoring wells, Sekhri finds that the north-western states of the country, including Punjab, Haryana, Rajasthan, Gujarat, western Uttar Pradesh, and New Delhi, have experienced the most substantial falls in the water table over this period. Three important facts emerge from the examination of the data. First, the decline in water tables in India is spatially heterogeneous, with the north-western region affected the most. Second, the bread basket states, including Punjab and Haryana, are experiencing a significant fall in water tables. Third, the decline has accelerated over time.

Against this backdrop, Sekhri seeks to understand what policies have helped conserve this vital resource. Pervasive usage of individual wells makes monitoring and demand enforcement extremely difficult, and hence impedes conventional policy design to check over-extraction. Therefore, the focus of public policy has mostly been on supply side interventions. This study uses data from observation and monitoring wells to evaluate the impact on water tables of the three policies that India has followed: rainwater harvesting mandates, subsidies for decentralized rainwater harvesting, and delaying paddy transplanting.

One of the first policies introduced across many Indian states was mandated rainwater harvesting. States selected the measures for mandating rainwater harvesting. These measures included construction of rainwater harvesting structures on the roofs of buildings that met specific size criteria.

Delhi was the first to pass this mandate in 2001. Other states that have mandated rainwater harvesting include Andhra Pradesh, Tamil Nadu, Kerala, Madhya Pradesh, Rajasthan, Bihar, and West Bengal. Sekhri analyses district level data to examine whether such mandates have had any short run impact on the decline of the water table. To circumvent selection bias, groundwater levels in districts in the states that passed the mandates earlier are compared to the states that passed them later. States that did not pass the law are not used in the analysis.

The paper also examines the impact of a policy pursued by the Gujarat government that promoted decentralized rainwater harvesting. Decentralized efforts to recharge groundwater began in the Saurashtra region of Gujarat after the drought of 1987, and continued to be used by farmers in later years. In 2000, the Gujarat government introduced the Sardar Patel Participatory Water Conservation Project in response to the work of farmers and NGOs. The program provided a subsidy for rainwater harvesting and was implemented in two phases, which commenced in 2000 and 2005. Sekhri's empirical analysis compares groundwater levels in districts in the regions that received the subsidy program in 2000 to the districts that received the program later in 2005.

One of the key initiatives undertaken in Punjab to slow down the decline in the water table has been a mandated delay of paddy transplanting. In 2006, the state government influenced the timing of paddy transplanting by changing the date on which free electricity was provided to the farm sector. The transplanting date was therefore delayed, thereby reducing the amount of intensive watering that the crop could receive during its production cycle. The delayed date was mandated in 2008 via an ordinance. This was later turned into a law—The Punjab Preservation of Sub-Soil Water Act, 2009—that penalizes farmers for violations of its clauses. Haryana followed suit and also mandated a delay in paddy transplanting in 2009. Haryana passed its Preservation of Sub-Soil Water Act in March 2009, an act that is very similar to the Punjab Act. The Sekhri paper uses the timing of the introduction of this policy in Punjab and Haryana to isolate the causal effect of the policy on water tables.

Each specification in the analysis of these three sets of policies controls for state and year fixed effects, annual average district precipitation, and demographic controls interacted with year indicators.

Sekhri's paper shows that while top-down rainwater harvesting mandates showed no beneficial effect, decentralized rainwater harvesting subsidies were more effective in Gujarat. Her analysis shows that the delayed paddy transplantation policy worsened the groundwater situation. Therefore, according to Sekhri, decentralized policies that involve grassroots stakeholders who are more informed about local conditions will be more effective at facilitating conservation.

The conclusion must be seen as tentative, however. According to Tushaar Shah, one of the discussants of the paper, urban water harvesting mandates have remained largely on paper, except in Chennai. He contends that even if the mandates were successfully implemented, their impact would not show up in the rural groundwater levels monitored by the Central Groundwater Board and used by the author as the dependent variable. Shah further notes that Punjab delayed implementing its paddy-sowing mandate until 2009, and, therefore, finds the author's choice of 2006 as the beginning date of the mandate incorrect. According to him, the mandate remains largely on paper. For these reasons, he suggests that it is perhaps premature to conclude that rainwater harvesting and paddy-delaying mandates are ineffective instruments for reversing the depletion of water tables.

Evidence on IT Investments and Productivity in Indian Manufacturing

India's manufacturing sector has remained small, approximately 16 percent of GDP, compared to that of other developing countries. Even though India's services sector, particularly in software and IT, has so far been successful in spurring the expansion of the economy, there are doubts about its capacity to maintain sustained growth in aggregate output and employment without a larger contribution from the industrial sector. Manufacturing in particular generates jobs across a wide range of skill levels, making it important that India focus on expanding the sector. In response, India's National Manufacturing Policy (NMP) has been recently introduced with the goal of generating 220 million new manufacturing jobs by 2025, and increasing this sector's share of GDP to 25 percent by 2022.

The paper by Shruti Sharma and Nirvikar Singh argues that growth of productivity and employment in the manufacturing sector can be potentially stimulated by using the country's advantage in IT services to boost efficiency and support innovation. This relationship is explored in their paper by examining the impact of IT investment on productivity in the manufacturing sector, as measured by gross value added (GVA). They analyze plant-level data spanning five years between 2003 and 2007, taken from India's Annual Survey of Industries (ASI). Although the ASI covers 15,000–50,000 manufacturing plants each year, the authors restrict the data to the plants that were surveyed in all five years. Accounting for missing observations and zero values, their sample consists of approximately 2,500 plants each year. The paper finds some evidence that plants with higher levels of IT capital stock have higher gross value added, controlling for other inputs. However, this effect is diminished when plant level fixed effects are included. One possible interpretation of this result is that unobserved managerial quality is an important factor in the impact of IT capital on productivity. The results are robust to the use of estimation methods that allow for endogeneity: in particular, Generalized Method of Moments estimates for different specifications are qualitatively consistent with those from OLS.

Sharma and Singh then proceed to evaluate the role of management by examining how firm ownership and organizational structure affect productivity. They find evidence that firms owned by the central government, despite having lower overall productivity, tend to benefit more from IT investment than privately-owned or jointly-owned firms. On the other hand, the results do not provide enough evidence to determine differences in the productivity of IT capital between plants with different organizational structures.

The authors also find a positive relationship between the use of intermediate goods imports and productivity, but weak evidence that IT capital and imported intermediates are substitutes in domestic manufacturing plants. Furthermore, their analysis suggests that the level of IT stock and the proportion of skilled workers (defined as salaried workers, as opposed to wage workers) are complementary. However, their results regarding the effect of labor skill intensity on the impact of IT capital on plant productivity are inconclusive.

Given regional differences in manufacturing plants, the paper examines the impact of geography, considering both plant location and possible agglomeration effects. Despite substantial differences in IT usage and other characteristics between plants across India's four regions, they do not translate into differences in the impact of IT capital on plant GVA. With regard to agglomeration effects, the authors' analyses result in no evidence of state-level agglomeration externalities, but do indicate that industry-level agglomeration has a positive impact. Based on these findings, Sharma and Singh suggest using industry-level policies targeted at encouraging IT use in manufacturing plants to achieve better impacts from IT investment. These recommendations are consistent with those presented in the recent report by the National Manufacturing Competitiveness Council and National Association of Software and Services Companies (NASSCOM).

Finally, the authors estimate an IT demand model to consider the factors that influence a plant's decision to invest in IT. As expected, plants that already invest in some level of IT capital and plants with higher financial capacities are more likely to increase their investments in IT. However, while controlling for potential selectivity biases based on the plants' existing levels of IT capital, they find little evidence to suggest that access to financial capital or skilled workers are important factors in decisions regarding IT investment.

Sharma and Singh's results are consistent with the existing literature in that investment in IT has a positive impact on productivity in manufacturing plants in India. They conclude that financial constraints may be the primary cause of the currently limited levels of IT capital in Indian manufacturing plants, and that industry-level policies targeted at encouraging increased levels of IT investment are necessary given their positive impacts on plant GVA. Finally, based on the indirect evidence for the important role that managerial capacity plays in determining the productivity of IT investment, the authors suggest that policies aimed at improving basic management skills may be useful.

Annual IPF Lecture and IPF Policy Roundtable

Though not included in this Volume, following the tradition set in 2004 when it started, the 2012 IPF also featured the annual IPF Lecture given this time by Dr V. Y. Reddy, former Governor of the Reserve Bank of India. Dr Reddy spoke about his by now much-cited talk on "India: New Strategies for Economic Development."

Since 2011, the IPF has also featured a Policy Roundtable to conclude the IPF. The panelists on the 2012 IPF Policy Roundtable took on the subject of "The Future of Economic Growth in India," a timely topic looking back at India's slipping GDP growth rate over the past year. The Roundtable was expertly chaired by Y. V. Reddy, and featured B. J. Panda (Member of Parliament from the Lok Sabha), Shankar Acharya (ICRIER), T. N. Ninan (*Business Standard*), and Rakesh Mohan (NTDPC and Yale University).

A video recording of the 2012 IPF Lecture and a transcript of the 2012 IPF Policy Roundtable are available on www.ncaer.org.

K A R T H I K   M U R A L I D H A R A N
University of California, San Diego,
NBER, NCAER, and J-PAL

Priorities for Primary Education Policy in India's 12th Five-year Plan[*]

ABSTRACT   India has demonstrated considerable progress in the past decade on improving primary school access, infrastructure, pupil–teacher ratios (PTRs), teacher salaries, and student enrollment. Nevertheless, student learning levels and trajectories are disturbingly low. The past decade has also seen a number of high-quality empirical studies on the causes and correlates of better learning outcomes based on large samples of data and careful attention paid to identification of causal relationships. The findings from this research are however, not being reflected in the current policy priorities of the Government of India. This paper seeks to bridge the gap by summarizing the research, making policy recommendations based on this research, and suggesting an implementation roadmap for the 12th Plan. The main findings reported in this paper are that there is very little evidence to support the notion that improving school inputs in a "business as usual" manner will improve learning outcomes. On the other hand, innovations in pedagogy (especially supplemental remedial instruction targeted to the level of learning of children) and governance (focused on teacher performance measurement and management) have shown large positive impacts on student learning. The research over the past decade suggests that increasing inputs to primary education in a "business as usual" way

* *karthik.muralidharan@gmail.com*   I am grateful to Abhijit Banerjee, Rukmini Banerji, Jean Dreze, and Parth Shah and to participants at the IPF for their comments. I thank Shekhar Shah for the invitation to write this paper, which grew out of a lecture at NCAER in December 2011. I especially thank Montek Ahluwalia, Narendra Jadhav, and Pawan Agarwal for incorporating several recommendations in this paper into the Education Chapter of the India's 12th Five-year Plan. This paper is based on primary research over the past decade that was enabled and supported by many. In particular, I thank the Government of Andhra Pradesh, the Azim Premji Foundation, the World Bank, and the UK Department for International Development for the papers made possible by the "Andhra Pradesh Randomized Evaluation Studies" project. I also thank Pratham, J-PAL, and the state governments that have supported their evaluations for generating several insights in this paper. I thank Abhijit Banerjee, Rukmini Banerji, Jishnu Das, Shanta Devarajan, Esther Duflo, Eric Hanushek, Caroline Hoxby, Devesh Kapur, Asim Khwaja, Geeta Kingdon, Michael Kremer, Pratap Mehta, Gulzar Natarajan, Lant Pritchett, Halsey Rogers, I. V. Subbarao, and Venkatesh Sundararaman for the comments, conversations, and collaborations that have informed my thinking on this subject over the past decade. All views expressed are my own.

is unlikely to improve student learning in a meaningful way unless accompanied by significant changes in pedagogy and/or improvements in school governance.

Keywords: *Primary Education, India, Research Summary, Policy Recommendations*

JEL Classification: *H41, H77, I21, I22, I25, I28, J41, M52*

1. Introduction

Investing in education is arguably one of the most critical components of enabling the "Inclusive Growth" agenda of the Government of India. Among the several studies carried out on the correlates of long-term economic growth in the 1990s, the correlation between average years of education in a country and its growth rate has been among the most robust (Barro 1991, and Benhabib and Spiegel 1994 provide evidence in a cross-country growth regression framework; Mankiw, Romer, and Weil 1992 do so in a growth accounting framework). Concurrently, micro-evidence on the returns to education consistently finds positive returns to primary education in developing countries ranging from 7 percent to 10 percent per extra year of schooling (Duflo 2001; Duraisamy 2002). Thus, investments in education are essential for aggregate economic growth as well as for enabling citizens to participate in the growth process through improved wages and employment.

At the same time, recent evidence suggests at both the macro and micro levels that what matters for both growth as well as employability are not years of education as much as the quality of education represented by learning outcomes and skills. In an influential set of papers, Hanushek and Woessmann (2008, 2010) show that cognitive skills as opposed to years of schooling are more robustly correlated with economic growth. They show that the share of basic literates as well as the share of high performers has independent and significant effects on growth and that these types of human capital complement each other. While the results above are based on cross-country regressions, Schoellman (2012) presents micro-evidence using wages of immigrants to the US and shows that cross-country differences in education quality are as important as cross-country differences in years of schooling in accounting for differences across countries in output per worker.

In addition to being an engine of productivity and growth, education quality also determines the extent to which citizens can broadly participate in the growth process. It is a common refrain among employers in India that the majority of college graduates are not "employable" due to a lack of skills commensurate with their paper qualifications. The weak correlation between years of education and actual knowledge is even more pronounced at the primary schooling level (see Section 2). However, while India has made considerable progress in improving primary education when measured by the quality of schooling inputs (including student enrollment and retention), the progress on learning outcomes has been minimal. It is therefore an urgent priority for primary education policy in India to improve the quality of education measured not just in terms of inputs and student enrollment/ retention, but also in terms of learning outcomes.

The past decade has also seen a growing body of high-quality empirical research on primary education in India that can inform primary education policy in a meaningful way. However, the current policy framework for primary education in India (including those in the Right to Education Act) does not reflect the insights from this body of research. The main purpose of this paper is to bridge this gap by distilling the insights from rigorous academic research based on large samples and careful attention to identifying causal relationships, and pointing out the policy priorities that the evidence points toward. This paper does not seek to conduct a comprehensive academic review of this literature with a detailed discussion of econometric identification issues. Rather, it seeks to present education policy-makers in India at both the Center and state-level with a succinct summary of the most credible quantitative research on education over the past decade and then focus on drawing out and discussing the policy priorities suggested by the evidence.[1] In the interests of keeping the scope of this paper manageable, one area that will not be covered is private schools and the optimal structure for leveraging and regulating non-state actors in primary education.[2]

---

1. The policy recommendations made in this paper reflect the author's judgment of the appropriate weight to be placed on various sources of evidence over the past decade as well as extensive field experience during primary education research in India over this period. For another recent policy paper that summarizes the recent evidence, see Mukerji and Walton (2012), who address similar issues with a more explicit focus on the Right to Education (RtE) Act.

2. The author has ongoing research in the field based on a large multiyear randomized experiment on the causal impact of private schools in India on learning outcomes, and would like to defer the discussion on private schools till we have better evidence. Suggestive evidence on private schools in India based on cross-sectional data is provided in Muralidharan and Kremer (2008) and Desai et al. (2009).

The paper is organized into four main sections. Section 2 provides a concise statement of the main facts regarding primary education in India; Section 3 reviews the evidence on the impact of various sets of education inputs (at the school, teacher, and student level) on learning outcomes, reviews the evidence on attempts to improve outcomes by reforming pedagogy and school governance, and finally briefly reviews the evidence on demand-side interventions; Section 4 outlines the policy priorities and approaches for primary education in the coming decade suggested by the evidence. Section 5 provides a discussion of implementation challenges and feasible strategies for overcoming these, followed by a brief conclusion.

2. Facts on Primary Education in India

2.1. School Quality as Measured by Inputs Has Improved Considerably in the Last Decade

A positive consequence of the substantial attention paid to primary education during the past decade by the Government of India as well as state governments under campaigns such as the Sarva Shikhsa Abhiyan (SSA) has been the considerable improvement in the quality of government schools as measured by the availability of various kinds of inputs. This can be seen in the trends in the District Information System for Education (DISE) data between 2004 and 2010.[3] In addition to seeing changes in school facilities and teacher quality and quantity in official government reported data, these improvements are also confirmed in data collected completely independent of the government.

Muralidharan, Das, Holla, Kremer, and Mohpal (2013) present results from an all-India panel study of village schools that revisited the rural sample of the nationally representative school survey conducted in 2003 as part of the nationwide study on teacher absence reported in Kremer, Muralidharan, Chaudhury, Hammer, and Rogers (2005). Muralidharan et al. (2013) report very significant improvements in input-based measures of schooling quality from this nationally representative panel data. For instance, pupil–teacher ratios have fallen by nearly 20 percent (from 47.4 to 39.8); the fraction of

---

3. Indeed, the investments in high quality administrative data on schools and the creation of the Education Management Information Systems (EMIS) under which the DISE data are made available has also been a significant positive feature in education administration in the past decade.

schools with toilets and electricity has more than doubled (from 40 percent to 84 percent for toilets and 20 percent to 45 percent for electricity); the fraction of schools with functioning midday meal programs has nearly quadrupled (from 21 percent to 79 percent); and the overall index of school infrastructure has improved by 0.9 standard deviations (relative to the distribution of the school infrastructure index in 2003). At the same time, school enrollment rates have increased steadily to the point that 96.7 percent of children aged 6–14 are now enrolled in school (Pratham 2012).

These are considerable achievements, and should not be regarded lightly given the scale of the Indian primary education system, which is the largest in the world. It highlights that the Indian state does have capacity to execute goals when undertaken in a "mission mode." These results also suggest ground for optimism that the Indian state is able to make progress on outcomes that are measured and made into a policy priority. However, as we will see below, these improvements in school quality as measured by inputs have not translated into improvements in learning outcomes, which may be partly explained by the fact that education policy in the past decade has not prioritized learning outcomes.

2.2. Student Learning Levels Are Disturbingly Low

While the most prominent set of public discourses on the state of Indian primary education (including those leading up to the RtE law) have focused on the low quality of school inputs and schooling conditions (most notable among these was the Public Report on Basic Education [PROBE] Report published in 1999), a new wave of discourse focused on the levels of learning was initiated by Pratham with the publication of the Annual Status of Education Report (ASER) in 2005. This has now become an annual exercise that measures learning outcomes of school-age children in nationally representative samples, with samples large enough to estimate learning levels precisely at the district level.

However, unlike measures of school quality based on inputs (which have shown an upward trend), the picture here is bleak. The most recent ASER report (Pratham 2012) finds that less than 50 percent of children who are enrolled in the fifth standard are able to read a simple paragraph at the second-standard level, and that less than 27 percent of children enrolled in the third standard are able to solve a two-digit subtraction problem with borrowing and less than 55 percent of children enrolled in the fifth standard are able to solve the same problem. Over the years, the ASER data suggest that not only are the levels of learning low, but that the trends in learning levels are in fact negative. Since basic reading and arithmetic are foundational skills, the low levels of learning suggested by the ASER data are especially alarming since they suggest that the Indian education system is doing well at enrolling children in school, but failing when it comes to teaching them even basic skills (Pratham 2012).[4]

The ASER testing tools are meant to enable a rapid assessment of learning levels and do not span the full range of question difficulty representing the syllabus. It is useful therefore to also look at results from the nationwide School Learning Study conducted in 2010 (Educational Initiatives 2010) by Educational Initiatives, who are one of India's leading testing and assessment firms. These assessments included a broad range of questions including publicly released items from the international Trends in International Mathematics and Science Study (TIMSS) tests, which would enable a global comparison. The main findings here are consistent with those from the ASER reports. Learning levels are low, and in particular scores on questions that require application of concepts are consistently lower than those on questions representing rote learning. The report also finds that the mean score across Indian public schools on the common TIMSS questions in the standard 4 language test is less than half that of the international mean (less than 30 percent compared to over 60 percent).[5]

Muralidharan and Zieleniak (2013) use a unique longitudinal data set in the state of Andhra Pradesh collected by following a cohort of students over five years and find that not only are learning levels low, but so are the learning trajectories over time. They use item response theory (IRT) to create item characteristics of a 3-parameter logistic model (difficulty, discrimination, and guessing parameters) for a database of over 900 questions each in math and language that were administered as part of the Andhra Pradesh Randomized Evaluation Studies (APRESt) studies over five years. Using overlapping questions over years and a set of identical questions that were administered simultaneously to students across grades 1 to 5, they estimate learning trajectories, defined as the probability of a typical student in a given grade getting a question correct over time as they progress through

---

4. These figures are based on representative household surveys, and present average achievement levels regardless of whether a student attends a private or a government school. When the figures are broken down by school type, the data consistently show that students in private schools score higher on every measure. Thus, the learning levels for students in government schools are even lower than the ones reported above.

5. The results are not reported in standard deviations (Educational Initiatives 2010).

the grades. Their findings suggest that for most questions of intermediate levels of difficulty, less than 20 percent of students who do not correctly answer a grade N-level question at the end of grade N, are able to answer it correctly at the end of grade N+1. These results suggest that spending additional years in school, while no doubt useful in terms of added learning, has remarkably low effectiveness in improving learning outcomes, especially given the considerable economic cost of an additional year in school. They also find evidence of increasing variance in absolute learning levels of students over time.[6]

The studies mentioned above are all unanimous in suggesting that learning levels in India are low by any absolute standard. But the magnitude of India's "learning deficit" is particularly stark when placed in an international comparative context. Das and Zajonc (2010) show that learning levels in the Indian states of Orissa and Rajasthan would fall below 43 of the 51 countries for which comparable TIMSS data are available. Even more striking is the finding of the recent Programme for International Student Assessment (PISA) assessments carried out in two of the more advanced Indian states in terms of learning levels—Himachal Pradesh and Tamil Nadu—which finds that the two tested Indian states ranked 72nd and 73rd out of a total of 74 tested entities for which results were reported (not all were countries). Combining these results with those of the SLS (2010) suggests that many of the more educationally backward states like UP, Bihar, and Jharkhand would lag even further behind in international comparisons (and drag down the population-weighted all-India means much further). It is worth highlighting that these results do not simply reflect the correlation between economic development and test scores because the top scoring entity was the city of Shanghai in China, which has the annual per-capita income of a middle-income country (approximately 13,000 US$ per head as of 2011, which is comparable to that of Brazil).

Thus, while the quality of schooling as defined by traditional notions of school inputs has been improving steadily due to increased government expenditure, quality as defined by learning outcomes is low both in absolute terms (measured by what competencies children in school are demonstrating) as well as in relative terms (as seen in the PISA scores).

---

6. Note that this probably understates the increase in variance because of a higher probability of students dropping out from the lower end of the learning distribution.

2.3. There Is an Increasing and Widespread Exodus to Fee-charging Private Schools

There is perhaps no greater indicator of the quality of government schooling as perceived by parents than the increasing extent to which parents are eschewing free government schools (in fact government schools have a "negative" cost once the various incentives such as midday meals, free text books, and other benefits are accounted for) and moving their children to fee-charging private schools. Desai, Dubey, Vanneman, and Banerji (2009) show, using nationally representative data from 2005, that 58 percent of students in urban India attended fee-charging private schools. The annual ASER reports show a steadily increasing trend in private school enrollment from 18.7 percent in 2006 to 25.6 percent in 2011, with these increases being broad-based across states. These numbers highlight that India has a share of private school enrollment that is comparable to a country like Chile that has a fully voucher-based school system.

It is beyond the scope of this paper to compare the effectiveness of private and government-run schools, but these data indicate that in spite of considerable increases in spending on government schools, parents do not perceive this spending to be generating enough quality in the government schooling experience for them to retain their children there. While it is true that parents value many things in schools (with learning outcomes being only one component in a vector of schooling attributes that parents care about), the trend toward increasing private school share in primary education combined with the low levels of learning outlined in the previous section suggest that there are considerable systemic weaknesses in translating increasing education spending into superior outcomes in government-run schools.

3. Reviewing the Evidence on Causes and Correlates of Learning Outcomes

The main factors that determine the performance of a school system include the level of inputs provided (facilities, teachers, and student inputs), the pedagogical processes employed in classrooms, and the overall governance of the school system. In addition to these supply-side factors, a further key determinant of educational attainment is the extent of demand for education from parents and students. Each of these areas has seen considerable empirical research in the past decade and this section briefly summarizes the evidence on these broad classes of issues that are relevant to the translation of spending into outcomes.

3.1. Inputs

The most important components of education spending in the past decade have been on improving school facilities and infrastructure, improving teacher salaries and training, hiring more teachers to reduce PTRs, and expenditure on student benefits such as textbooks, and midday meals. The Planning, Allocations and Expenditures, Institutions: Studies in Accountability (PAISA) Report (Accountability Initiative 2012) shows that these three categories of expenditure account for 90 percent of the SSA budget (in the most recent year, 44 percent was spent on teachers, 36 percent on schools, and 10 percent on students, though the last category does not include spending on midday meals). However, as the discussion below shows, the empirical studies to date do not find significant correlations between these investments and either intermediate measures of system performance (such as teacher absence) or measures of outcomes (such as student test scores).

3.1.1. SCHOOL INFRASTRUCTURE   In the absence of rigorous randomized evaluations studying the impact of infrastructure improvement on learning outcomes in India, the broadest evidence to date comes from Muralidharan et al. (2013). Using village-level panel data from a nationally representative sample of over 1,250 villages across 19 Indian states, they find no correlation between changes in average village-level school infrastructure (between 2003 and 2010) and changes in enrollment in government schools, though they do find a small positive effect on the number of students attending school. They also find no correlation between changes in average village-level school infrastructure and either teacher absence or student test scores, even though as noted earlier, they find significant improvements in almost all measures of school infrastructure.

One experimental evaluation of an infrastructure intervention is Borkum, He, and Linden (2010) who study the impact of a school-library program in Karnataka. They find that even though the program provided schools with several new books as well as a librarian, the program had no impact on student reading scores. Analysis using the five-year panel data set of student learning outcomes collected as part of the APRESt project also finds no correlation between the infrastructure index in the school and measures of student test-score gains.[7]

Thus, almost all the existing evidence points to a limited impact of improvements in school infrastructure on learning outcomes. The reasons for this are not obvious. One possibility is that these investments make schools more appealing to teachers and students, but have no impact on the teaching and learning process, which may be the main determinant of learning. Another possibility is that infrastructure may be built but not used. For instance, the APRESt project collected matched data between school facilities and household behaviors and the data suggests that over 75 percent of children who attend schools that have a toilet still report relieving themselves in the open in school.[8] A final possibility is that the returns to infrastructure investments need to be evaluated over the depreciation lifecycle of the corresponding infrastructure. It is possible that the cumulative impact of investments in buildings over a 30-year depreciation lifecycle may be significantly positive, while the annual effect on learning outcomes is too small to be measured statistically.

This last possibility should caution us against interpreting the results to date as suggesting that infrastructure investments should not be made. More broadly, the results should not be interpreted as saying that school infrastructure does *not* matter for improving learning outcomes (they may be necessary but not sufficient), but the evidence does suggest that investment in infrastructure by *itself* is unlikely to have a significant impact on improving learning levels and trajectories. This is essential to point out because the staffing patterns of education department offices around the country suggest that the dominant concern for the department is typically infrastructure and facilities, while there are almost no staff at the district and block levels whose main task is to focus on academics and pedagogy.[9]

3.1.2. TEACHER QUANTITY AND QUALITY The other major component of investment in inputs has been increasing teacher salaries and training, and reducing

---

7. Calculations by author using the APRESt data. Note that these are not experimental results, but by controlling for lagged test scores, this analysis mitigates several of the usual omitted variable concerns.

8. This could be for logistical reasons such as lack of water in the school toilet or the lack of staff to clean the toilet, due to which teachers may prefer to keep the toilets closed. Alternatively, these results could reflect the difficulty of changing behavioral norms with respect to sanitation.

9. Thanks to Rukmini Banerjee for highlighting this point in her discussion.

pupil–teacher ratios. The evidence summarized below again points to very limited impacts of these investments on improved learning outcomes.

While there has been no experimental evaluation of the impact of varying individual teacher characteristics in India, there have been quite a few studies that control for lagged test scores and estimate the impact of teacher characteristics on learning outcomes in a value-added framework. The first point to highlight is that *none of these studies* to date finds a significant positive relationship between teacher training and increases in test scores of students taught by the corresponding teacher (see Kingdon and Teal 2010; Muralidharan 2012; Muralidharan and Sundararaman 2011b, 2013). Similarly, there is no correlation between teacher salary and student test score gains (Kingdon and Teal 2010; Muralidharan 2012; Muralidharan and Sundararaman 2011b),[10] and if anything, the correlations typically point to a *negative* relationship between teacher salaries and gains in student test scores.

The evidence on the impact of reducing PTRs on improved learning outcomes is also quite mixed, with most studies not finding much of an impact. Banerjee, Cole, Duflo, and Linden (2007) report results from an experimental evaluation that provided remedial instruction to children with low test scores by taking them outside the regular classroom for remedial instruction provided by a volunteer. However, while the test scores of the children who received this remedial instruction went up significantly, they find no impact on the test scores of the students who remained in the original classroom with a smaller class size. These results suggest that reducing class-size may have a limited impact on improving test scores.

Muralidharan and Sundararaman (2013) study the impact of school-level PTR on test score gains by using longitudinal data on test scores and changes in PTR over time and find significant but modest gains from reducing the school level PTR. Their estimates imply that reducing school level pupil–teacher ratio by half would at most yield gains in test scores of 0.25 standard deviations per year. Jacob, Kochar, and Reddy (2008) study the impacts of class size on learning outcomes on Andhra Pradesh using a control-function approach and also find significant but small effects of class-size reductions on test scores.

---

10. The results from Muralidharan and Sundararaman (2011b) and Muralidharan (2012) referred to here are based on the tables of heterogeneous treatment effects of the performance-pay interventions as a function of teacher characteristics. The specifications used our standard value added specifications and the results reported above are the coefficient on the linear term (the main effect of the characteristic) and not the interaction term (which measures the heterogenous impact of the performance pay program as a function of the characteristic).

Further, the panel data analysis conducted by Muralidharan et al. (2013) finds no correlation between changes in mean PTR in a village and changes in normalized mathematics test scores. They also find evidence of a possible mechanism for this finding, which is that there is a very robust *negative* relationship between PTR and teacher absence. In other words, *reductions* in PTR over time were strongly correlated with *increases* in teacher absence. Thus, the impact of reducing class size by hiring additional teachers was mitigated by increased levels of teacher absence in the schools. This is consistent with the experimental evidence presented in Muralidharan and Sundararaman (2013) where they find that schools that were randomly selected to receive an additional contract teacher saw a significant increase in the absence rates of the regular teachers.[11] In other words, the marginal rate of teacher absence may be considerably higher than the average, which could limit the impact of reducing PTR on improving learning outcomes.

Finally, a related issue is the one of distribution of teachers across schools. While budgetary considerations lead to a focus on average PTRs, in practice there is wide variation in PTRs across schools. Chin (2005) shows that Operation Blackboard in India which redistributed teachers from large to small schools led to a significant increase in primary school completion rates for girls and the poor even though there was no increase in the average number of teachers per school and no reduction in mean class size.

Summarizing the research on PTR on learning outcomes, we see that the best studies do find some positive impacts of class-size reduction on student test scores. Nevertheless, these estimated impacts are modest in magnitude, and given the high cost of class-size reductions, it may not be very cost-effective to aim to improve test scores by reducing class sizes. Thus even a 20 percent reduction in PTR (which is a very expensive intervention) would not yield large test score gains (around 0.05 standard deviations/year) and would be considerably less cost-effective than achieving the same class-size reduction using contract teachers (Muralidharan and Sundararaman 2013) or introducing modest amounts of performance linked bonuses (Muralidharan 2012; see Section 3.3.4). The evidence also suggests that in addition to average PTRs, it may also be important to pay attention to the distribution of teacher resources across and within schools, and that it may be possible to improve learning outcomes at no additional cost simply by rationalizing the allocation of teachers across schools, and by providing smaller class sizes to earlier grades.

---

11. Similar findings are reported by Duflo, Dupas, and Kremer (2012) in an experimental study of contract teachers in Kenya, suggesting that this may be quite a general result.

3.1.3. STUDENT GRANTS AND MIDDAY MEALS   The final major category of inputs is student-based spending including textbooks, uniforms, and midday meals. Again, studies to date do not find any significant positive relationship between these categories of spending and improved learning outcomes.

Das, Dercon, Habyarimana, Krishnan, Muralidharan, and Sundararaman (2013) present experimental evidence on the impact of a school grant program that stipulated that the funds should be spent on inputs directly used by students. The program was implemented over two years in the major categories of spending were books, stationery, and writing materials (~50 percent); workbooks and practice books (~20 percent); and classroom materials (~25 percent) with similar patterns of expenditure in both years of the program. They find that this program had a significant positive impact on student test scores at the end of the first year, but that the impact in the second year was close to zero, with the cumulative two-year effect being positive but not significant. They show the most likely mechanisms of this result is that households considerably reduce their own spending on their child's education in the second year of the program.

Thus, when the program was unanticipated and when the money arrived after parents had already incurred their educational expenditures on books and materials for the school year (as in the first of the program), there was a significant net increase in materials which translated into significant improvements in test scores. However, when these inputs were anticipated, households were able to re-optimize and reduce their own spending. Thus, there was no significant increase in net inputs in the second year which would explain why there was no impact on test scores either. These results highlight the importance of accounting for household re-optimization in response to public spending programs in thinking about the long-term impacts of increased spending, and suggest a possible mechanism for the lack of correlation between increased spending on inputs and improved outcomes.[12]

A similar concern exists in the context of midday meals, because it is possible for households to adjust the allocation of food within the household in response to the fact that the school-going child now has access to one meal in the school. Afridi (2010a) studies the impact of midday meal provision and finds that the program substantially increases the total caloric intake of

---

12. In technical terms, these results highlight that it is possible for the production function effect of additional inputs on test scores to be positive (this is a partial derivative of the impact of additional inputs holding other factors constant), while the policy effect might be considerably lower (since this includes re-optimization by other agents). This is clearly a very general theme since the discussion in the previous section of increased absence among pre-existing teachers in response to the addition of a new teacher is an illustration of the same point.

school-going children in rural Madhya Pradesh, by 50 percent to 100 percent. Using a difference-in-difference estimation strategy that relies on a staggered rollout across schools, attendance rates for girls are estimated to increase by 12 percentage points in rural Madhya Pradesh (Afridi 2010b) and 5 percentage points overall in Delhi (Afridi, Barooah, and Somanathan, 2010). However, these papers do not study the impact of midday meals on test scores. Jayaraman, Simroth and Vericourt (2010) use data from 13 states to construct triple-difference estimates using private schools as a control group and find that the midday meal program is associated with a 6.8 percent increase in enrollment, but had no impact on test scores. Finally, the panel data analysis in Muralidharan et al. (2013) finds that there is a *negative* (though not always significant) correlation between changes in the midday meal status of schools in a village, and changes in normalized math test scores. One possible mechanism for this result may be the diversion of teacher time to manage and oversee the midday meal process. Analysis of teacher time use data in Andhra Pradesh using the APRESt data, suggests that government school teachers report spending around 10 percent of their daily time in school overseeing the midday meal.

Another student input that has been found to have a significant impact on enrollment, but insignificant impact on learning outcomes is the bicycles that have been provided to girls in several states to improve secondary school enrollment. Muralidharan and Prakash (2013) study the impact of the Chief Minister's Bicycle Program that provided girls in Bihar with a bicycle conditional on enrolling in 9th grade. They use a triple difference approach (using boys and the neighboring state of Jharkhand as comparison groups) and find that being in a cohort that was exposed to the Cycle program increased girls' age-appropriate enrollment in secondary school by 40 percent (a five percentage point gain on a base enrollment rate of 13 percent). They find that the impact of the program was significantly greater in villages where the nearest secondary school was further away, suggesting that a key mechanism for program impact was the reduction in the "distance cost" of school attendance induced by the bicycle. However, they do not find any significant impact of the cycle program on girls' learning outcomes as measured by their passing rates in the 10th-standard board exam.

To summarize, it appears that most of the investments in improving school quality as measured by inputs (regardless of whether these are at the school, teacher, or student level) are either not correlated with improved learning outcomes or only weakly so. There may well be other important reasons for making these investments (such as child welfare), and student inputs that reduce the marginal cost (or increase the marginal benefit) of attendance do seem to have a positive impact on school participation. But the evidence to date does not suggest any reason to be optimistic that "improving" school quality in a "business as usual" way will lead to a substantial improvement in learning outcomes.

3.2. Pedagogy

While there have been significant increases in schooling inputs, a key determinant of how these investments translate into learning outcomes is the structure of pedagogy and classroom instruction. Getting aspects of instruction right is particularly challenging in a context such as India where several millions of first-generation learners have joined a rapidly expanding national schooling system. In particular, standard curricula and teaching practices that may have been optimal at a time when education was more limited may not fare as well under the new circumstances. The discussions in this section focus on some key aspects of classroom structure and pedagogy that are relevant for the South Asian context—including remedial instruction, and the use of technology in the classroom.

3.2.1. REMEDIAL INSTRUCTION   A fundamental challenge for pedagogy in a context of several millions of first-generation learners is the large variation this creates in the initial preparation of children when they enter school. Also, as Muralidharan and Zieleniak (2013) show, the variance in student learning levels increases over time. How does a teacher effectively teach a classroom where students are so varied in their skill level? Remedial schooling interventions have been one method to attempt to reduce the variance of achievement in the classroom and ensure that all students are progressing. Remedial programs offer the possibility of focusing on those students who are lagging behind and teaching at a level that is appropriate for their achievement. Ideally, such an intervention would increase their progress, and decrease the heterogeneity of student learning levels in a given grade.

The evidence confirms that this may be the case, with several high-quality studies finding strong impacts of remedial instruction programs on learning outcomes, even when implemented by volunteers or informal teachers with little formal training and paid only a modest stipend that is several times lower than the salary of regular government teachers.

First, Banerjee, Cole, Duflo, and Linden (2007) report results from an experimental evaluation of a program run by Pratham specifically targeted at the lowest performing children in public schools in the Indian cities of Mumbai and Vadodara. The program provided an informal teacher hired from the community (known as a Balsakhi or "friend of the child") to schools, with an explicit mandate to focus on children in 3rd and 4th grade who had not achieved even basic competencies in reading and arithmetic. These children were taken out of the regular classroom for two hours a day, and were provided with remedial instruction targeted at their current level of learning. The program improved student test scores by 0.28 standard deviations, with most of the gains coming from students at the lower end of the learning distribution.

Second, Banerjee, Banerji, Duflo, Glennerster, and Khemani (2010) report results from several interventions designed to improve community participation in education. Of all the interventions tried, the only one that was found to be effective at improving learning outcomes was a remedial instruction program implemented by youth volunteers hired from the village who were provided a week of training and conducted after school reading camps for two to three months. These effects were substantial (albeit off a low base) with the average child who was not able to read anything at the baseline and who attended a camp being 60 percentage points more likely to be able to read alphabets than a similar child in a control village.

A third piece of experimental evidence is provided by Lakshminarayana, Eble, Bhakta, Frost, Boone, Elbourne, and Mann (2012), who study the impact of a program run by the Naandi Foundation that provided remedial education program run by community volunteers to a randomly selected set of villages in Andhra Pradesh. After an initial sensitization to households regarding the program, the volunteers provided two hours a day of remedial instruction after normal school hours in the school itself (on a daily basis). The subject matter covered in these sessions was tailored to students' class-specific needs and learning levels, and aimed to reinforce the curriculum covered in school. At the end of two years of this intervention, student test scores in program villages were 0.74 standard deviations higher than those in the comparison group, suggesting a large impact of the after-school remedial instruction program.

Finally, Banerjee, Banerji, Duflo, and Walton (2012) study the impact of a program implemented by Pratham in partnership with the state governments of Uttarakhand and Bihar that attempted to scale up remedial instruction in public schools, and find that summer camps conducted by regular teachers transacting the learning-appropriate remedial materials were effective in raising test scores. However, they find that there was no impact of other models that attempted to incorporate this pedagogy in the regular school day. The authors interpret their findings as suggesting that the remedial pedagogy was successful, but that it was difficult to get teachers to implement new curriculums during school hours.

3.2.2. TECHNOLOGY-AIDED INSTRUCTION Greater use of technology in classrooms is commonly thought of as a promising way to rapidly improve education outcomes in developing countries (including India). Posited channels of impact include (*a*) cost-effective replication and scaling up of high-quality instruction using broadcast technology (such as radio and television-based instruction); (*b*) using technology to overcome limitations in teacher knowledge and training (for instance for teaching more advanced concepts in science and mathematics or for teaching a new language like English—for which there is growing demand but a limited supply of teachers with the requisite competence); (*c*) using technology to provide supplemental instruction at home; (*d*) using technology to engage children better in the learning process through the use of interactive modules (such as educational games and puzzles); and (*e*) using technology to customize individual student learning plans. These interventions also range from being quite inexpensive on one hand (radio-based instruction for instance) to very expensive (individual laptops for students such as envisaged under the "One Laptop per Child" or OLPC initiative).

While the promise of enhanced use of technology in instruction is clear, and there are many advocates for doing so, the evidence on the effectiveness of technology in instruction remains limited and a few rigorous studies have evaluated the benefits of such interventions. Skeptical scholars have even argued that the promotion of technology is fueled more by the prestige and symbol of modernity than any actual evidence of the effectiveness of the interventions (Shields 2011). While many continue to champion educational technology, there may be adverse consequences of their implementation, the simplest of which would be an ineffective technology that does not increase achievement and takes time away from other more effective teaching techniques. Understanding the efficacy of technology is especially important as technology is often relatively expensive compared to other activities; if they do not lead to superior learning outcomes, then it is likely that there are more cost-effective methods than technology to improve educational outcomes.

Linden (2008) evaluates the impact of a computer-aided instruction program implemented by a nongovernmental organization (NGO) in Gujarat (Gyanshala) that was implemented both in an after-school supplemental instruction model as well as in a model where computer-aided instruction replaced a period of regular instruction. The paper finds that the supplemental program led to significant positive effects on test scores (0.28 standard deviations), while the in-school model led to significantly lower test scores (−0.57 standard deviations), suggesting that a blanket use of "computers in school" may not only not be effective, but could also be harmful if it replaces otherwise productive instructional time.[13]

Further evidence on the importance of design details is provided by He, Linden, and MacLeod (2008) who analyze an intervention aimed at improving English skills in which part of the intervention is directed by teachers and the other component is a self-paced machine. While both components led to positive gains in test scores, the study found that stronger students fared better using the machine, while weaker students benefited more from the guidance of a teacher. Thus, technology may be an effective teaching aid, but it may require higher initial levels of learning to be used effectively.

Banerjee et al. (2007) find that a computer remedial program increases test scores twice as much as the remedial teacher. However, because of the high expense of the computer-based program, scaling up the teacher-based remedial program would be five to seven times more cost-effective than the computer assisted learning program. The experiment illustrates that while certain technologies may be effective, it still may be more cost-effective to use non-technology–based programs.

Finally, while set in a different middle-income context, it is worth highlighting results from an experimental evaluation of the much-publicized "One Laptop Per Child (OLPC)" program in Peru (Cristia, Ibarraran, Cueto, Santiago, and Severin 2012). The paper finds that while the program increased the ratio of computers to students in schools from 0.12 to 1.18 in treatment schools, there was no impact on either school enrollment or test scores in Math and Language. The paper does find some positive effects on general purpose measures of intelligence such as the Raven's Progressive Matrices but the overall results suggest need for caution in believing that the introduction of computers in classrooms will by itself lead to improvements in learning levels.

These cautionary results are especially relevant in a context such as India where it is tempting to scale up interventions like "tablet computers for all" as a potential shortcut for addressing the challenges of education quality. To summarize, there are many good reasons to be excited about the *potential*

---

13. While set in a different context, a well-identified study on the impact of providing 14-year-old students with computers at home in Romania also found negative effects of the computer on test scores (Malamud and Pop-Eleches 2011)—again serving to caution that a naïve attempt to provide students with more technology can have negative effects and that interventions need to pay careful attention to what activities are being crowded out by the additional computer time.

for technology-enabled instruction to improve learning outcomes significantly. However, the evidence on the impact of greater use of technology in the classroom is mixed and seems to depend crucially on the details of the model by which it is implemented. A lot more careful research is needed (on both process and impacts) before committing resources to scaling up these programs, especially those involving expensive investments in hardware.

3.3. Governance

Beyond pedagogy, another explanation for the low correlation between increases in spending on educational inputs and improved learning outcomes may be the weak governance of the education system and limited effort on the part of teachers and administrators to improve learning levels. This section reviews the evidence on some of the key themes relating to school governance in India.

3.3.1. TEACHER ABSENCE   Perhaps the most striking measure of weakness of school and teacher governance in India is the high rate of teacher absence from schools. Kremer et al. (2005) present results from a nationally representative all-India survey of schools where enumerators made unannounced visits to schools to measure teacher attendance and activity. They find that on any given day, around 25 percent of teachers were absent from work, and less than half of the teachers on the payroll were found to be engaging in teaching activity. The absence rate was the second highest in a similar survey across eight low- and middle-income countries.

Muralidharan et al. (2013) present results from a nationally-representative panel survey that revisited the villages visited in the study above, and find that there has been a reduction in teacher absence rates from 26.3 percent to 23.7 percent.[14] While this is a significant reduction in teacher absence rates, the magnitude of improvement in measures of governance such teacher absence is considerably lower (0.26 standard deviations relative to the 2003 distribution of teacher absence) than the magnitude of improvement in physical inputs such as school infrastructure (0.91 standard deviations relative to the 2003 distribution).

In addition to these two nationally representative studies, several other studies have also noted the high rates of teacher absence in India. Duflo, Hanna, and Ryan (2012) find teacher absence rates in excess of 40 percent in informal schools run by an NGO in Rajasthan. Muralidharan and

---

14. The absence rate of 25 percent includes both the rural and the urban sample, whereas the absence rate in the rural sample in 2003 was 26.3 percent (for the villages in the panel data set).

Sundararaman (2011b, 2013) and Muralidharan (2012) regularly document teacher absence with multiple unobserved visits to a representative sample of rural government-run primary schools in Andhra Pradesh and find teacher absence rates to steadily range between 24 and 28 percent over the five-year period from 2005–06 to 2009–10.

3.3.2. MONITORING Muralidharan et al. (2013) use their nationally representative panel data set on teacher absence to estimate the correlations between changes in various school and management characteristics from 2003 to 2010 and changes in teacher absence. Among all the variables they study, there are only two robust correlates of teacher absence that are significant under all specifications (with and without state/district fixed effects). The first is the negative correlation between pupil–teacher ratio and teacher absence (described in Section 3.1.2), and the second is the strong negative correlation between school inspections and teacher absence. They find that increasing the probability of a school having been inspected in the past three months from 0 to 1 is correlated with a 7 percentage point reduction in teacher absence (or 30 percent of the observed absence rates). This estimate is similar in both cross-section and panel estimates, bivariate as well as multiple regressions, and with and without state/district fixed effects. Using the most conservative of these estimates, Muralidharan et al. (2013) calculate that increasing inspections/monitoring could be over 10 times more cost-effective at increasing teacher-student contact time (through reduced teacher absence) than hiring additional regular teachers.

On the other hand, the correlations between "bottom up" measures of governance and monitoring such as the frequency of Parent–Teacher Association (PTA) meetings and teacher absence is also negative but the magnitude is always lower than that of the "top down" inspections and is not always significant. These results highlight that there may be significant collective action problems that may make community-based monitoring less effective than top-down administrative monitoring (a result consistent with the experimental findings of Olken (2007) in the context of monitoring corruption in Indonesia). Banerjee et al. (2010) provide experimental evidence on the challenges of using community mobilization to improve school quality. They find no impact of various programs to build community involvement in schools in Uttar Pradesh on community participation, teacher effort, or learning outcomes.

Duflo, Hanna, and Ryan (2012) conduct an experimental evaluation of an intervention that monitored teacher attendance in informal schools in Rajasthan using cameras with time-date stamps to record teacher and student attendance. The program also paid teacher salaries as a function of the number of valid days of attendance. They find that this program reduced teacher absence by half, but structural estimates of a model of labor supply suggest that the mechanism for this result was not the "monitoring" per se, but rather the incentives tied to the attendance. Muralidharan and Sundararaman (2010) study the impact of a program that provided schools and teachers with low-stakes monitoring and feedback and find that this program had no impact on either teacher attendance or test scores. These results suggest that while "monitoring" is an important tool in reducing teacher absence, "low-stakes" monitoring is unlikely to be very effective, and that it is "high-stakes" monitoring with positive/negative consequences for presence/absence that is more likely to be effective.

3.3.3. Contractual Structure A widespread but highly controversial aspect of primary education policy in India during the past couple of decades has been the use of locally hired contract teachers on fixed-term renewable contracts, who are not professionally trained, and who are paid *much lower* salaries than those of regular teachers (often less than one-fifth as much).[15] Supporters consider the use of contract teachers to be an efficient way of expanding education access and quality to a large number of first-generation learners, and argue that contract teachers face superior incentives compared to tenured civil-service teachers. Opponents argue that using under-qualified and untrained teachers may staff classrooms but will not produce learning outcomes, and that the use of contract teachers de-professionalizes teaching, reduces the prestige of the entire profession, and reduces motivation of all teachers.[16] However, as seen below, there is no evidence to support the view that contract teachers are less effective than regular teachers.

Muralidharan and Sundararaman (2013) present experimental evidence from a program that provided an extra contract teacher to 100 randomly chosen government-run rural primary schools in the Indian state of Andhra Pradesh. At the end of two years, students in schools with an extra contract teacher performed significantly better than those in comparison schools by 0.16 and 0.15 standard deviations, in math and language tests respectively.

---

15. Contract teacher schemes have been widely employed in several states of India (under different names such as Shiksha Karmi in Madhya Pradesh and Rajasthan, Shiksha Mitra in Uttar Pradesh, Vidya Sahayak in Gujarat and Himachal Pradesh, and Vidya Volunteers in Andhra Pradesh). The salary differentials are even more pronounced if we account for the present discounted value of the pension and other retirement benefits offered to civil-service government teachers.

16. See Kumar et al. (2005) for an example of these criticisms.

They also find that contract teachers were significantly less likely to be absent from school than civil-service teachers (16 percent vs. 27 percent). Finally, they implement four different non-experimental estimation procedures (using both within and between-school variation as well as variation over time in pupil–teacher ratios in the same school) and find that they can never reject the hypothesis that contract teachers are at least as effective in improving student learning as regular civil-service teachers. In fact, their point estimates typically suggest that the contract teachers are more effective than regular teachers who are more qualified, better trained, and paid five times higher salaries.

Atherton and Kingdon (2010) use data from Uttar Pradesh and estimate the relative effectiveness of contract and regular teachers using a student fixed-effects approach (exploiting variation in the contract/regular teacher status of teachers who are teaching different subjects to the same student) and find that the contract teachers produced better learning outcomes. Finally, Goyal and Pandey (2011) use data from Madhya Pradesh and Uttar Pradesh and find that contract teachers exert higher levels of effort than regular teachers with employment security (on measures of teacher attendance and engagement).

It is also relevant to this discussion to highlight that all the four studies discussed in the previous section that found large positive effects on student learning outcomes of remedial instruction programs, used volunteer/informal/contract teachers with minimal formal training who were paid stipends that were at most one-fifth of the salary of regular teachers. These results suggest that the superior work incentives of contract teachers may more than make up for their lack of formal teacher training. They also suggest that the binding constraint in translating increased education spending into improved learning outcomes may not be teacher training and qualifications (as is commonly believed) but teacher effort, which is (relatively) weaker for civil-service teachers with lifetime employment security because there is no reward for effort and performance under the status quo (and conversely, few consequences for poor performance).

3.3.4. PERFORMANCE-LINKED PAY The discussions in this section suggest that improving governance is not just a matter of making better policies but also requires enhancements in the capacity of the government to effectively *implement* policies. Since the effort exerted by public sector employees is a key determinant of state effectiveness, a natural set of policy options to enhance governance in education would be to consider linking compensation of teachers as well as education administrators to measures of performance.

Muralidharan and Sundararaman (2011b) present experimental evidence on the impact of a program in Andhra Pradesh that provided bonus payments to teachers based on the average improvement of their students' test scores in independently administered learning assessments (with a mean bonus of 3 percent of annual pay). At the end of two years of the program, students in incentive schools performed significantly better than those in control schools by 0.27 and 0.17 standard deviations in math and language tests respectively. Students in incentive schools also performed better on subjects for which there were no incentives, suggesting positive spillovers between improved performance on math and language and the untested subjects (science and social studies). Since the performance pay programs were implemented as part of a larger set of experimental evaluations costing the same amount, the authors are able to compare the relative effectiveness of input and incentive-based approaches to improving learning outcomes. They find that the incentive schools performed significantly better than other randomly chosen schools that received additional schooling inputs of a similar value.

Also, as discussed earlier, Duflo, Hanna, and Ryan (2012) find that paying teachers on the basis of the number of days they attend work (as opposed to a flat salary that does not depend on performance) led to a halving of teacher absence rates (from 42 percent to 21 percent) and significant increases in student test scores (by 0.17 standard deviations).

Finally, Muralidharan (2012) presents evidence from the longest running experimental evaluation of a teacher performance pay program (spanning five years), and finds that students who completed their full five years of primary school under the individual teacher incentive program performed significantly better than those in control schools by 0.54 and 0.35 standard deviations in math and language tests respectively. The group teacher incentive program also had positive (and mostly significant) effects on student test scores, but the effect sizes were always smaller than those of the individual incentive program, and were not significant at the end of primary school for the cohort exposed to the program for five years. The paper estimates that the individual teacher performance pay program would be around 15 to 20 times more cost-effective (including administrative costs) at improving learning outcomes than the default policy of reducing pupil–teacher ratios by hiring more teachers (even assuming the most generous estimates of the impact of PTR reductions on test scores from the discussion in Section 3.1.2).

Taken together, these results suggest that even modest changes to compensation structure to provide reward and recognition to teachers on the basis of objective measures of performance (such as attendance or increases in student test scores) can generate substantial improvements in learning outcomes at a fraction of the cost of a "business as usual" expansion in education spending.

3.4. Demand Side Interventions

The discussion so far has focused mainly on the supply side of education, since this is what typically concerns what the government does in terms of running schools. However, the amount of education obtained by a child typically reflects a decision made by parents that considers the costs and benefits of education as well as other considerations (including credit, information, discount rates, risk preferences, and time horizon). Indeed, it is possible that the sharp increases in school enrollment over the past decade have been driven not so much by the education policies of the government as much as they have been by rapid economic growth and increasing real and perceived *returns* to education, which in turn have boosted the demand for education.[17] Nevertheless, it is possible that there is still under-investment in education because of demand-side failures including incorrect perceptions on the returns to education, and high discount rates of parents.

3.4.1. PROVIDING BETTER INFORMATION ON RETURNS TO EDUCATION Since household decisions regarding education investments are made on the basis of *perceived* as opposed to actual returns to education, interventions that provide better information about education options and the mean and distribution of outcomes at different levels of education may improve decision-making regarding education investments. In a randomized evaluation in the Dominican Republic, Jensen (2010) found that providing eighth-grade boys with information on the returns to secondary education increased the years of education completed by 0.25 to 0.30 years. In an experimental study in Madagascar, Nguyen (2008) finds similarly large effects on student test scores of simply providing better statistics to students on the mean wages at different levels of education. These gains are remarkable given the simplicity of the intervention, which involved reading a simple statement to students. However, one challenge is that the returns to education are typically not very credibly estimated (especially in countries with rapidly transforming economies

---

17. While there is no research that credibly quantifies the relative importance of supply and demand side factors in improving education attainment in India, there are several studies that highlight the importance of increasing returns to education in household decision-making with respect to educational attainment including Munshi and Rosenzweig (2006), Jensen (2012), and Shastry (2012).

such as India). Also, returns to education are likely to be heterogeneous, and accurate estimates of the distributions of returns to education are even more difficult to obtain. These complications raise the risk of providing incorrect information to households regarding returns to education, which may make them worse off.

A good way to address this concern (and still provide useful information) is demonstrated by Jensen (2012) who presents the impact of a program in North India where recruiters for call centers visited villages and hired girls who met the job requirements for working in call centers. He finds that women in treatment villages were significantly less likely to get married or have children during this period, and more likely to either enter the labor market or obtain more schooling. But this intervention provides information on returns to education not by showing average returns calculated from a (potentially incorrect) Mincer regression, but by demonstrating to village residents that girls with a high-school education can get hired by call centers. This is important because the recruiting standards were *not* changed, and so no (potentially) incorrect information was provided. But the intervention did provide accurate new information to village residents regarding the job possibilities for educated girls because the recruiters would typically not have visited the village (since the expected number of recruits would not justify the fixed costs of the recruiters going to the village).

The success of all these information-based interventions suggests that this may be a particularly useful avenue to explore for increasing education participation, especially since information interventions can be carried out relatively inexpensively.[18]

4. Policy Recommendations

While there has been a considerable amount of high-quality research in the past decade on what does and does not seem to matter for improving learning outcomes in India, it is not obvious that each of these individual

---

18. Another source of a demand-side market failure can be the high discount rate of parents who may choose to not send their children to school because the benefits are too far in the future while the costs (both monetary and opportunity costs) are immediate. While the Right to Education Act seeks to limit this concern by making schooling compulsory till age 14, there may still be a role for demand-side interventions such as conditional cash transfers at later ages. However, we do not discuss this topic here because (*a*) the focus of this piece is on primary education, and (*b*) there is not much good evidence on the impact of conditional transfer programs in India.

research findings should directly translate into policy. Policy formulation needs to consider technical, administrative, ethical, as well as political factors and even the best technical studies can only provide inputs into one dimension of policy-making. For instance, many programs which may not be "cost-effective," such as education for children with special needs, may nevertheless be consistent with normative principles of a just and humane society. Nevertheless, given budgetary pressures and the existence of several sectors that can claim an ethical basis for increased spending in a fiscally constrained environment (including health and food security), it becomes both morally and practically imperative to account for cost-effectiveness in questions of public policy. Improving the cost-effectiveness of social sector spending will allow a fiscally constrained state to do more in the social sector and improve both efficiency of spending as well as achieve greater equity in outcomes.

The collection of evidence presented in the previous section suggests that there are several "low-hanging" fruits for education policy that can improve learning outcomes at low cost. Since the majority of disadvantaged children (especially in rural India) still attend government-run schools, the focus of this section is on the policy priorities that are most relevant to the running of the government-school system. The paper makes four main policy recommendations in this regard (from easiest to most challenging in terms of practical implementation as well as political feasibility). Implementation issues are discussed in the next section.

4.1. Make Learning Outcomes an Explicit Goal of Primary Education Policy

The evidence on the key role of learning outcomes for both components of the "inclusive growth" agenda of the Government of India combined with the evidence on low levels and trajectories of learning presented in Section 2.2, should make it almost obvious that a key goal of primary education policy in India should be to measure and improve learning outcomes.

Nevertheless, this seemingly obvious point is necessary to highlight because the current education policy framework pays almost no attention to it. Nowhere is this more visible than in the "Results Framework Document (RFD)" of the Ministry of Human Resource Development (MHRD). The RFD serves as the document that outlines the goals of MHRD for the year, and places weights on different priorities including access, equity, quality, and departmental processes. While these are all important goals to aspire toward, it is striking that there is *no mention of learning outcomes in the most recent RFD* for 2012–13.[19] While "quality" of education is given prominence, the document defines quality exclusively in terms of improving the "inputs" into education—with most of the focus being on teacher training. This formulation is consistent with standard input-based conceptions of quality of education, but has almost no support in the data. In particular, there is *no study* that finds a positive correlation between a teacher possessing a formal teacher training credential and measures of gains in learning of students taught by the teacher. This is not to suggest that teacher training and other inputs *cannot* be contributors to improving learning outcomes but to highlight that these inputs *in their current form* do not seem to matter for improved learning outcomes. However, since there is no reason to think that the current policy framework envisages anything other than expanding training and other inputs in their current form, the evidence points to expecting that the future will not be very different from the past experiences.

Of course, there is no guarantee that measuring learning outcomes will by itself lead to an improvement (for instance, six years of ASER reports showing consistently low levels of learning have not led to any noticeable changes in policy). But it is almost certain that not measuring outcomes will encourage the system to continue on its current course with poor transformation of inputs into outcomes. Several studies have documented that organizations (especially bureaucracies) are more likely to deliver on outcomes that get measured (Wilson 1989). India's own experience in education over the past decade supports this point, since there has been a significant improvement in input-based measures of quality (which were the stated policy goals). Thus, the starting point in the education policy agenda needs to be an inclusion of improving learning outcomes as an explicit goal of primary education policy with immediate effect.

Opponents of this view raise four sets of objections to this approach. The first is that frequent testing and measurement makes education stressful for children and is therefore not child-friendly (Raina 2013). A second objection is that the Indian education system is already obsessed with exams and test performance to the exclusion of higher-order thinking and critical reasoning, and that Indian education needs less testing and not more. A third objection is that education is a complicated process involving several sets of actors (including parents and the community) and that the Government cannot be

---

19. http://mhrd.gov.in/sites/upload_files/mhrd/files/Modified percent20RFD percent202012–13_after percent20ATF percent20meeting.pdf. The closest component of the RFD that relates to learning outcomes is "Assessment of Learners under Saakshar Bharat"; however, this is an adult education scheme.

held responsible for outcomes (while it can be held accountable for inputs that it is obligated to provide). Finally, even if the principle of outcome-based monitoring is accepted, there is skepticism regarding its administrative feasibility—with a particular concern being the issue of maintaining integrity of measurement if officials will be monitored on the basis of these measures. Each of these points is addressed below.

The first point is well-taken, and it is worth highlighting the difference between assessment *of* learning (which is the normal view of testing), and assessment *for* learning (which is what I have in mind). The former approach emphasizes the role of "testing" what a student knows with a view to ranking and classification (and is inevitably stressful), whereas the latter approach emphasizes the role of assessments as diagnostic tools to teachers and administrators to measure student "understanding" of concepts to be followed up with targeted instruction (and additional resources where necessary) to bridge learning gaps at an early stage. The entire point of this approach is not to "stress" the child but to meaningfully "care" for the child's learning by paying attention to it. This aspect of measurement is in fact consistent with the "Continuous and Comprehensive Evaluation (CCE)" framework envisaged by the RtE. The recommendation, therefore, is simply to take this more seriously and require the measurement and reporting of individual student-level learning outcomes over time.

The second objection is based (in my view) on extrapolating the experiences of children in elite high-pressure urban settings (which are the settings experienced by the children of those in policy-making roles) to the entire country. Theory and evidence suggest that optimal policy is different at different levels of learning (see Lazear 2006 for a clear illustration of the relevant issues), and while it is true that excessive testing can narrow the intellectual development of high-achieving students, the opposite is true at low levels of learning (especially given the default policy of automatic promotion through grades regardless of levels of learning). In a setting where 60 percent of school-aged children cannot read, the evidence suggests that basic and higher-order skills are complements and not substitutes (see Muralidharan and Sundararaman 2011b). Further, there is also evidence to suggest that testing helps with processing learned materials and even in the learning of untested materials (Chan, McDermott, and Roediger III 2006). Finally, there is also evidence that parents of rural children (especially those who are not literate themselves) would like to have more objective measures of how their children are doing in school (Andrabi, Das, and Khwaja 2012). The evidence, therefore, points to there being *too little* reliable measurement of learning in rural government schools as opposed to too much measurement.

The third objection sounds reasonable but goes completely against the spirit of the RtE Act, which places the responsibility of ensuring that every child obtains a quality basic education on the State. If education quality depends on actual learning outcomes as opposed to simply spending time in school, then a natural corollary of the RtE Act is that the state takes some responsibility for providing learning skills to all children. Of course, outcomes cannot be guaranteed, but at the very least, measuring and documenting learning levels and gaps provides a basis for differential targeting of additional resources to disadvantaged children to bridge these gaps. Finally, while administrative concerns are very real, these exist with the implementation of almost any policy and different administrative structures can be experimented with at the state and district levels to provide feasible templates for implementation (see Section 5.2 for more discussion of this point).

4.2. Undertake Curricular Reform to Adjust for the Vast Variation in Learning Levels and Provide Additional Instructional Resources in Early Schooling Years to Disadvantaged Children

Muralidharan and Zieleniak (2013) show that the learning trajectories of students over time are substantially flatter than the rate of growth envisaged by the curriculum. It is therefore not surprising that a very large fraction of school-aged children complete primary education without having achieved even basic levels of learning. They also show that there is not only a large amount of variation in student learning levels at the end of grade 1, but that this variance grows over time.

The hypothesis that is most consistent with these findings is the one articulated in Chapter 4 of Banerjee and Duflo (2011) and also in Pritchett and Beatty (2012), which is that the curriculum has been designed by highly educated elites and reflects a period of time when there was no expectation of universal primary education. Indeed, as they note, the historical purpose of education systems in many developing countries may not have been to provide "human capital" to all students as much as to screen-gifted students for positions of responsibility in the state and the clergy. Since the teachers continue to follow the textbook as the default mode of instruction, and define their goals in terms of completing the curriculum over the course of year, it is not surprising that they are effectively "teaching to the top" of the distribution and that a large number of children are in the class but not learning because the lesson is too advanced for them.

While there is no direct test of this hypothesis in the Indian context, it is consistent with the findings of a large body of experimental evaluations of education interventions in India in the past decade. In particular, the finding that targeted remedial instruction programs have been highly effective in improving test scores in spite of being implemented by untrained and poorly paid volunteers, while large investments in teacher qualifications and training, PTR reductions, and other investments in school infrastructure have not been found to be effective suggest that the "business as usual" pedagogy is not conducive to improving learning outcomes effectively.[20]

A natural implication of this theory is that there may be large returns to reforming curricula to move at a different pace for students of different levels (Banerjee and Duflo 2011), or perhaps to even slowing down the pace of the general curriculum (Pritchett and Beatty 2012). However, modifying curricula is a time-consuming and arduous process and waiting to do this could risk the educational experiences of children in the coming years at a time when there is a very narrow time window left for India's "Demographic Dividend." Thus, while curricular reform to account for variation in learning levels should be a high priority, it may make sense to start immediately with programs that provide supplemental remedial instruction to children who are falling behind in early grades (who would be identified early though a system of CCE as mentioned above).

Banerjee et al. (2012) experiment with different models of incorporating learning materials targeted to the initial levels of children into the regular schooling system in Bihar and Uttaranchal. They find that the only model that was successful was one where the instruction was provided in a summer camp, and conclude that the behavior of teachers in the classroom appears to be so deeply ingrained toward completing the "regular" curriculum that

---

20. This view is also consistent with evidence from multiple studies in Africa. Glewwe, Kremer, and Moulin (2009) provide experimental evidence on the impact of a program that provided free textbooks to children in Kenya. They find that the program had no impact on average test scores, but students at the top 20 percent of the baseline test score distribution did significantly better with the textbooks. This would clearly make sense if it was only the top 20 percent of students who could read well enough to benefit from possessing a textbook. Duflo, Dupas, and Kremer (2011) present evidence from a program in Kenya that compared test score growth of students in the regular classroom to those of students who were tracked according to initial learning levels. They find that students in the tracked classrooms do significantly better at all initial levels of learning suggesting that reducing the variance of learning levels in the classroom allowed teachers to target the level of the instruction much more effectively.

it is difficult for them to deviate from that and modify their behavior toward incorporating the new materials in the classroom. Thus considerable additional work needs to be done to pilot and evaluate effective models of modifying pedagogy to reflect the need to cater to students who are falling behind. There is, however, already enough evidence to warrant the scaling up with public funds of programs that provide *supplemental* remedial instruction to children who need it through either after-school programs or through summer camps. The exact implementation models should be left to individual states to determine with the lessons from existing models and evaluations made available to them (see Section 5.2 for more on this).

4.3. Expand the Use of Locally-hired Contract Teachers, Especially for Remedial Instruction

The perception that contract teachers are of inferior quality and that their use is a stop-gap measure to be eliminated by raising education spending enough to hire regular teachers is deeply embedded in the status quo education policy discourse (and has been formalized in the RtE). The results discussed in this paper suggest that this view is not supported by the evidence. The fact that all the remedial instruction programs evaluated in this paper used young local volunteers (typically women) who were not trained as teachers and had only a 12th standard qualification (or in some cases even 10th), suggests that motivation and using appropriate pedagogy may be more important determinants of teacher effectiveness than qualifications or training. The results on contract teachers suggest the same conclusion (especially since they are found to be no less effective than regular teachers even with the regular pedagogy).

The combination of low-cost, superior performance measures than regular teachers on attendance and teaching activity, and positive overall impact of adding contract teachers to schools suggest that expanding the use of contract teachers could be a highly cost-effective way of improving primary education outcomes in India. In particular, expensive policy initiatives to get highly qualified teachers to remote areas (where they are often absent) may be much less cost-effective than hiring *several* local contract teachers to provide much more attention to students at a similar cost. Also, as Kingdon and Sipahimalani-Rao (2010) show, there is a surplus of educated unemployed youth (even graduates) who apply for contract and para-teacher jobs even though these jobs pay only a fraction of the salary of a regular teacher. Thus, the supply elasticity of contract teachers appears to be quite high and does not seem to be a binding constraint to expanding the use of locally hired contract teachers.

The expanded use of contract teachers could address several social challenges at the same time. It would provide employment (and the prestige of a "white collar" job) to educated unemployed youth, who are not skilled enough for formal sector jobs, but have more than adequate skills to impart basic instruction to first-generation learners. Given that the majority of these teachers are young women, the income and autonomy provided by these jobs could improve the intra-household bargaining positions of these women as well as outcomes for their children (as is suggested by many studies). Most important of all, such an initiative could lead to substantial improvements in learning outcomes of school-aged children, especially if several contract teachers are hired for the cost of one regular teacher.

Opponents of the use of contract teachers worry that their expanded use may lead to a permanent second-class citizenry of contract teachers, which in the long run will erode the professional spirit of teaching and shift the composition of the teacher stock away from trained teachers toward untrained teachers. Thus, even if expanding the use of contract teachers is beneficial in the short run, it might be difficult to sustain a two-tier system of teachers in the long run. Finally, the political economy concern is that hiring larger numbers of contract teachers will lead to demands to be regularized into civil-service status, which may be politically difficult to resist given the strengths of teacher unions and if such regularization were to happen, it would defeat the purpose of hiring a large number of contract teachers in the first place.

One possible course of action is to hire all new teachers as contract teachers at the school-level, and create a system to measure their performance over a period of time (six to eight years for example) that would include inputs from parents, senior teachers, and measures of value addition using independent data on student performance. These measures of performance could be used in the contract-renewal decision at the end of each fixed-term contract (or to pay bonuses), and consistently high-performing contract teachers could be promoted to regular civil-service rank at the end of a fixed period of time (see the next section for more details). In other words, contract teachers need not be like permanent adjunct faculty, but can be part of a performance-linked tenure track. Continuous training and professional development could be a natural component of this career progression, and integrating contract and regular teachers into a career path should help to address most of the concerns above, including the political economy ones. The recommendation for a career ladder is also made by Kingdon and

Sipahimalani-Rao (2010), and by Pritchett and Murgai (2007), who also provide an excellent discussion of how such a system may be implemented in practice.[21]

4.4. Invest in Governance, Especially Teacher Performance Measurement and Management

Research over the past decade in the US confirms what is intuitive to most observers of education, which is that the most important determinant of education quality that is in the locus of control of policy-makers is teacher quality (Rivkin, Hanushek, and Kain 2005; Rockoff 2004). Good teachers can really make a difference, and a sequence of good teachers can significantly alter the educational trajectory of students and often make up for socioeconomic disadvantages (Hanushek and Rivkin 2006). Thus the good news is that education policy-makers can have a substantial impact on learning outcomes by hiring and retaining good teachers.

The less good news is that teacher quality as measured by value-addition (which is a statistical measure of the extent to which a teacher is able to improve student learning during the period of time that they are responsible for teaching the concerned student) cannot be predicted by most observable characteristics of teachers (including the factors that are commonly considered to be proxies for quality such as experience, education, and training). Thus, the factors that are rewarded in the status quo may not be the ones that matter for teacher quality. While research on teacher value-added using Indian data is still in early stages, Kingdon and Teal (2010) find very similar results, and preliminary results using the longitudinal data from the APRESt project suggest that the same patterns hold in India.

These results suggest that a better way to identify effective teachers may be to directly measure their value-addition on a regular basis. But, before doing this, it is important to ask if these measures of teacher value-addition are just statistical constructs based on test scores, or if they are useful measures of gains in student human capital. A pathbreaking recent paper by Chetty, Friedman, and Rockoff (2011) helps answer this question, by doing a long-term follow- up of 2.5 million children in the US and linking their adult outcomes to measures of teacher value-added in grades 3 to 8. They find that teacher quality measured by value addition is strongly predictive of adult outcomes including college attendance, quality of college attended,

---

21. Pritchett and Murgai (2007) discuss how such a structured career leader for teachers can be embedded within a more decentralized education system that provides local communities more autonomy on managing schools.

and wages. Teacher quality in school is also positively correlated with social outcomes such as reduced teenage pregnancy and improved quality of neighborhood lived in. A final striking result is that they estimate that a policy that would replace highly ineffective teachers (those in the bottom 5 percent of the value-addition distribution over a period of time) with an average teacher would increase lifetime income of students by US$300,000.

While these long-term results are not replicable in any Indian dataset at present, preliminary analysis using five years of longitudinal student data in Andhra Pradesh that is matched to teachers, shows that the consequence of variation in teacher quality may be even more pronounced in India. In particular, the difference in mean annual value-added between a teacher who is 1 standard deviation below the mean teacher and one who is 1 standard deviation above the mean is considerably larger than the corresponding fig-ure in US data.[22] Thus, teacher performance measurement and management could be especially high-return activities in the Indian context.

There are two ways to improve average teacher quality: the first is to not hire low-quality teachers and to hire and retain high-quality teachers (the selection margin), the second is to design systems that encourage teachers to exert greater effort in a continuous manner—including upgrading their human capital over the course of their career in ways that improve their teaching ability (the effort margin). However, employing the selection mar-gin effectively under the status quo would be very difficult since the existing selection criteria (especially teacher training) do a very poor job of predicting teacher quality. Thus, it is necessary to measure teacher effectiveness on the job before being able to effectively assess their quality.

A career ladder of the sort proposed in the previous section, whereby all new teachers are hired as contract teachers, provided small annual bonuses on the basis of annual measures of performance, and are then promoted to regular teacher status at the end of a period of time that is long enough to evaluate their performance accurately, would have the dual advantage of improving teacher quality on both the selection as well as the effort margin. Such an initiative could also build a foundation for treating teaching as a true profession where highly effective teachers are rewarded, recognized, and promoted into positions of leadership and mentoring; while ineffective teachers are identified early for coaching and support (and if they are unable

---

22. The exact figures are not quoted here since the results are preliminary, but the inter-quartile range of the teacher value-added distribution in the APRESt data is so much larger than those in US data that the main point is likely to be robust to any changes in the point estimates. Note that a simple explanation for this may be that teachers play a disproportionately large role in test-score gains in a context where many parents are illiterate.

to improve even with such support, counseled into other jobs that they may be better suited for). Further details of how such a ladder might work are provided in Pritchett and Murgai (2007).

Finally, while putting in place such a system will take time and experimentation to refine the implementation details (see next section), the evidence suggests that even modest investments in better governance can have large returns. A case for optimism in the finding that increased frequency of inspection is correlated with a significant reduction in teacher absence (Muralidharan et al. 2013) is that these represent "business as usual" inspections as currently done by the system. Of course, these are not experimental estimates of the effect of increasing inspections, but the very robust findings of negative correlations between increased inspections and lower absence, suggests that even at the margins of the *current* system, increasing the frequency of supervisory visits to schools is likely to be a more cost-effective way of increasing effective teacher–student contact time than hiring more teachers (as seen earlier).

5. Moving from Recommendations to Implementation

While the research to date suggests the four policy recommendations made here, it does not provide adequate guidance as to a possible implementation roadmap. There is perhaps no better proof of the primacy of the implementation challenge than the fact that many of the policy recommendations made in this paper (especially that of a career ladder) are similar to those made five years ago in Pritchett and Murgai (2007) in this *same forum*. There is now more and better evidence to support these recommendations, but the issues have not changed much in the past five years and have been clearly visible to experts in this area. The ASER reports have been saying essentially the same thing for seven years now—that learning levels are low in spite of high enrollments—but not much has changed in India's national education priorities (as starkly illustrated by an RFD that has no mention of learning outcomes). The rest of this section outlines some of the key themes that may be relevant to being able to implement an education reform agenda along the lines suggested here.

5.1. Ideas Matter

Even before discussing issues of practical implementation and political economy, it is worth admitting that the status quo as represented by the formulations in the RtE suggest that the insights from the careful empirical work done on education in India over the past decade using large-scale datasets and paying attention to identification issues, have either not been communicated to or not been accepted by the education "establishment" in India. To the extent that the reform agenda being suggested by the quantitative research on the economics of education is seeking to reform the "conventional" wisdom on input-based policies, it is worth thinking about where this conventional wisdom gets formed. At present, it comes from Schools of Education (and related disciplines) where there is a limited amount of quantitative training of students, and where there is a greater emphasis on the history and philosophy of education and of the role of education in shaping society.

These are very important issues, but it has meant that the discourse in education schools and in the "Education for All (EFA)" and "RtE" communities has focused on historical injustices in education access and has typically (and probably correctly) interpreted the lack of universal primary education in India as a failing of the state, representing, at best, elite apathy toward mass education, and at worst an elite conspiracy to make sure that their educational advantage was maintained over generations. Attempts by the "Rights Community" to secure more opportunities for the disadvantaged naturally focus on the most visible symbols of inequity including school buildings, and teachers, which in turn leads to an input-based approach being the default demand of those seeking to secure the rights of disadvantaged children.

Attempts by education economists to bring cost-effectiveness into the discourse are then strongly resisted as an attempt by elites to defund public schools at a time when their own children have all moved to private schools. For instance, one reaction in an education ministry meeting where we presented evidence that locally hired volunteers and contract teachers may be as (or more) effective than regular trained teachers was that "this will be used by the finance ministry to cut the budget for education." So perhaps one way to bring cost-effectiveness into the conversation is to assure education advocates that the total funding will not be cut even if more cost-effective policy options are followed, and *that any resulting savings will be used to improve education outcomes further.* Of course, the setting of annual departmental budgets is a deeply political process, but such a commitment can serve as a starting point in moving the conversation from "how can we maximize the budgetary allocation for education" to "how can we maximize the quality of education delivered at any given budget"—with an assurance that being efficient will not hurt the sector's budget allocation.

More broadly, active attempts need to be made to disseminate and discuss the insights from the quantitative research over the past ten years with members of the education community and to incorporate some of the tools and methods of modern quantitative research into curricula and syllabi of education schools, so that their graduates are better equipped to engage with this research and its findings. This is a long-term project, but is an important investment in building dialogue and engagement with regards to priorities for education policy across stakeholders from an "education" perspective and those from a "cost-effectiveness/public finance" perspective.

5.2. Allow States More Autonomy to Experiment and Innovate with Reform Ideas

Even those who agree in principle with the recommendations here would (reasonably) worry about the feasibility of implementing such reforms. While they might seem promising theoretically and be supported by the evidence, there is still no guarantee that these reforms might succeed in practice. But implementation is a tactical and administrative issue that needs to account for local conditions and it would therefore be optimal to give states (and even districts) a substantial amount of autonomy with respect to how they may implement the ideas above. In addition to autonomy with regards to implementation of specific initiatives, it would also make sense to give states more autonomy with respect to how they may use their education budgets to best achieve learning goals.

It is, therefore, a matter for concern that the RtE in its current form mandates uniformity across a broad range of criteria including detailed specifications for building codes and playgrounds, pupil–teacher ratios, teacher qualifications, and teacher salaries. While these norms may be well-intentioned and have the goal of raising education in all states to a minimum standard, there are two problems with this approach. The first problem, which is a conceptual one, is that mandating these norms across the country magnifies the risk of making well-intentioned mistakes because the jurisdiction over which the mistake is being made would be all of India (which is the largest education system in the world). The second problem, which is an empirical one, is that these are *all* input-based standards, and *none* of these inputs appear to matter much for learning outcomes. Even if experts at the Central-level were to feel that input-based standards are a good starting point for improving education quality, both theory and evidence from other contexts suggests that a better approach would be for the central government to issue *guidelines* on suggested inputs (as opposed to mandates) and targets on outcomes, but then allow states to take the lead in innovating with respect to ways of achieving these outcomes.[23]

Using states as laboratories for education policy innovation makes sense for several reasons.[24] The first is simply that this provides 28 settings for experimentation as opposed to just one, allowing a greater diversity of ideas and implementation models to be tried out at lower risk. Second, Indian states are large (the 10 most populous Indian states would each rank in the top 25 countries in the world by population) and have enough scale to be autonomous policy-making entities on almost all issues related to primary education. Third, there is great diversity among states' political leaders, and corresponding variation in their priorities and their abilities to build political support for specific education policies, which is likely to result in a broader range of ideas being tried. Finally, the locus of political accountability is increasingly shifting to the states, which provides an incentive for states to copy good ideas from each other.[25]

A more productive role for the central government would be to support experimentation by states to better understand the impacts of specific initiatives in assessment, pedagogy, resource use, and governance and to then facilitate knowledge transfers across states that enable scaling up of successful reforms. Under the suggested framework for center–state relations, the Center would not be looking to institute mandates and police the fulfilling of individual line items, but rather to look to learn from state-level experiences in achieving improvements in learning outcomes, and play a facilitating role in evaluating and transferring knowledge about best practices.[26] This would also be consistent with the first principles of the optimal allocation of roles across levels of government in a federal structure, which suggest that

23. Of course, there is a trade-off here as well, and it may be important for the central government to reserve the right to intervene in the cases of states that are not making adequate progress in achieving universal education goals. Nevertheless, the importance of experimentation with solutions and customization of solutions to local contexts suggests an overall approach of centrally determined minimum goals on education outcomes, with considerable autonomy to states on how to achieve these goals.

24. This paragraph is based on Muralidharan (2011).

25. A good example of this is the wide imitation of the Government of Bihar's program to provide bicycles to girls entering secondary school.

26. An example where such an approach would have been useful is the case of Tamil Nadu shifting to a system of Activity-Based Learning (ABL) that features mixed age classrooms and organizing students by learning levels. In principle, the idea of ABL addresses some of the key pedagogical challenges of dealing with variation in learning levels that we discussed earlier. But ABL was rolled out across the Tamil Nadu with very little evaluation of the impact of this state-wide change in pedagogy on learning outcomes, which was a missed opportunity for other states (and also for Tamil Nadu) to learn more about the impact of this change.

functions having more economies of scale should reside in higher levels of government, whereas those that need to respond to local information and variation in local conditions should reside in lower levels of government (see Pritchett and Pande 2006 for further discussions on this theme).

In his public remarks at the release of the most recent ASER report in January 2012, the honorable minister for HRD, Shri Kapil Sibal, said that Pratham should take the message to chief ministers and engage with them to improve outcomes. This is exactly the right approach, but needs to be accompanied with more autonomy for states, untied funds for innovation, and more structured sharing of best practices across states. Even states might be too large a unit for making comprehensive changes quickly, and the appropriate administrative unit for experimenting with some of these ideas may be a district. In fact, a promising approach may be for a committed NGO that can bring the requisite expertise together to work in partnership with an interested state government at the level of one district (or perhaps one district each in a few states) to bring about systemic changes across the district by following the recommendations laid out here. This should be accompanied by careful evaluations of both processes and outcomes to allow comparison of the status quo and the suggested reforms to subject these reform ideas to rigorous testing and evaluation.[27]

5.3. Political Economy: Bringing Teachers on Board

Naturally, many of the reforms outlined here, especially those relating to use of contract teachers, can be expected to be met with opposition from teachers and unions. Nevertheless, it is also true that many teachers are not satisfied with the status quo (as documented in Pritchett and Murgai 2007). This view is supported in the data on teacher absence: Kremer et al. (2005) show that in Indian government schools, teachers reporting high levels of job satisfaction are *more likely* to be absent. In subsequent focus group discussions with teachers, it was suggested that this was because teachers who were able to get by with low efforts were quite satisfied, while hard-working teachers were dissatisfied because there was no difference in professional outcomes between them and those who shirked. In such a context, the provision of even small amounts of bonuses based on objective measures of performance

---

27. This is something that Pratham is already doing as seen in the results presented in Banerjee et al. (2012), but is something that can be considered and attempted more, especially by the larger nonprofits that have dedicated endowment-based funding, which will allow them to make longer-term investments in personnel and capacity needed to support governments in pilots for "systemic" transformation.

that are transparently and fairly applied could *increase* intrinsic motivation, and teacher satisfaction, which may lead to teachers favoring such a system. It could also explain how average bonuses of only 3 percent of annual pay could elicit the teacher responses that led to large gains in student learning outcomes in the APRESt experiment.

Muralidharan and Sundararaman (2011a) analyze teacher opinions on performance-linked pay and find that over 80 percent of teachers had a favorable opinion about the idea of linking a component of pay to measures of performance with over 45 percent of teachers having a *very favorable* opinion. Over 75 percent of teachers report an increase in motivation as a result of the program and 68 percent responded that the government should scale up the program implemented in Andhra Pradesh. Finally, when asked about their preferences over a series of mean-preserving spreads of pay based on performance, 75 percent of teachers reported support for at least a small portion of pay being linked to performance. What is especially interesting is that levels of teacher support for performance-pay in all these questions were significantly higher in the treatment groups than in the control groups, and thus exposure to a well-designed and communicated program increased teacher support for the idea.

Of course, the opinions of individual teachers could differ from those of teachers as a group and those of union leaders who would wield a disproportionate influence in policy conversations.[28] But, these results suggest that a well-structured career ladder based on objective measures of teacher performance supplemented by inputs from parents and community members may be implementable, especially if total compensation for existing teachers goes up as a result.

More broadly, it is essential for conversations on education reform to bring teachers on board and avoid an adversarial framing of the sort implied by discussions of "teacher accountability." Rather, it is important to highlight that all high-performing organizations have well-defined goals and feature personnel policies that reward and recognize strong performers. Thus, reforms that improve measurement of learning outcomes promote effective school leadership and management, and create career rewards for high-performing teachers which are likely to increase the professionalism of the education system and increase the respect accorded to the teaching profession.

---

28. Unions have a strong history of being against attempts to differentiate pay on the basis of productivity (Ehrenberg and Schwarz 1986).

6. Conclusion

This paper has provided a summary of the insights from a decade of high-quality empirical research on primary education in India and seeks to help bridge the gap between what we are learning from this research and the status quo of primary education policy in India.

The combination of ASER data over time and the international benchmarks provided by the latest PISA results unambiguously establish that the Indian primary schooling system is not doing an adequate job in preparing the generation of children that represents India's "Demographic Dividend" with even the basic skills that will enable them to participate in the process of India's economic growth. The research summarized in this paper highlights that simply increasing the inputs to primary education in a "business as usual" way are unlikely to change the trajectories of student learning in a meaningful way unless accompanied by significant changes in pedagogy and/or improvements in governance.

The reform agenda suggested in this paper includes some ambitious components. One is the suggestion for reevaluating the entire curriculum to see if the pace at which the school syllabus is expected to move is a feasible one for all children and to see if slowing down the curriculum and/or introducing some kind of tracking might make sense. The other is to take teacher performance measurement and management seriously. Both of these will take time to figure out the details for and the prudent approach would be to consider serious experiments at the district (or even block) level before trying to implement these ideas on a larger scale.

But there are also items in the list of recommendations that can be done more immediately. For instance, given what we now know about the low levels of learning, it is unconscionable to not make improving learning outcomes a central objective of education policy in India; a good start would be to give it prominence in the "Results Framework Document (RFD)" of MHRD. The good news is that given the (relatively) positive track record of the Indian state in making headway on numbers that are actively monitored, this step alone may catalyze creative thinking in states and districts on ways to improve indicators on learning levels. The research also strongly supports scaling up supplemental instruction programs using locally hired short-term teaching assistants that are targeted to the level of learning of the child—which should be more easily implementable.

The best approach for implementing this reform agenda would be for the central government under the 12th Plan to prioritize learning outcomes and provide states with pools of flexible funding that will allow them to experiment with ways of improving learning outcomes in a cost-effective way. The Planning Commission can help in knowledge-sharing by convening state education departments and providing them with summaries of relevant research; guidelines on what the research points to as effective ways of improving learning outcomes; and in working with states and other partners to design, implement, and evaluate district (or block) level pilots in reorienting pedagogy and governance toward a better functioning education system.

The next 10 years will see the largest ever number of citizens in the Indian school system at any point in the country's history (or future), and it is critical that this generation that represents the demographic dividend be equipped with the literacy, numeracy, and skills needed to participate fully in a rapidly modernizing world. In a fiscally constrained environment, it is also imperative to use evidence to implement *cost-effective* policies that maximize the social returns on any given level of public investment. The growing body of high-quality research on primary education in the past decade provides an opportunity to put this principle into practice.

References

Accountability Initiative. 2012. PAISA Report. New Delhi: Center for Policy Research.

Afridi, Farzana. 2010a. "Child Welfare Programs and Child Nutrition: Evidence from a Mandated School Meal Program in India," *Journal of Development Economics*, 92 (2): 152–65.

———. 2010b. The Impact of School Meals on School Participation: Evidence from Rural India. Indian Statistical Institute.

Afridi, Farzana, Bidisha Barooah, and Rohini Somanathan. 2010. School Meals and Student Participation in Urban India. Delhi School of Economics.

Andrabi, Tahir, Jishnu Das, and Asim Khwaja. 2012. Report Cards: The Impact of Providing School and Child Test-scores on Educational Markets. Harvard Kennedy School.

Atherton, Paul and Geeta Kingdon. 2010. The Relative Effectiveness and Costs of Contract and Regular Teachers in India. Institute of Education, University of London.

Banerjee, Abhijit, Rukmini Banerji, Esther Duflo, Rachel Glennerster, and Stuti Khemani. 2010. "Pitfalls of Participatory Programs: Evidence From a Randomized Evaluation in Education in India," *American Economic Journal: Economic Policy*, 2 (1): 1–30.

Banerjee, Abhijit, Rukmini Banerji, Esther Duflo, and Michael Walton. 2012. Effective Pedagogies and a Resistant Education System: Experimental Evidence on Interventions to Improve Basic Skills in Rural India. MIT.

Banerjee, Abhijit, Shawn Cole, Esther Duflo, and Leigh Linden. 2007. "Remedying Education: Evidence from Two Randomized Experiments in India," *Quarterly Journal of Economics*, 122 (3): 1235–64.

Banerjee, Abhijit and Esther Duflo. 2011. *Poor Economics*: MIT Press.

Barro, Robert J. 1991. "Economic Growth in a Cross Section of Countries," *Quarterly Journal of Economics*, 106 (2): 407–43.

Benhabib, Jess and Mark M Spiegel. 1994. "The Role of Human Capital in Development: Evidence from Aggregate Country Data," *Journal of Monetary Economics*, 34 (2): 143–74.

Borkum, Evan, Fang He, and Leigh Linden. 2010. School Libraries and Language Skills in Indian Primary Schools: A Randomized Evaluation of the Akshara Library Program. Columbia.

Chan, Jason C. K., Kathleen B. McDermott, and Henry L. Roediger III. 2006. "Retrieval-Induced Facilitation: Initially Nontested Material Can Benefit From Prior Testing of Related Material," *Journal of Experimental Psychology: General*, 135 (4): 553–71.

Chetty, Raj, John N. Friedman, and Jonah E. Rockoff. 2011. The Long-Term Impact of Teachers: Teacher Value-Added and Student Outcomes in Adulthood. Harvard.

Chin, Aimee. 2005. "Can Redistributing Teachers Across Schools Raise Educational Attainment? Evidence from Operation Blackboard in India," *Journal of Development Economics*, 78: 384–405.

Cristia, Julian P., Pablo Ibarraran, Santiago Cueto, Ana Santiago, and Eugenio Severin. 2012. Technology and Child Development: Evidence from the One Laptop Per Child Program. IZA Discussion Paper 6401.

Das, Jishnu, Stefan Dercon, James Habyarimana, Pramila Krishnan, Karthik Muralidharan, and Venkatesh Sundararaman. 2013. "School Inputs, Household Substitution, and Test Scores," *American Economic Journal: Applied Economics*, 5 (2): 29–57.

Das, Jishnu and Tristan Zajonc. 2010. "India shining and Bharat drowning: Comparing two Indian states to the worldwide distribution in mathematics achievement," *Journal of Development Economics*, 92 (2): 175–87.

Desai, Sonalde, Amaresh Dubey, Reeve Vanneman, and Rukmini Banerji. 2009. "Private Schooling in India: A New Educational Landscape," in *India Policy Forum*, Volume 5, edited by Suman Bery, Barry Bosworth, and Arvind Panagariya, pp. 1–58. New Delhi: SAGE Publications.

Duflo, Esther. 2001. "Schooling and Labor Market Consequences of School Construction in Indonesia: Evidence from an Unusual Policy Experiment," *The American Economic Review*, 91 (4): 795–813.

Duflo, Esther, Pascaline Dupas, and Michael Kremer. 2011. "Peer Effects, Teacher Incentives, and the Impact of Tracking: Evidence from a Randomized Evaluation in Kenya," *American Economic Review*, 101 (5): 1739–74.

———. 2012. School Governance, Teacher Incentives, and Pupil-Teacher Ratios: Experimental Evidence from Kenyan Primary Schools, National Bureau of Economic Research. Working Paper 17939.

Duflo, Esther, Rema Hanna, and Stephen Ryan. 2012. "Incentives Work: Getting Teachers to Come to School," *American Economic Review*, 102 (4): 1241–78.

Duraisamy, P. 2002. "Changes in Return to Education in India, 1983–94: By Gender, Age-cohort and Location," *Economics of Education Review*, 21: 609–622.

Educational Initiatives. 2010. School Learning Study. Educational Initiatives.

Ehrenberg, Ronald G., and Joshua L. Schwarz. 1986. "Public-Sector Labor Markets," in *Handbook of Labor Economics*, edited by Orley Ashenfelter and Richard Layard. Elsiever.

Glewwe, Paul, Michael Kremer, and Sylvie Moulin. 2009. "Many Children Left Behind? Textbooks and Test Scores in Kenya," *American Economic Journal: Applied Economics*, 1 (1): 112–35.

Goyal, Sangeeta and Priyanka Pandey. 2011. "Contract Teachers in India," *Education Economics*: 1–21.

Hanushek, Eric and Steve Rivkin. 2006. "Teacher Quality," in *Handbook of the Economics of Education*, edited by Eric Hanushek and Finis Welch. North-Holland.

Hanushek, Eric and Ludger Woessmann. 2008. "The Role of Cognitive Skills in Economic Development," *Journal of Economic Literature* no. 46 (3): 607–68.

———. 2010. Do Better Schools Lead to More Growth: Cognitive Skills, Economic Outcomes, and Causation. CESIfo, Munich.

He, Fang, Leigh Linden, and Margaret Macleod. 2008. Teaching What Teachers Don't Know: An Assessment of the Pratham English Language Program. UT Austin.

Jacob, Verghese, Anjini Kochar, and Suresh Reddy. 2008. School Size and Schooling Inequalities. Stanford.

Jayaraman, Rajshri, Dora Simroth, and Francis De Vericourt. 2010. The Impact of School Lunches on Primary School Enrollment: Evidence from India's Mid-Day Meal Scheme. Indian Statistical Institute.

Jensen, Robert. 2010. "The (Perceived) Returns to Education and the Demand for Schooling," *Quarterly Journal of Economics*.

———. 2012. "Do Labor Market Opportunities Affect Young Women's Work and Family Decisions? Experimental Evidence from India," *Quarterly Journal of Economics*, 127 (2): 753–92.

Kingdon, Geeta and Vandana Sipahimalani-Rao. 2010. "Para-Teachers in India: Status and Impact," *Economic and Political Weekly*, XLV (12): 59–67.

Kingdon, Geeta and Francis Teal. 2010. "Teacher Unions, Teacher Pay and Student Performance in India: A Pupil Fixed Effects Approach," *Journal of Development Economics*, 91 (2): 278–88.

Kremer, Michael, Karthik Muralidharan, Nazmul Chaudhury, F. Halsey Rogers, and Jeffrey Hammer. 2005. "Teacher Absence in India: A Snapshot," *Journal of the European Economic Association*, 3 (2–3): 658–67.

Kumar, Krishna, Manisha Priyam, and Sadhna Saxena. 2005. "The Trouble with Para-Teachers," *Frontline*, 18 (22).

Lakshminarayana, Rashmi, Alex Eble, Preetha Bhakta, Chris Frost, Peter Boone, Diana Elbourne, and Vera Mann. 2012. Support to Rural India's Public Education System: the STRIPES Cluster Randomised Trial of Supplementary Teaching, Learning Material and Additional Material Support in Primary Schools.

Lazear, Edward. 2006. "Speeding, Terrorism, and Teaching to the Test," *Quarterly Journal of Economics*, 121 (3): 1029–61.

Linden, Leigh. 2008. Complement or Substitute? The Effect of Technology on Student Achievement in India. Columbia.

Malamud, Ofer and Christian Pop-Eleches. 2011. "Home Computer Use and the Development of Human Capital," *Quarterly Journal of Economics*, 126 (2): 987–1027.

Mankiw, Gregory, David Romer, and David Weil. 1992. "A Contribution to the Empirics of Economic Growth," *Quarterly Journal of Economics*, 107 (May): 407–37.

Mukerji, Shobhini and Michael Walton. 2012. Learning the Right Lessons: Measurement, Experimentation and the Need to Turn India's Right to Education Act upside down. Harvard Kennedy School.

Munshi, Kaivan and Mark R. Rosenzweig. 2006. "Traditional Institutions Meet the Modern World: Caste, Gender, and Schooling Choice in a Globalizing Economy," *American Economic Review*, 96 (4): 1225–52.

Muralidharan, Karthik. 2011. "India's States Can be Laboratories for Policy Innovation." *Business Standard*, December 12.

———. 2012. Long Term Effects of Teacher Performance Pay: Experimental Evidence from India. UC San Diego.

Muralidharan, Karthik, Jishnu Das, Alaka Holla, Michael Kremer, and Aakash Mohpal. 2013. The Fiscal Costs of Weak Governance: Evidence from Teacher Absence in India. UC San Diego.

Muralidharan, Karthik and Michael Kremer. 2008. "Public and Private Schools in Rural India," in *School Choice International*, edited by Paul Peterson and Rajashri Chakrabarti. Cambridge: MIT.

Muralidharan, Karthik and Nishith Prakash. 2013. Cycling to School: Increasing Secondary School Enrollment for Girls in India. UC San Diego.

Muralidharan, Karthik and Venkatesh Sundararaman. 2010. "The Impact of Diagnostic Feedback to Teachers on Student Learning: Experimental Evidence from India," *Economic Journal*, 120 (546): F187–F203.

———. 2011a. "Teacher Opinions on Performance Pay: Evidence from India," *Economics of Education Review*, 30 (3): 394–403.

———. 2011b. "Teacher Performance Pay: Experimental Evidence from India," *Journal of Political Economy*, 119 (1): 39–77.

Muralidharan, Karthik and Venkatesh Sundararaman. 2013. Contract Teachers: Experimental Evidence from India. UC, San Diego.

Muralidharan, Karthik and Yendrick Zieleniak. 2013. Meauring Learning Trajectories in Developing Countries with Longitudinal Data and Item Response Theory. UC San Diego.

Nguyen, Trang. 2008. Information, Role Models, and Perceived Returns to Education: Experimental Evidence from Madagascar. MIT.

Olken, Ben. 2007. "Monitoring Corruption: Evidence from a Field Experiment in Indonesia," *Journal of Political Economy*, 115 (2): 200–49.

Pratham. 2012. *Annual Status of Education Report.*

Pritchett, Lant. 2012. The First PISA Results for India: The End of the Beginning. edited by Ajay Shah.

Pritchett, Lant and Amanda Beatty. 2012. The Negative Consequences of Over-Ambitious Curricular in Developing Countries. Harvard Kennedy School.

Pritchett, Lant and Rinku Murgai. 2007. "Teacher Compensation: Can Decentralization to Local Bodies Take India from Perfect Storm through Troubled Waters to Clear Sailing?" in *India Policy Forum*, Volume 3, edited by Suman Bery, Barry Bosworth and Arvind Panagariya, pp. 123–77. SAGE Publications.

Pritchett, Lant and Varad Pande. 2006. "Making Primary Education Work for India's Rural Poor: A Proposal for Effective Decentralization," in *Social Development Papers: South Asia Series.* New Delhi: World Bank.

PROBE Team. 1999. *Public Report on Basic Education in India.* New Delhi: Oxford University Press.

Raina, Vinod. 2013. Tests are Torture. *India Today*, January 25.

Rivkin, Steven G., Eric A. Hanushek, and John F. Kain. 2005. "Teachers, Schools, and Academic Achievement," *Econometrica*, 73 (2): 417–58.

Rockoff, Jonah E. 2004. "The Impact of Individual Teachers on Student Achievement: Evidence from Panel Data," *American Economic Review*, 94 (2): 247–52.

Schoellman, Todd. 2012. "Education Quality and Development Accounting," *Review of Economic Studies*, 79: 388–417.

Shastry, Kartini. 2012. "Human Capital Response to Globalization: Education and Information Technology in India," *Journal of Human Resources*, 47 (2): 287–330.

Shields, Robin. 2011. "ICT or I See Tea? Modernity, Technology and Education in Nepal," *Globalization, Societies, and Education*, 9 (1): 85–97.

Wilson, James Q. 1989. *Bureaucracy.* New York: Basic Books.

Comments and Discussion

Rukmini Banerji
Pratham

While empirical research on different aspects of education in India is rising, the evidence does not seem to be informing or influencing policy-making at the national level, particularly with respect to "what works" to improve student learning outcomes. In this context, Karthik has to be congratulated for putting the growing body of high quality empirical research in one place and for thinking about how to extract suggestions/inform policy in a meaningful way. It is unusual to have academics take the time to translate research to recommendations for implementation.

Placing the findings from the available recent empirical research alongside the norms stated in the Right to Education Act is an interesting exercise. The Act emphasizes inputs; it focuses on stipulated teacher–student ratios and teacher qualification norms. The Act also stresses that "age grade mainstreaming" is desired and during the school year, the "curriculum should be completed on time." The Act also assigns a major role to School Management Committees for improving the functioning of schools. The available empirical evidence summarized in the review paper suggests that none of the factors above seem to be linked to improvement of learning outcomes. While inputs and infrastructure may be a necessary condition for developing education, the evidence does not indicate that these factors will be sufficient to bring about a sea change in teaching–learning in Indian schools. At this stage, after reviewing the empirical literature, it would be fair to reach the conclusion that "more of the same" or "business as usual" is not going to lead to any major changes in one of the most critical challenges facing India today—that of dismal basic learning levels of children.

Children in Indian schools have a range of learning needs—"remedial education" is certainly needed but this needs to be placed against a broader landscape of what primary education should achieve if a child spends five continuous years in school. The learning needs of children in primary school in India can be categorized in the following way:

- Preschool year(s) : School readiness skills are needed (reading readiness, number readiness) for getting ready to enter into Grade 1.

- Grade 1–2: Foundational skills—basic reading, basic arithmetic, expression—need to be built in these early years so that the foundations of learning are strong and children can build on these basic skills in later years and other domains.
- Grade 3 to 5: A large majority of Indian children who have reached these grades have learning levels that are not even at the standards expected of them in Grade 2. Large-scale, serious "catch up" action is needed across the country to give these children a fighting chance to complete elementary education in a meaningful way.
- Grade level capability: Especially in Grade 3, 4, and 5, children need to be helped not only to reach Grade 2 level but also to get to capabilities expected of them at their grade.

Against the backdrop of what needs to be done, how do we see the current realities of our schools and classrooms? Three structural elements stare at us in the face in any typical rural school in India:[29]

- Mixed age group: It is assumed that children in a given grade/class are homogenous. The Right to Education Law refers to age-grade mainstreaming assuming again that children of a particular age are to be in a particular grade. The reality is that our classrooms are very diverse. Let us take an example: Grade 4 in Bihar. Based on the assumption that children enter school at age six (which in itself is a faulty assumption), we presume that the "right age" for Grade 4 is about nine or ten. Annual Status of Education Report (ASER) 2012 data from Bihar shows that 51 percent children in Standard 4 are of the "right age" (nine or ten), about one quarter are older and another one quarter are younger. If the rationale for ensuring that children of the right age are in the right grade is based on principles of child development, then half of all children in Bihar are not in the "right grade at the right age."
- Mixed grades: The Right to Education (RTE) assumption that children must be "mainstreamed" into an age-grade appropriate class again is built on the notion of homogeneity by grade. Data from ASER surveys 2009 to 2012 indicate that the proportion of children sitting in mixed-grade classrooms is rising over time. (Approximately 14,000 to 15,000 government schools with primary sections in rural areas are visited during each year's ASER survey.) For example, in 2009, the

29. For a detailed discussion of these issues, see http://ideasforindia.in/article. aspx?article_id=63.

percentage of Grade 2 children sitting in a class which had at least another grade if not more was close to 59 percent. That figure has gone up to almost 63 percent by 2012. Similar figures for Grade 4 (that is, Grade 4 children sitting with children of other grades) has risen from about 51 percent in 2009 to 57 percent in 2012.

- Mixed learning levels in any grade: The reality of Indian classrooms is that children in the same grade at often at vastly varying levels of learning. Take for example Grade 5 according to ASER 2012 for rural India: The highest level of the ASER reading test is a long paragraph at Grade 2 level of difficulty. We find that 47 percent of children in Grade 5 are able to read this text fluently. It is possible that some of these children are reading at a higher level as well. However, we should be seriously concerned about the half that in Grade 5 not yet able to read at Grade 2 level. Looking carefully at this half, we find that in Grade 5 there are 17 percent children who are as yet not able to do more than simply recognize letters. Another 15 percent can read simple words but cannot effectively tackle simple sentences. 21 percent children can read simple sentences but cannot read as yet fluently read at Grade 2 level. The "age-grade" assumption also implies that a child in any grade/class has mastered content and skills expected in previous grade/class. But ASER and other data shows that this is not the case; most children are at least two grades behind, if not more.

Weighing the needs and the realities, it is critical that as a country we think about what policies are needed to immediately influence practice. Two immediate actions come to mind: first, we need to clearly articulate phase-wise learning goals rather than grade-wise standards or expectations. For example, as a country we need to know what children should be able to do by end of the second year of schooling and then again by the end of the fifth year of schooling. Second, in the early years in school, the focus of all teaching–learning activity needs to be on basic skills (like reading, number recognition, operations, problem solving, expression) as learning goals rather than "knowledge" or subject matter.

The review paper outlines and summarizes learnings from several important domains of research—on teachers and on parents.

Karthik's paper has reviewed the empirical evidence on teachers in terms of class size, student–teacher ratios, absenteeism and incentive/performance. Given the thrust in RTE and actions that are visible in many states, especially educationally backward states, on teacher recruitment, preparation and capacity building, it is clear that much more research and evidence is needed on a variety of issues that connects the capability of teachers to teach with the classroom processes and learning outcomes. For example, how to measure and understand teachers' capability to teach?[30] How to raise the efficacy of training on teachers' ability to translate what they have learned into effective action in the classroom? Almost all states have carried out teacher eligibility tests in the last few years; this data is now available and needs to be analyzed. The large outlays on teachers by central and state governments needs to be matched by much more research that can help us understand how teacher training can lead to better student performance.

On parents, the literature that has been reviewed in the paper has been mostly on parental decision-making—tuition, school choice (vouchers, cash transfers), participation in accountability/governance. Here too, there is need for deeper investigations on a number of related topics. For example, we do not know much about how different kinds of parents in India understand and interpret "what learning means" or how to support their children to learn better. Earlier work done by Banerjee et al. in rural Jaunpur district in Uttar Pradesh indicated how parents overestimate what their children know.[31] Recent research with young mothers in low-literacy areas of Purnia district in Bihar and Ajmer district in Rajasthan suggests that illiterate mothers or mothers with little schooling have very little idea of what their children do or learn in school and rarely engage with issues of learning either with their children or with the schools.[32]

Today India has close to universal school enrollment of children. This is the result of years of work with schools and communities: parents demanding schooling and government providing access. Extensive efforts on the demand and supply side of the equation have led to clear outcomes and clear understanding of what schooling means. Even illiterate parents in remote areas of India will be explained that schooling is important. But as the country moves beyond schooling toward learning, we are all at the early stages of the learning curve—in our understanding of what "learning" implies and of how to get there. In this context, parents are extremely important. It is their understanding and their aspirations that will drive the future of educational quality in India.

---

30. See work done by Geeta Kingdon and Rukmini Banerji in the SchoolTELLS study that studied teaching and learning in government and private schools of Uttar Pradesh and Bihar and assessed teacher capability for teaching.

31. See http://www.povertyactionlab.org/evaluation/can-informational-campaigns-raise-awareness-and-local-participation-primary-education-ind.

32. See http://www.povertyactionlab.org/evaluation/impact-mother-literacy-and-participation-programs-child-learning-india.

Toward the end of his paper, Karthik bravely tackles another fundamental question on the thorny path from research to action: Why does evidence not translate into policy or practice? He points to the lack of culture of quantitative research in the education community as a possible reason. This question is a bigger one that needs wider discussion. Perhaps part of the answer is that the country has been focused for such a long time on providing and tracking inputs and there is no history of thinking of outcomes as important nor is there any priority given to measuring outcomes. Perhaps this is why there is not much openness to learning how different paths may lead to better outcomes.

Parth J. Shah
Centre for Civil Society

Shekhar asked me last night whether I would fill in for Abhijit Banerjee, who is likely to be delayed in getting to the conference. I thought that I have two things common with Abhijit, we both are PhDs and we have a recently born child, so we have personal interest in education. So I said yes! I read the paper only last night. Karthik and I have been talking about education reform ideas for a while and as he says, most of these ideas have been presented before, by Lant Prichett for example. The School Choice Campaign that we have been running since 2007 also offers similar reform ideas. Of course in 2007 we did not have the benefit of much of the research that Karthik himself has done and cited in the paper. A couple of ideas that the School Choice Campaign talked about but the paper does not—one, school vouchers and charter schools, and two, converting all government funding of schools to a per student basis. Instead of giving lump-sum grant, the funding of government schools and private-aided schools should be based on the number of students in the school.

I fully agree with Karthik on all his reform ideas. I would focus on the politics of reform—the weight of empirical evidence on the one hand versus the ideology on the other. The most challenging issue is how we can take empirical evidence either done in India or abroad and begin to engage with educationists and policy-makers and how could that then begin to change the discourse on the issue of outcomes, on the issue of teacher accountability and many of those which are highlighted in this paper.

I highlight a couple of things which could help the discussion in terms of the politics of reform. This is based on the public policy courses and seminars that we run for college students, journalists, and NGO leaders.

The first learning is the story you tell around the empirical evidence. People remember stories, and through that the evidence, hopefully! And I will give you one example of it. I have presented much of the evidence that Karthik cites to various audiences, educationists, editors of newspapers, and magazines and I ask them a few days later, what do they remember from the discussion of the data that was presented to them. The one story they always remember, which unfortunately is not in the paper, is this Jishnu Das study in Pakistan. One question people have about reforms that rely on parental choice is how wise the parents are in their ability to make decisions about which schools are good for their children. So, the capacity to choose schools and does that capacity exist among mostly illiterate and semi-literate parents that we have in much of India. Jishnu Das had this study in Pakistan where he asked parents in a small town to rank schools in that town in terms of what they thought was the quality of the school. After he got the ranking from the parents, he sent education experts to the same set of schools and got them to rank the schools by their expert standards. Once he got the two sets of rankings, one from the parents and the other from the experts, he then compared those two sets of ranking and it turned out that the coefficient of correlation was close to 0.9. That kind of story and evidence is always remembered. So the challenge is how we convert much of the evidence in Karthik's paper in a format that appeals to the instinct and the first principles of many of the players in the policy-making process. That is a bigger challenge not just in terms of translating into Hindi and taking it to larger audiences but also finding ways of making them more appealing, more intuitive to the audience and so that they will remember that evidence when they sit down at the table to discuss and debate policy ideas. The story-telling is critical in using research and evidence to further more reform-oriented discourse in education.

Educationists are focused on inputs, and not on learning outcomes. Among the many reasons that Karthik provides for the focus on inputs, one more is the genuine belief that in a vast country like India, the only way to guarantee education of quality is to standardize it, make it uniform. The RTE Act is the culmination of that belief. So whether you are in Bombay or Bolangir you would have the same kind of school, the infrastructure would be the same, the teacher qualification and training would be the same, the teacher salary and remuneration would be the same. It is the old-factory model of production. Standardize all inputs and you will be able to assure same quality across this vast land. I think that belief is the central part of the debate in terms of quality. Karthik points out that all the evidence goes against the input focus. But then educationists wonder, how else one could standardize and make all schools uniform, since that is the way to provide equal quality across diverse India.

How do we promote the idea of diversity and liberalization as a way to achieve quality, is the key question in this debate. I think that is where we don't really have as much research and evidence as to what are the ways in which we can diversify, what are the ways in which we can allow the people to make decisions on their own and thereby create better competitive environment and hopefully create better quality education at more affordable prices. The private sector provision of education is diverse; there is a range of schools from ₹50 a month to ₹50,000 a month! There is no uniformity or standardization. That's the reason educationists detest private provision. If we had convincing evidence that private sector delivers better quality education at lower cost then how much weight and effort do you want to put on improving the state education system? Since we have finite intellectual and advocacy resources, the question I struggle within our School Choice Campaign is how much do we focus on improving the state system versus the efforts to liberalize and support the private provision of education. As we know, we have the largest private sector education system in the world. What kind of evidence would help us decide this question? Need Karthik's expert help!

Maybe the last couple of points are in terms of the specifics of the reforms in the paper. One is about contract teachers versus civil service teachers. Karthik argues that all new teachers should be contract teachers and only after a certain period of performance and assessment, the successful ones should be made permanent. Lant Prichett talks about decentralization of teacher hiring. The question I have is why not go all the way and empower individual schools to hire their own teachers? The schools may be required to follow some common norms but the final decision remains at the school level.

Would all the proposed reforms, including that of hiring at the school level, achieve the ultimate goal of quality if they are not accompanied by more autonomy for schools in running their day-to-day affairs? In private schools, principals are leaders of the school. Don't we need to make state school principals genuine school leaders as opposed to simply higher-level bureaucrats? Is there any evidence, national or international, that can help us build the case for hiring at school level and of more autonomy and school leadership?

I agree with Karthik's idea that states should be the laboratories for experimentation and then taking the evidence and convincing larger audience about what works and what does not work. However we need to go one step further. My experience with different audiences suggests that people habitually discount evidence by either "India is not US or Sweden," or even for Indian data, by "India is not Delhi, or Andhra Pradesh!" So, one step further is how we can encourage schools of education, of Economics and other social science departments to actually generate evidence at the local level in their own ways. These studies may not be as sophisticated as randomized controlled trial (RCTs), the new gold standard, but it could generate evidence locally which would become more acceptable to local participants in the debate and thereby could have more influence on the final decisions on policy.

On the issue of parents, as Rukmini pointed out, not much has been said in the paper. The only tool we have under RTE to improve state schools is the School Management Committees (SMCs), where parents are supposed to play a dominant role. The question I have is: What evidence do we have on whether state education systems have improved by increased parental involvement? To the best of my knowledge, there is little evidence. Would SMCs actually make any difference in the quality of state schools?

The last point, different pedagogies and different learning styles of students. There are multiple pedagogies/curricula—Rishi Valley, Montessori, Waldorf-Steiner, IB, CBSE, and several elite private schools claim to have their own unique approach. Children also have different ways of learning. Can we go completely outside the box and allow children to choose what kind of school they want to go to, meaning which pedagogies they find more suitable to their learning preferences? Is there a way of matching pedagogy with learning style of the student? Does that then allow more experimentation, more liberalization, and more diversity within the education system?

I hope I have raised enough interesting questions for Karthik to stay busy! Thank you.

Abhijit Banerjee
Massachusetts Institute of Technology

This is in many ways a model of how a policy paper should be written. The issue is important and sharply posed. The evidence is discussed and some clear and sharp conclusions are drawn. The policy recommendations build on these, but also try to be realistic, and toward the end, Karthik, drawing on his experience of working within the system, lays out some specific recommendations for how to reform primary education.

The evidence he summarizes offers a simple but somewhat frightening message. The education establishment In India whose views are embodied in the RTE Act is obsessed with school inputs—better buildings, higher paid teachers and so on. Yet there is no evidence of correlation between school inputs and school outcomes. This is consistent with quasi-experimental evidence such as that in Banerjee et al. (2007) on Mumbai and Vadodara, showing that doubling the teacher–student ratio without changing pedagogy has no effect on test scores, as well as evidence from randomized control trials in Rajasthan and Kenya. In both of these cases class sizes were quite large to start with—40 in India and 80 in Kenya—so the lack of an impact was not because class size was already very small. Nevertheless a part of the reason why teacher availability does not matter is probably misallocation—teachers put a lot of effort into making sure that they get posted to urban locations, with the consequences that some schools have no teachers and some have more teachers than they probably need. Operation Blackboard, the one major educational initiative taken by the central government in the 1980s, was a lot about trying to reduce the number of one-teacher schools by reallocating teachers: Chin (2005) shows that this lead to greater school completion rates among girls and the poor.

However another factor behind the lack of correlation between school inputs (such as the teacher–student ratio) and school outcomes is almost surely teacher effort. In India the private schools that attract the most motivated children from poor families are often inferior to the government schools in terms of both buildings and teacher pay, but generate better learning outcomes. Of course this could be purely because of selection—clearly parents need to be especially motivated to spend money when free schooling is available. However, Karthik and co-authors have shown in a paper, which is not yet public, that this is not the whole story. Their preliminary results from an experiment where some families got vouchers to send their children to private schools suggest that there are no systematic differences between public and private schools in terms of learning outcomes, but private schools are much cheaper to run. It follows that the extra inputs that the government schools are provided with are either useless or at least less useful than the benefits from whatever teachers are doing differently in private schools.

Karthik has an answer to the question of what they are doing differently—they are working harder. Teacher absence rates are clearly lower in private schools than in government schools and other measures of effort are also consistent with this view. Karthik's own work suggests that a part of the reason is incentives. Muralidharan and Sundaram (2013) show that contract teachers in government schools in Andhra Pradesh who still face the risk of being fired are about 40 percent less likely to be absent than civil service teachers who have secured jobs. They also show that the estimates of test score gains from adding a contract teacher to a government school are substantial, suggesting that these teachers are no less effective than the civil service teachers in terms of learning gains and despite being less trained, less experienced, and paid only about twenty percent of what the latter get paid. In other words, the whole push toward better paid teachers under the RTE Act is a waste of money—these teachers are already dramatically overpaid relative to their outside options as Lant Pritchett and Rinku Murgai have shown in an earlier issue of this journal, and deliver no more than their much less paid colleagues. Karthik rightly discusses the possible routes to changing the contracting environment for teachers.

However the most striking fact that Karthik's work unearths is that much of traditional incentives discussion somewhat misses the point. Muralidharan and Sundaraman (2011) show that very small incentives (3 percent of the annual salary) have very large effects on test scores, especially over the longer run. But then why don't teachers in private schools who presumably face much stronger incentives—there are many schools in the average village and parents can vote with their feet—adopt whatever these incentivized government teachers were doing and therefore do much better than the average government school? The same question can also be asked with respect to the various pedagogical interventions that Pratham carries out with the help of unpaid volunteers—broadly described as teaching at the right level—which also seem to generate very large gains in test scores at minimal cost. Why doesn't every private school adopt these and substantially boost performance?

My best guess is that the answer lies in the tyranny of the syllabus. Both teachers and parents seem to be sold on the idea that schools are primarily responsible for covering the syllabus, even if that means that children don't learn anything. Given that many of the students in Indian schools are some approximation of first-generation learners, one would imagine that a lot of the time in the early grades are devoted to making sure that everyone is up to speed on the basic skills, but this seems not to be the case: data suggests that a lot of the children fall behind almost immediately and progressively lag further and further till they finally give up and drop out. Whenever I have asked teachers why they do not do anything about it, their standard excuse is that the syllabus needs to be covered—while this may not be literally true, school systems allow little or no time or encouragement to step outside the curriculum and pursue learning for every child.

But if devotion to the syllabus all around is the main reason why children are not learning much even in private schools (since this is what parents want and private schools have to be oblige them, there is no reason to expect private schools to teach very differently from government schools and indeed the evidence suggests that they don't), then what do we do about it? A part of the answer is to set aside some time in the current program to focus on basic skills. The fact that this is easy enough to do even without a radical reform of the program is suggested by the fact that Karthik's incentivized teachers could do it while working within the existing system. Indeed both Punjab and Haryana have now implemented something along these lines. However, ultimately we would want a more thoroughgoing reform of the system, which puts universal acquisition of basic skills front and center. Getting parents to reset their expectations from the school system would be an important first step here. The obsession with the syllabus has a lot do with the focus on the final school-leaving exam that has historically been the gateway to good jobs. This is an exam where children are supposed to be examined on the entire syllabus.

Poor parents, however, do not seem to realize that very few children from their kinds of families will get far enough through the system to get to striking distance of the job that requires an educational qualification, especially these days when its common to go to college as well before looking for a job. A vast majority will drop out long before that. For these children, the fact that the syllabus was covered is neither here nor there—it is much more important to acquire basic skills. Persuading these parents as well teachers and educational administrators to recognize that these basic skills have value and therefore deserve their attention has to be central to any attempt to reform the system, as much as the reform of incentives and pay that Karthik emphasizes.

General Discussion

Narendra Jadhav (Chair) kicked off the session by congratulating NCAER for choosing education to start the 2012 Indian Policy Forum (IPF) with. This would be very timely, since the Planning Commission was putting together the final set of documents for the 12th Five-year Plan and the guidance from the paper, the discussants comments, and the floor discussion would be very important for finalizing the plan relating to education. Having heard the presentation by Karthik Muralidharan, he felt that the paper would be a game-changer.

Karthik Muralidharan replied that in many ways it was most appropriate that NCAER was sponsoring this paper. This research agenda had started for him exactly 10 years ago with the first NCAER–NBER Neemrana Conference that he attended, in December 2001 when he was a first-year graduate student. And it was exactly 10 years ago this summer that he had come to India to start his fieldwork, the first round of which got him interested in service delivery in education.

Meeta Sengupta asked, assuming that teacher abilities are central to the learning process, if there was any evidence relating teacher cohorts to learning outcomes. Teachers learn from their peer group, whether they learn absenteeism or how to be a better teacher. Is there anything that correlates this group learning to student learning outcomes?

T. N. Srinivasan asked the question: Why does India not experiment at the provincial or state level in education? In China, this is what they have done, right from the household responsibility system. Systems developed from the bottom-up rather than from the top-down. Going further, he asked why not experiment at the panchayat level, given how big the Indian states are? He suggested that if the ultimate aim is to improve learning outcomes, the paper could go even beyond what it has done, and frame its questions in even broader terms such as these and recommend policies and actions. He felt this was a time to be bold.

Govinda Rao suggested it would be useful to look at the Bihar experiment of appointing para-teachers or *Shiksha Mitras*. Elementary school teachers are appointed at the village panchayat level, middle school teachers at the block level, and high school teachers at the district level. This has virtually killed the "industry" of ad hoc teacher appointments and transfers in Bihar. A second question is what the standardization that is part of the Sarva Shiksha Abhiyaan is doing to the cost of providing education at the state level. Third, work that Rao was doing shows that states are substituting their resources in education and healthcare using the transfers from the Center.

Sheetal Sekhri wondered, given that there is a lot of heterogeneity in what students know in a classroom, whether there was student tracking that would shed light on learning trajectories. Why are teachers not routinely evaluated by students in India as happens in many other countries? This could make the teachers more accountable, could help to curb absenteeism, could help in how they teach, and could be a very low-cost intervention.

Devesh Kapur asked if learning outcomes would be better or worse if there was no Human Resource Development (HRD) ministry? Narendra Jhadav in the Chair asked tongue-in-cheek if he would like to also add the Planning Commission to the question.

Sonalde Desai asked if we had any evidence on variance within schools versus variance across schools. We know that kids from certain backgrounds—dalits, adivasi, Muslim, children with parents with little education—suffer substantial disadvantage. It is not clear what is happening: Is it that they are going to the wrong schools, is it that schools are discriminating, or is it that parental input is relatively low, so that the returns to education are lower? This should be easy to address by looking at variance within and between schools.

Dilip Mookherjee wondered how nationally representative was the Andhra Pradesh evidence. To what extent are the findings about the lack of impact of inputs and curriculum valid nationally— a question that is important before we start deciding on national education policy. Second, if you transfer some responsibility to states and local governments for experimentation, aren't there the usual concerns about willingness as well as capacity of local communities to monitor or improve educational standards? Don't we need some kind of centralized monitoring and perhaps the threat to take over from local communities the schools that are falling behind?

Karthik Muralidharan thanked discussants for their excellent comments. Education is probably the most critical enabler of inclusive growth, contributing both to inclusion and to growth. Education and human capital are needed for aggregate growth and you need to make sure that education is widely available for the poorest to access the fruits of this growth. There was also a growing literature showing that what matters for both components of this inclusive agenda is not so much years of schooling as much as actual knowledge and skills. There is a growing body of high-quality empirical research in India over the past 10 years on all this. The motivation in many ways for this paper was that the *status quo* education policy simply does not reflect what we have learnt. There is, of course, good reason for this because it takes times for ideas to permeate from research into the policy domain. This is my attempt to try and bridge this gap between where the research and the policy is.

On Rukmini Banerji's comments, Karthik agreed completely about the importance of the early ages. One result he did not talk about is that even though the pupil–teacher issue overall did not seem to matter that much, they find very strong correlation between the PTR and value addition in Grade 1, and thereafter a very clear declining impact between Grade 1 and Grade 5. So, even within the existing framework, a relatively low-hanging fruit would be to have much smaller class sizes in Class 1 where the children would be socialized into the process of learning. Currently, the way workload gets allocated, multigrade teaching situations can often mean Grade 1 and Grade

5 are combined because teachers and schools are allocating kids to equalize load amongst the teachers, not thinking of learning impacts.

Karthik agreed with Banerji that there were many very-low–cost ways of identifying effective teachers. Focus groups in Andhra Pradesh under the sponsorship of the district collector of Hyderabad show that teachers most often think that if they are qualified they must be a good teacher, whereas in practice there are simple things that can be done to identify whether somebody is a good teacher.

What are the two things that should feature centrally on primary education in the 12th Five-year Plan? Karthik suggested, first, that there is enough evidence that it would be unconscionable for learning outcomes not to be a central objective of the 12th Plan. In bureaucracies, what gets measured is what gets done. Second, the Plan must emphasize incentives for government staff and experimentation at different levels of government to spur innovation. In China, incentives are incredibly central for government workers and their entire career trajectory depends on their performance. The centrality of experimentation across jurisdictions is also remarkable. India needs to marry central guidelines that Delhi thinks are warranted with a certain amount of flexible money for states and districts to pursue something that they feel will work better as long as it is well-documented and the government continues to monitor outcomes at the Central level.

Responding to the issue raised by Abhijit Banerjee about children also as an input into schooling, Karthik noted that there is a set of interventions at the student and parent level that can have high returns. The traditional view has been that parents matter but policy-makers don't control parents. Increasingly, the literature is finding that relatively low-cost interventions on the parental side, that provide them information and some opportunities for meeting and some training, can have a big impact. A way of thinking about this is that the reason the marginal return to parental training is higher than the marginal return to teacher training is that the parents have much better incentives to act on their knowledge than the teacher.

Addressing Dilip Mookherjee's point on external validity, Karthik noted that on remedial instruction, there are now four different studies in Uttar Pradesh, Uttaranchal, Mumbai, and Baroda that are finding similar results.

On Abhijit Banerjee's question about why small incentives sometimes produce such big results, Karthik suggested that the qualitative research can give useful insights. External incentives are sometimes thought of as crowding out intrinsic motivation. In India, the lack of differentiation based on teacher performance has been highly demotivating. Teachers are enthusiastic when they join, but 10 years later it is all gone. In such circumstances, even modest increases in pay that reward teachers on some objective measure of outcomes can have deep impact. It is actually crowding in intrinsic motivation. The framing is important because the framing of the incentive programs we implemented was framed less in terms of "accountability," which would create an adversarial framing between administrators and teachers, but more in terms of "recognizing and rewarding excellent teaching," which appears to have crowded in intrinsic motivation for teachers.

Narenda Jadhav concluded the session by noting that with this thought-provoking session, the challenge now is to convert this empirical research into policy-making, starting with the 12th Plan. He said he was going to take a lot with him and this would involve a lot of rewriting of the education chapter in the 12th Five-year Plan. He again thanked Karthik for an outstanding, game-changing paper.

References

Banerjee, A., Shawn Cole, Esther Duflo, and Leigh Linden. 2007. "Remedying Education: Evidence from Two Randomized Experiments in India," *The Quarterly Journal of Economics*, 122 (3): 1235–64.

Chin, A. 2005. "Can Redistributing Teachers Across Schools Raise Educational Attainment? Evidence from Operation Blackboard in India," *Journal of Development Economics*, 78, December.

Muralidharan, K. and V. Sundararaman. 2011. "Teacher Performance Pay: Experimental Evidence from India," *Journal of Political Economy,* 119 (1): 39–77.

———. 2013. *Contract Teachers: Experimental Evidence from India.* UC San Diego.

Murgai, R. and L. Pritchett. 2006–07. "Teacher Compensation: Can Decentralization to Local Bodies Take India from the Perfect Storm through Troubled Waters to Clear Sailing?" India Policy Forum.

DEAN SPEARS
Princeton University, NCAER, and Delhi School of Economics

Policy Lessons from the Implementation of India's Total Sanitation Campaign*

ABSTRACT Ending widespread open defecation and pursuing feasible methods of safe excreta disposal must be the top policy priorities for India. This paper draws policy lessons from the first 10 years of latrine construction under India's Total Sanitation Campaign (TSC), which was a flagship program of the Indian government. The TSC improved average health and human capital among Indian children where it was implemented, but sanitation coverage remains substantially incomplete. Indeed, the first 10 years of the TSC, on average, prevented an infant death for a few thousand dollars, a comparatively very inexpensive average cost. This initial success is in part due to the Clean Village Prize or Nirmal Gram Puraskar (NGP), an incentive for village governments. Heterogeneity in the intensity and effectiveness of TSC implementation suggests that the additional benefits of extending effective TSC implementation to the many remaining Indian children would probably substantially exceed the additional costs. Therefore, as the TSC becomes the Nirmal Bharat Abhiyan, India should not miss the opportunity to invest in successful principles of total sanitation: quality data, effective monitoring, and motivational ex post incentives.

Keywords: *Health, Sanitation, Infant Mortality, Child Height, Open Defecation, Total Sanitation Campaign*

JEL Classification: *O12, I15*

1. Introduction

Open defecation is a large global problem, but it is substantially and importantly an Indian problem. About 60 percent of the approximately 1 billion people worldwide who defecate openly live in India.[1]

1. According to internationally standardized DHS data, open defecation in India in 2005 occurred at a comparable rate to in Namibia in 1992, and was much more common than in Zimbabwe in 1994 or Zambia in 1992.

* *dspears@princeton.edu*

Although open defecation may seem remote in some parts of India's modern cities, 600 million people in India—over half of the population—defecate openly. Without a toilet or latrine, they simply go outside. Widespread open defecation has major consequences for health and human capital in India.

This paper draws policy lessons from the first 10 years of latrine construction under India's TSC, from 2001 to 2011. The TSC was a "flagship" program of the central Indian government and represented a large effort to improve rural sanitation: over the approximately 10-year period studied, it reported building one latrine per 10 rural people in India. The TSC was designed to improve upon perceived shortcomings of earlier programs: instead of emphasizing subsidies for building infrastructure, it included an ex post monetary incentive[2] for local political leaders to eliminate open defecation and made use of village social structures.

Ending widespread open defecation and pursuing feasible methods of safe excreta disposal must be top policy priorities for India. TSC was been able to improve health and human capital among Indian children, on average, where it was implemented, but sanitation coverage remains substantially incomplete. Indeed, the first 10 years of India's TSC, on average, prevented an infant death for a few thousand dollars, a comparatively very inexpensive average cost. This initial success is in part due to the Clean Village Prize or Nirmal Gram Puraskar (NGP), the incentive for village governments to eliminate open defecation. Heterogeneity in the intensity and effectiveness of TSC implementation suggests that the additional benefits of extending effective TSC implementation to the many remaining Indian children would probably substantially exceed the additional costs. Therefore, as the TSC becomes the Nirmal Bharat Abhiyan, India should not miss the opportunity to invest in successful principles of total sanitation: quality data, effective monitoring, and motivational ex post incentives.

1.1. Policy Lessons

This paper will explain and review evidence for seven policy lessons drawn from data about sanitation in India and econometric analysis of the impact of the TSC. These conclusions are presented alongside their evidence throughout the paper, and are summarized here:

---

2. Some government TSC documents about the TSC refer to what economists call "subsidies" as "incentives"; this paper will follow standard economics terminology in calling the NGP—a conditional, ex post reward—an incentive.

Policy Lesson 1. Improving sanitation—meaning safe excreta disposal—must be a top priority for India. Because open defecation has negative externalities, it is everybody's problem, and requires government action.

Policy Lesson 2. By promoting and incentivizing latrine use, the TSC has had positive initial impacts on children's health and human capital.

Policy Lesson 3. Publicly supported sanitation with an ex post incentive to motivate use can be a comparatively very inexpensive way to save babies' lives.

Policy Lesson 4. Villages are a critical level of governance for sanitation intervention.

Policy Lesson 5. Incentives to local leaders for outcomes are useful and should be strengthened by both increasing the monetary incentive and devoting resources to ensure accurate evaluation and adjudication.

Policy Lesson 6. The additional benefit of extending effective sanitation implementation to remaining Indian children would probably substantially exceed the additional cost.

Policy Lesson 7. Achieving total sanitation coverage will require both safeguarding the quality of administrative data—perhaps by providing resources for data sources that bypass bureaucratic interests—and investing in large datasets about health outcomes.

1.2. Overview

This paper reviews and integrates recent papers by the author about sanitation in rural India and adds several new analyses. Therefore, this paper will cover a wide range of topics important to rural sanitation policy in India. Table A in the Appendix briefly summarizes the prior papers incorporated here.

Section 2 presents evidence on the importance of sanitation for health and human capital, and the costs of open defecation. Section 3 reviews research on the effects of the TSC on health and human capital, and computes that the first ten years of the TSC will have prevented an average infant death for only a few thousand dollars. Section 4 documents that villages are a critical level of governance for the implementation of sanitation improvements. Section 5 studies heterogeneity among Indian states in the effectiveness of TSC latrines, and concludes that there is still much room and need for further effort. Section 6 concludes, reviewing policy opportunities as the TSC becomes the Nirmal Bharat Abhiyan (NBA).

2. The Primacy of Sanitation

When this paper refers to "sanitation," it will mean safe excreta disposal in particular (not, for example, water supply or disposal of household trash). There are many constraints on health and development in rural India; among these, why should open defecation be a priority? First, sanitation coverage is particularly poor in India, relative to other countries at similar levels of development. Second, germs from unsafely disposed of feces cause chronic illness and adverse changes in the lining of the intestines of small children, importantly keeping them from growing and developing at critical early ages. Third, these early life health deficits have life-long consequences for human capital, including for achieving adult cognitive potential. Each reason will be considered in turn.

2.1. Suggestions from Aggregate Comparisons

Historians have long used height as a measure of well-being (Steckel 2009). However, a puzzle has recently emerged: modern differences across developing countries in GDP per capita do not very well explain differences in average height (Deaton 2007). In particular, people in Africa are taller than their level of economic development would predict, and people in India are much shorter. This puzzle does not appear to be explained by international differences in genetic height potential: although the median Indian child is two standard deviations below the international reference population, the best-off Indian children meet international norms (Bhandari et al. 2002).

Spears (2012b) observes that international variation in open defecation offers one solution to the puzzle. The analysis collapses each of the 140 Directorate of Health Services (DHS) survey rounds with height and sanitation data into one observation, so a country-year is an observation. The analysis finds that sanitation coverage alone explains 54 percent of the cross-country variation in the height of children under three years old. India, with relatively short children and high levels of open defecation, falls squarely on the regression line. Moreover, open defecation may be particularly dangerous in India because—even in rural India—population density is very high.

Across DHS survey-years, each additional percentage point of household sanitation coverage is associated with an increase in height approximately equal to 0.01 standard deviations of height in the international reference population. This result is not driven by time trends, fixed heterogeneity across countries, or any single world region, and is robust to the inclusion of a range of control variables, including for gross domestic product (GDP). No similar effect is found of other plausible cross-country differences, such as electrification, water supply, political autocracy, and Food and Agriculture Organization (FAO) estimates of average calorie deficits.

Figure 1 reports a similar analysis, comparing Indian states in a cross section using the NFHS-3, the 2005–06 round of India's DHS. Rural and urban parts of states are collapsed separately, so each circle is either the rural or urban population of a state, with the area of the circle proportional to the size of the population it represents. There is a clear negative slope: within India, in places with more open defecation, children are shorter, on average. The two circles well above the line are urban and rural Tamil Nadu. The largest circle, at the bottom-right, is rural Uttar Pradesh.

FIGURE 1.   Differences in Sanitation across Indian States Explain Children's Height

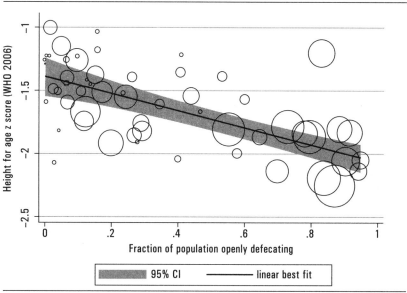

Source: Author.

Table 1 verifies the statistical significance of this relationship. The association between open defecation and children's height-for-age is essentially unchanged when state fixed effects are added, so the regression is focused on the difference between rural and urban parts of the same state. This suggests that the result is not driven by unobserved state-level heterogeneity in genetic potential, governance, or other differences. Heterogeneity in sanitation coverage appears to be an important determinant of difference in height across Indian states. Of course, this correlation is not itself enough to establish a causal effect of sanitation; that will be the goal of Section 3.

TABLE 1. Height-for-age of Children under 3 and Sanitation, OLS

Height-for-age z-score:	(1)	(2)	(3)
Open defecation	−0.660***	−0.598***	−0.555***
	(0.164)	(0.110)	(0.0701)
State fixed effects			ü
Weights	population	none	population
n (rural/urban state parts)	58	58	58
R²	0.391	0.326	0.961

Source: Author.
Note: Standard errors in parentheses; 29 states; * $p < 0.05$, ** $p < 0.01$, *** $p < 0.001$.

2.2. The Lasting Consequences of Early Life Health

Disease early in life has lasting consequences for human capital (Almond and Currie, 2011). Evidence is accumulating that poor health and inadequate nutrition in early life cause persistent deficits in cognitive development and ability (e.g., Case and Paxson 2010). Cunha, Heckman, and Schennach (2010) advocate that policy invest in very young children's cognitive skills, based on evidence of temporarily high returns on such investment at early ages.

Much of this research has focused on rich countries, but the life-long health and human capital costs of early life disease may be even greater in a developing country such as India. Spears (2012c) considers the correlation between height-for-age and cognitive achievement using National Council of Applied Economic Research's (NCAER's) 2005 India Human Development Survey (IHDS) data. Although there is a positive slope between height and cognitive achievement among children in the US—taller eight- to eleven-year-olds are a little more likely to be able to read—this slope is at least twice as steep among Indian children. The analysis then controls for matched household-level data from the 1990s, which suggests that household-level sanitation and hygiene may be an important omitted variable explaining this slope. Because childhood cognitive skills predict adult cognitive skills, these results imply a detrimental effect of widespread open defecation in India on adult labor productivity (Hanushek and Woessmann 2008).

3. Effects of India's TSC

Has the Total Sanitation Campaign improved children's health and human capital? Many recent accounts of the TSC have focused on *process* evaluations. Such evaluations ask, for example, whether the TSC is actually constructing the latrines it claims to be constructing, or in which states the TSC is better meeting its spending targets. In contrast, this section reports results of *impact* evaluations, which attempt to determine whether the activities of the TSC are achieving the intended final outcomes. Here the question is not so much whether the TSC is spending money or as promised, but whether whatever activities it *is* doing are having an effect on the final outcomes that policy-makers care about. Is the TSC causing children to be healthier?

3.1. Difficulties in Documenting Effects of Sanitation

Estimating the causal effect of a program or policy is always difficult, but sanitation presents its own special challenges. The first difficulty is that one person's open defecation imposes "external" harmful effects on other people. Statistically, this means that it might not be helpful merely to compare health among people who do and do not have latrines, even if the latrines were randomly distributed. The second difficulty is in measuring the right outcome. Recent medical research suggests that fecal germs can importantly harm children's growth and development without necessarily causing diarrhea. However, counts of diarrhea episodes reported in surveys are the most commonly studied outcome by which sanitation is statistically evaluated. Taken together, these challenges suggest that policy-makers should handle research on sanitation with care.

3.1.1. EXTERNALITIES   In economics, an activity carries an externality if it has consequences for somebody else, consequences other than those taken into consideration by the person who chose the activity. So, pollution has negative externalities because it harms people other than the people who elect to pollute. In contrast, scientific research can have positive externalities because future engineers might use findings to make something helpful that the original researcher did not intend. Externalities are important for two reasons. First, externalities can make effects of a program or policy more difficult to measure. Second, externalities are a central rationale for government intervention.

Figure 2 illustrates the negative externalities associated with open defecation. Health does not only depend on whether one's own household defecates openly; it also matters what others do. Feces from other households can make children sick and stunt their growth. The figure plots average heights-for-age of rural children under five in various categories, using the National Family Health Survey-3 (NFHS-3). The figure splits children into those whose households do (light bars) and do not (dark bars) openly defecate. Unsurprisingly, on average the children whose households do not openly defecate are taller than those whose households do. (All of the bars are negative because the average Indian child is shorter than the international reference population.)

FIGURE 2. Height-for-age z-score of Children by Own Household's and Community Sanitation

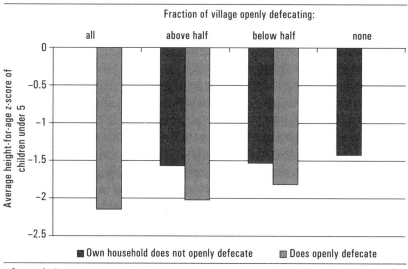

Source: Author.

The graph further separates children by the fraction of the households in their village included in the survey who openly defecate. This village-level factor adds explanatory power beyond the household's own behavior: within both groups, children who live in villages where fewer households openly defecate are taller, on average. By itself, this figure is only suggestive of a causal relationship: we cannot rule out that otherwise disadvantaged children also sort into neighborhoods with more open defecation. However, the graph is consistent with other evidence that open defecation has negative externalities. If so, then a household's own open defecation matters, but other households' do, too.

Externalities complicate statistical measurement of causal effects because they require that causes be studied at the appropriate scale. That is, is it household, village, or state open defecation that matters most? Many papers have attempted to estimate the effect of sanitation by comparing health outcomes between households (in the same village, often) that do and do not have latrines. Although those two papers find positive effects of sanitation, this approach is likely to underestimate the effect of latrines: households with latrines make children in households without them healthier, and households without latrines make children in households with them sicker, bringing both groups closer together.[3] Partially because of this problem, our research, reviewed below, studies variation in sanitation coverage at the district level. Identifying the key level of aggregation is an important open research topic.

In addition to complicating measurement, according to public economics, the involvement of negative externalities is exactly what makes open defecation society's problem and the government's problem, rather than merely a private issue for each household. Exactly because the external health effects of open defection are on other people, they are underappreciated (if appreciated at all) by those who openly defecate. Because open defecators fully appreciate their own benefits, but not other people's costs, they openly defecate "too much" from a socially optimal perspective. Thus, the theory of public economics holds that in the case of externalities, private decision-making will never achieve the optimal outcome. Government action is necessary to reduce open defecation.

Section 2 presented aggregate evidence of the importance of sanitation and reviewed studies documenting the impact of early life health on human capital. That evidence provides the motivation for *somebody* pursuing safe sanitation; it is the involvement of negative externalities that indicates that the responsibility must importantly be the government's or other public actors'.

Policy Lesson 1. Improving sanitation—meaning safe excreta disposal— must be a top priority for India. Because open defecation has negative externalities, it is everybody's problem, and requires government action.

3.1.2. WHAT SURVEY-REPORTED DIARRHEA MISSES A second difficulty in statistically measuring effects of sanitation is that the health consequences of open

---

3. Miguel and Kremer (2004) demonstrate that prior studies had missed the effect of deworming medicine on children's academic performance by randomizing at the individual level, allowing treatment and control children to reinfect one another.

defecation may be difficult to detect in the variables commonly measured in household surveys. In particular, the outcome variable most commonly associated with sanitation in large-scale health surveys is diarrhea morbidity, usually as reported to a surveyor by a child's mother. However, this data could be misleading.

In general, survey-reported disease can be systematically biased when poorer people perceive and report disease differently than richer people do (Das et al. 2012). Moreover, measuring diarrhea with surveys may be particularly difficult (Schmidt et al. 2011). In a field experiment, Zwane et al. (2011) show that households who are surveyed more frequently report less child diarrhea. If diarrhea data is very noisy, it might be difficult to detect the signal of an effect of sanitation, creating the false impression that sanitation has no effect.

Perhaps even more importantly, recent medical literature suggests that large and lasting effects of disease caused by poor sanitation can occur without necessarily causing diarrhea. Humphrey (2009) suggests that chronic but subclinical "environmental enteropathy"—a disorder caused by overwhelming fecal contamination which increases the small intestine's permeability to pathogens while reducing nutrient absorption—could cause malnutrition, stunting, and cognitive deficits without manifesting clinically as diarrhea. Mondal et al. (2011) document this phenomenon in Bangladesh. Again, therefore, a study only of the effects of sanitation on diarrhea—even if they were perfectly measured—could incorrectly conclude that sanitation has no effect on human capital.

3.2. Effects of the TSC

Two recent papers have documented an important average effect of the TSC, using existing large-scale data sets. This evidence suggests that the TSC has made children healthier, taller, and better able to reach their cognitive potential. Indeed, the first 10 years of the TSC prevented an average infant death for only a few thousand dollars, a very low cost compared with other interventions in the literature.

Development economists have recently shown that important lessons for policy can be drawn from randomized, controlled experiments evaluating policies and programs (Banerjee and Duflo 2011). However, the studies of the TSC reviewed here are a reminder of the continuing potential for rigorous and informative program evaluations using large, observational datasets and research strategies grounded in the details of a program's design.

3.2.1. EFFECTS ON INFANT MORTALITY Perhaps the most important effect of sanitation is on infant mortality. Spears (2012a) documents an average, overall beneficial effect of the TSC on infant mortality using three complementary econometric methods. All three methods give approximately similar answers: given the stock of household latrines produced by the TSC by 2011, at the end of its first 10 operational years, it had caused a large but plausible decline in infant mortality of about 4 infant deaths per 1,000 live births. This effect is slightly smaller than the effect found by Galiani et al. (2005) of a water privatization program in Argentina, and comparable to the effect of a water source improvement program studied by Kremer et al. (2011) in Kenya. This section will review the first two econometric methods used to identify this effect; the third will be explained in Section 4.2.1.

The first empirical strategy compares infants born in different years within a district with children born in different years and in different districts, using district and year fixed effects. This approach identifies an effect of the TSC on infant mortality in the District Level Household and Facility Survey-3 (DLHS-3) data by the differences in the year-to-year profile of TSC implementation across districts. The analysis finds an apparent effect: the more TSC latrines that had been built in a child's district by its first year of life, the more likely it is to survive to its first birthday.

The work of the analysis is to demonstrate that this correlation indeed reflects a causal effect of the TSC, and not simply a spurious correlation of child health improving more quickly in the same district-years where the TSC is becoming better implemented. This is done through a series of falsification tests. First, an effect is seen only on rural children, not urban children, which is what would be expected because the TSC is a purely rural program. Second, there is no "effect" on a child's survival of her first year of life of the stock of TSC latrines existing in her second year of life. This is evidence of a causal effect: if the TSC were indeed *causing* the decline in infant mortality, latrines would not be expected to reach "back in time" to influence infant survival. However, if the results were merely a spurious correlation of good district-level trends with other good district-level trends, the exact timing might not have been expected to matter.

Other tests verify that the effect of the TSC works through plausible mechanisms. For example, the effect of the TSC is mainly on post-neonatal mortality (infant mortality after the first month of life) not neonatal mortality, which is what would be expected if the TSC operated by improving the disease environment. Moreover, the effect of the TSC is greatest for children who were given non–breast-milk food earlier in their lives. These children would have been more exposed to fecal pathogens in the absence of the TSC, so a larger effect on them would be expected. Finally, the effect of the TSC is greatest in districts with higher population density, plausibly suggesting that the TSC is more protective in places where people would have been more likely to encounter others' feces.

The second empirical strategy used a long difference-in-differences method, comparing aggregate, district-level census data on infant mortality from 2001 to 2011, the first 10 years of TSC implementation. This strategy asks whether rural infant mortality fell by more in districts where more TSC latrines were built in this period. The results essentially replicate the individual-level results from the first strategy, and again no "effect" is found on urban infant mortality. Importantly, this approach allows the data to pass a test that could have rejected "parallel trends"—the critical assumption that infant mortality would have evolved in similar ways without the program—by showing that TSC intensity in the 2000s is not correlated with changes in infant mortality in the 1990s or the 1980s.

Importantly, these results do not imply that the TSC has worked well throughout India, nor that the TSC has even been implemented throughout India; these are average effects. Indeed, these findings would have been statistically impossible to produce if there were not districts with more and less TSC coverage to compare. Section 5.1 will explore the heterogeneity of the effect of the TSC across Indian states.

3.2.2. EFFECTS ON CHILDREN'S HEIGHT The TSC reduced infant mortality by improving the disease environment in children's early lives. It is well documented in the literature that this would very likely also improve growth and development, allowing children to reach their height potentials. For example, Coffey (2012) matches survey data on women's height from the 2000s to Sample Registration System mortality data from the years of their births to show that women born in years and states with lower infant mortality grew taller as adults.

Section 2.1 showed that children grow taller in states with less open defecation, but it is difficult to draw a causal conclusion from this correlation alone. Variation in the implementation of the TSC allows a better justified inference of a causal effect of sanitation on children's height. Spears (2012a) applied the same individual-level identification strategy used to show an effect of the TSC on infant mortality to NCAER's IHDS data about the height of children under age five. Heights of Indian children must be studied with care because their height-for-age is falling relative to the international reference population until about age two; this is accounted for with a complete set of age-in-month dummy variable controls by sex.

Indian children born in districts and years in which more TSC latrines had been built grow taller, on average, than children born in other years in the same district, or other districts in the same year. At the mean intensity of the TSC across India, the TSC caused children's height-for-age to increase by about two standard deviations. This is slightly smaller than the size of the effect that Barham (2012) found for a health and family planning program in Bangladesh. This result suggests that widespread open defecation is indeed part of the explanation for the large average height deficit among Indian children.

3.2.3. EFFECTS ON CHILDREN'S COGNITIVE ACHIEVEMENT   The same early life environmental conditions that encourage children to reach their genetic height potentials also allow them to better reach their genetic cognitive and human capital potentials. Recall from Section 2.2 that Spears (2012c) found that the correlation between height and cognitive achievement that had been well-documented in developed countries is even steeper among Indian children. Because the TSC helped children grow taller, and because taller children are better able to read and perform other cognitive tasks, it is reasonable to ask next whether the TSC has caused an improvement in children's cognitive achievement.

Spears and Lamba (2012) investigate this question using Pratham's individual-level Annual Status of Education Report (ASER) data. The ASER data is generated by a large annual survey in each rural district that gives children academic achievement tests. In particular, the ASER survey tests reading, starting from letter recognition, and math, starting from number recognition.

The analysis follows the same individual-level identification strategy as before: Are children born in districts and years in which more TSC latrines had been built better able to subsequently recognize letters and numbers when they are six years old than children born in other districts or years? Because the TSC only started building latrines in 2001, and because ASER test data are not available after 2009, Spears and S. Lamba are able to study six-year-olds in 2007, 2008, and 2009 born in 2001, 2002, and 2003.

As expected, children exposed to better sanitation coverage in their first year of life showed greater cognitive ability at age six. Figure 3 illustrates a simplified form of the analysis. Only some districts received any TSC coverage at all in the first three years of the program. As the figure shows, cognitive achievement moves in parallel for districts that did and did not receive TSC latrines in this period for children born in 2001 and 2002, when the program intensity was very low. However, cognitive achievement increases by more for children born in districts with TSC latrines in 2003, when some latrines started being built on a wide scale.

FIGURE 3. Difference-in-differences in Cognitive Achievement due to the TSC

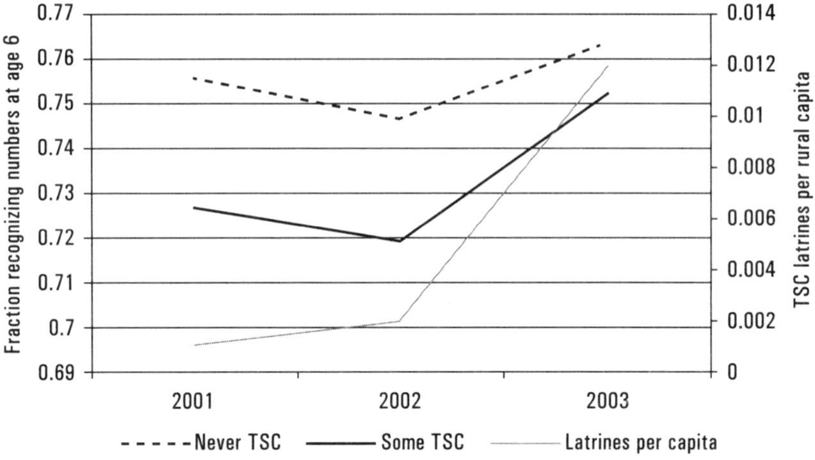

Source: ©Spears and Lamba (2012), reprinted with permission.

As before, details of the analysis suggest that this outcome was, indeed, a causal effect of the TSC. The effect of the TSC remains despite a range of controls in household and village characteristics and parents' education. There is no "effect" of the TSC on children who took the same ASER tests in the same years, but were too old to be exposed to the program, suggesting the finding is not merely a spurious result of district-level trends.

This result importantly indicates that widespread open defecation may not only be a substantial threat to health in India, but also carries a large economic cost in failure to meet human capital potentials.

Policy Lesson 2. By promoting and incentivizing latrine use, the TSC has had positive initial impacts on children's health and human capital.

3.3. Cost-effectiveness of the TSC

The effect of the TSC was moderately large, but perhaps more important is that it was purchased cheaply. Accountability Initiative (2011) reports annual TSC expenditure totals, computed from government accounts (George [2010] independently presents similar figures) and divided among central government, state government, and "beneficiary" expenditures. Sometimes cost-benefit analyses of policies only include government expenditures, but household and village spending on latrines is an important part of the full economic cost of the TSC.

Table 2 combines these cost figures with Spears's (2012a) estimates of the effects of the TSC to compute the 2010 US$ cost of an infant death averted. The computations follow the procedure recommended by Dhaliwal et al. (2011), and therefore are comparable to Abdul Latif Jameel Poverty Action Lab cost-effectiveness figures. These computations exclude all benefits of the TSC other than infant survival, such as the health or human capital of the children who live, and any direct utility gained from access to a latrine.

T A B L E 2 . Average TSC Expenditure per Expected Infant Death Averted

Latrine life		10% discounting		No discounting	
(years)	Effect	Total	Government	Total	Government
10	Low	4334	3666	2551	2188
10	Medium	3435	2906	2022	1734
10	High	1853	1568	1091	935
15	Low	3555	3007	1701	1458
15	Medium	2817	2383	1348	1156
15	High	1520	1286	727	624
20	Low	2234	1890	1276	1094
20	Medium	1770	1497	1011	867
20	High	955	808	545	468

Source: Author.
Note: Costs in 2010 US$. Expenditure data from Accountability Initiative for 2001–11.

Cost-effectiveness estimates are always based on a set of assumptions; Table 3 presents a range of results based on different assumptions. First, the table takes low, medium, and high estimates of the effect of the TSC from various tables in Spears (2012a). Second, the table presents estimates assuming that each latrine lasts 10, 15, and 20 years from the year of its construction before instantly fully depreciating. Franceys et al. (1992) explain

T A B L E 3 . Discontinuities on the NGP Incentive Rules

	Village population in the 2001 Census				
	Below 1,000	1,000 to 1,999	2,000 to 4,999	5,000 to 9,999	10,000 or more
Rupees:	50,000	100,000	200,000	400,000	500,000
Dollars (market):	1,000	2,000	4,000	8,000	10,000
Dollars (PPP):	3,400	6,800	13,600	27,200	34,000

Source: Author.

that "pits designed to last 25–30 years are not uncommon and a design life of 15–20 years is perfectly reasonable" (44). The computations include all expenditure and construction through the 2010–11 budget year, and ignore all expenditure and construction beyond this point.

Third, because costs and benefits are spread over time, cost-effectiveness depends on the discount rate. Results implement Dhaliwal et al.'s (2011) recommended 10 percent annual discount rate; results are also included without any discounting of costs or benefits as a sensitivity analysis (cf. Nordhaus 2007). Unsurprisingly, the computed cost of saving a life with this capital investment is lower at a zero interest rate; market discount rates likely fall between these two extremes.

Taken together, the results suggest that the TSC prevented an average infant death for a few thousand dollars. Importantly, this is an average cost, not a marginal cost. These estimates average over initialization and fixed costs, returns to scale, and the heterogeneity of a large country. Therefore, they almost certainly do not represent the marginal benefit of a US$2,500 donation to the Indian government. The marginal cost of saving the next infant life could be low if fixed, start-up costs were important, or high if latrines were put in the easiest or most effective places first.

The TSC has achieved its effects inexpensively relative to other programs and to some standards for the value of a statistical life. Ignoring, again, any benefits in addition to averting infant death and using the median discounted total cost estimate from Table 2, the TSC saved a life year for around US$35, a very rough figure that assumes an infant would have otherwise lived 65 to 70 years. Like similarly computed estimates, this one should be used only with extreme care (Hammer 1997). This figure should not be taken literally; the point is that it is well below common thresholds of US$100 or US$125 per life year saved. This estimate is comparable to some of the lowest figures in the literature, such as Ahuja et al.'s (2001) estimate of US$40 for household water chlorination or US$20 for point-of-collection chlorination in Kenya.

Although corruption is a common problem in low-capacity governments, many academic impact evaluations study programs that were implemented by high capacity nongovernmental organizations (NGOs) or motivated governments, potentially biasing estimates of effectiveness and complicating policy implications (Duflo et al. 2007; Coffey 2011). As Ravallion (2012) explains, "a small program run by the committed staff of a good NGO may well work very differently to an ostensibly similar program applied at scale by a government or other NGO for which staff have different preferences and face new and different incentives" (110). Projects in developing countries often suffer from "missing expenditures": discrepancies between official project costs and the actual value of the resources used (Olken 2007). Unlike some estimates of cost-effectiveness in the literature, this paper's are inclusive of all costs of administration and losses to corruption, under actual implementation at scale.

Policy Lesson 3. Publicly supported sanitation with an ex post incentive to motivate use can be a comparatively very inexpensive way to save babies' lives.

4. Explaining Sanitation Coverage and TSC Take-up

As Section 3 discussed, properly used and constructed pit latrines are a safe way of disposing of excreta. So, why do some rural places in India achieve better sanitation coverage than others? This section reviews evidence that sanitation take-up is importantly determined at the village level.

4.1. A Village-level Process

In conversations about the TSC, government officials and NGO staff at state, district, and village levels have all emphasized the importance of decisions made by village-level officials, that is, the *pradhan* or the *sarpanch*.

I recently met a District Magistrate (DM) in his large office in an old house, far from the commercial center of the district capital. I asked the DM if he had ever heard of the TSC, worrying that the answer might be no. "Heard of it?" he leapt out from behind his desk to sit next to me. On the way, he had pulled out from under his desk a stack of booklets in Hindi: these had his picture on the cover with the district official responsible for village councils, and were full of detailed instructions for how a *pradhan* should implement the TSC, complete with diagrams for latrine construction. He proudly explained that he had written much of it himself. Like many Indian Administrative Service (IAS) officers, he was originally trained as an engineer, a civil engineer in his case. "Distributed to everybody!" he beamed about the books.

Apparently, this DM had taken a special, personal interest in the TSC. He put together these booklets and summoned the district's *pradhan*s to a series of special meetings to encourage them to comply, enough meetings so that he could interact with them all. (A *pradhan* whom I later met confirmed the DM's story.) The DM explained to them the externalities of infectious disease: if you have a toilet and your neighbors do not, "the germs will not differentiate between them and you." Grinning, he recounted how he attempted to shame them, reminding them that they spend so much money on festivals as a matter of pride, but apparently do not have enough pride to keep their daughters-in-law from openly defecating.

At least in this district, all *pradhans* supposedly have special TSC accounts on which they can draw for the subsidy money, to organize construction with contractors of their choice. As the DM told me "everything is there, only the willpower is needed." But, not all of the *pradhans* had implemented the program. When I asked, he guessed—now sadly—that maybe 20 percent in his district were trying. Strikingly, the chief executive of this district of over 4 million people felt ultimately powerless to do much more than advocate and exhort, even for a program so clearly important to him.

This account was echoed by a TSC specialist working in a state headquarters of an international NGO. He was quite familiar with the pitfalls of rural sanitation programs. The office building in which we met had been constructed with an extra bathroom attached to his shared office. The bathroom was being used as a closet. When he went in to find pamphlets detailing the proper construction of latrines, he joked, "we are learning from them"—meaning villagers, who sometimes store tools and food in their latrine superstructures.

In his view, a key source of heterogeneity in implementation was "the P factor: the *pradhan* factor." He elaborated: "Where the *pradhan* was good, the opportunity [to implement the program] was good." He described that it is up to the *pradhan* to sort out how the latrines will be constructed: for example, will the work for the whole village be contracted out as one job? Often, "*pradhan* simply finds a mason." In short, "if the person is good he can make a difference. Lots of the program has depended on the *pradhan*'s influence."

This section reviews three sets of econometric evidence that village governance represents a key level of organization in determining sanitation take-up. First, relative to other household goods, latrine use is highly correlated at the village level. Second, randomized village-level political reservations predict TSC take-up. Third, variation in the size of the NGP incentive caused by a discontinuity in the rule linking population to prize size predicts village-level TSC intensity.

Policy Lesson 4. Villages are a critical level of governance for sanitation intervention.

4.1.1. A COORDINATION GAME? One possibility is that idiosyncratic household preferences or constraints are the primary determinants of take-up of pit

latrines, rather than open defecation. If so, one might expect some households within a village to have latrines and others not to; in different villages these household-level determinates would be differently distributed, so a large set of villages would exhibit a wide range of levels of sanitation coverage.

Another possibility is that properties of villages are the primary determinants of sanitation take-up. Perhaps in certain villages local leaders have encouraged safe excreta disposal, or perhaps social or biological complementarities cause people in a village to switch from open defecation to latrine use approximately together. If so, one would expect there to be many villages with full sanitation coverage and many villages where everybody openly defecates, with few villages in between.

Kishore and Spears (2012) formalize this intuition and test whether safe rural sanitation is primarily determined at the household or village level. The analysis uses the 2008 DLHS-3—a large survey with over 20,000 rural villages—and collapses the data to the village level to produce an estimate for each village of village-level sanitation coverage.

Figure 4 shows the strikingly bimodal distribution of village-level sanitation coverage: 31 percent of villages are at 0 percent or 100 percent open defecation among surveyed households. Using a looser standard, 37 percent

F I G U R E 4 . **Bimodality in the Distribution of Village-level Sanitation Coverage, DLHS-3**

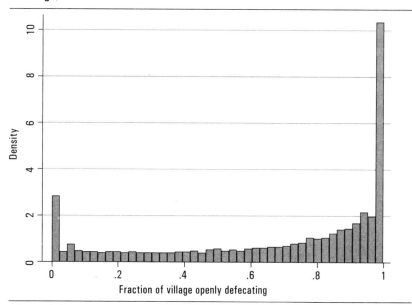

Source: Author.

are below 5 percent or above 95 percent. Visibly fewer villages have sanitation levels below these extremes. Because these are simple pit latrines, not linked sewer systems, the result is not mechanically driven by the natural monopoly of laying pipes (the result is the same if tiny fraction of rural households with piped sanitation is dropped).

Although this appears to be evidence for the importance of village-level determinants of sanitation, another possibility is that household wealth determines latrine take-up, and household wealth just happens to be highly correlated within villages. However, a similar pattern is not seen for other household assets. For example, in 53 percent of villages, no surveyed households use clean cooking fuel, and in 72 percent of villages less than 10 percent do. Similarly, in 28 percent of villages, no surveyed households have a *pucca* or well-constructed house, and in half of villages less than one in eight do. In neither of these cases is there a second mode of villages with near-universal take-up of clean cooking fuel or *pucca* houses. That said, more evidence is needed to explain the processes leading to this bimodal distribution in the light of economic theory, given possible theoretical explanations.

One explanation that Kishore and Spears explore is that village-level sanitation coverage is the outcome of a coordination game. In this game theoretic situation, the value of an action depends on whether other people are doing it, and there are incentives for doing what everybody else is doing. These incentives could be social—if the value of having a latrine depends on a social reference point, or if the pleasantness of visibly walking to openly defecate depends on whether others are doing so—or biological, if sanitation coverage is most effective when universal. In either case, extremely high and extremely low sanitation coverage will both be stable equilibria. Coordination from a village leader could change expectations in such a way as to move behavior from the low take-up stable equilibrium to the high take-up stable equilibrium.

4.1.2. EFFECTS OF VILLAGE GOVERNANCE If village governance were an important determinant of TSC take-up, then the preferences and efficacy of the village chairman would be expected to matter for TSC take-up. Village governance positions are reserved for women and for members of low castes, and these reservations are randomly assigned. Following on Chattopadhyay and Duflo's (2004) investigation of villages in West Bengal and Rajasthan being randomly assigned to have female *pradhans*, S. Lamba and Spears (2012) study the effect of random reservation of a village to have a scheduled caste (SC) *pradhan* on TSC implementation. The results indicate that villages randomly assigned to have an SC *pradhan* are about two percentage points less likely to have won the NGP for having an open defecation free village, a 25percent reduction. In principle, many mechanisms could account for this apparent effect. Strikingly, under SC *pradhans*, villages construct just as many latrines per capita as under unreserved *pradhans*. However, conditional on having a latrine for each household, SC *pradhans* are less than half as likely to win. This could illustrate the gap between latrine *construction* and latrine *use*, if SC *pradhans* are less able to motivate their villages to use the latrines. Alternatively, latrine use—unobservable in this data—could be just as high in villages with SC *pradhans*, but they are nevertheless less likely to ultimately receive the prize for other reasons. Whatever the explanation, the existence of this effect highlights the importance of village-level determinants of sanitation coverage.

4.2. Effects of the Clean Village Prize

The NGP, or clean village prize, is an ex post cash incentive awarded to villages that have achieved open defecation free status. The prize is large for rural India: one lakh rupees or about US$2,000 for the median village, or about US$6,800 at purchasing power parity.

In order to give a larger prize to larger villages (in which achieving open defecation free status would presumably be more difficult), the NGP incentive amount was designed as a "step function" of village population (Alok 2010). Table 3 presents the rule behind the prize.

Presumably, it is more difficult to achieve open defecation free status in a larger village. However, this difficulty is likely to be continuously increasing in population size: it is not much more difficult to get everybody in a village of 1,001 people to use latrines than to get everybody in a village of 999 people to use latrines. Given the discontinuities in the reward, however, this means that there are large discontinuities in a village leader's motivation to try to win the prize. Two *pradhans*, one of a village with 999 people and one of a village with 1,001 people, face similar costs in trying to win the NGP, but the one with 1,001 people will receive much greater benefits. Therefore, the simple economics of incentives predicts that the TSC will be implemented more vigorously, on average, in villages with populations just above the incentive discontinuities than in villages with populations just below the incentive discontinuities.

If these discontinuities in local leaders' incentives to try to win the NGP indeed predict TSC implementation, then this would be further evidence of the importance of local governance to sanitation policy. Spears (2012a) offers implicit evidence. In districts with many villages with populations just above the incentive discontinuities, rural infant mortality rates were lower in 2011, on average, than in districts with many villages with populations below the discontinuities. However, the incentives do not predict district-level infant mortality in 2001, before the program. This all indicates that greater incentives motivated village chairmen to put more effort into the TSC, leading to better child health. However, these results at the district level can only *imply* a village-level effect of the program. Section 4.2.1 presents village-level evidence.

4.2.1. VILLAGE-LEVEL EFFECTS OF DISCONTINUITIES IN THE NGP INCENTIVES Is there village-level evidence that the discontinuities in the NGP incentive have impacted TSC intensity? This exercise faces important data constraints. A crucial step is matching the TSC village-level administrative data on latrine construction (the outcome variable) to 2001 Census population data. This must be done by hand, using village names, without knowing what block the village is in. Village names are often spelled differently, or are altogether different (for example, perhaps a surveyor accidentally wrote down the name of a hamlet instead, or Hindus and Muslims may use different names for the same place).

Even if it were easy to match 2001 Census data to TSC administrative data, it may not have been very valuable. The village construction dataset is not a panel; there is one number recorded per village, which is replaced when a new number is eventually entered. However, the village dataset it is not a cross section either, because it has been updated irregularly. Village-level data is entered locally, and, although the data is required to be current, many villages have not updated their data in some time. Data were updated in 2011 for some villages, but not since 2008 for others. Figure 5 shows the large fraction of villages with out-of-date data when the data were accessed in early 2012. An official in the central government unit responsible for the TSC told me about it as directly as one could expect not to trust this data much.

Despite the important limitations of the data, it would be very important for policy-making to know whether the NGP incentive has motivated TSC latrine construction in villages. Although it will not be possible to estimate *quantitatively* the motivating effect of a marginal rupee of incentive on village effort, it may be possible to indicate *qualitatively* whether a greater incentive has caused better TSC performance.

FIGURE 5.   Distribution of Villages by Year TSC Administrative Data
Last Updated

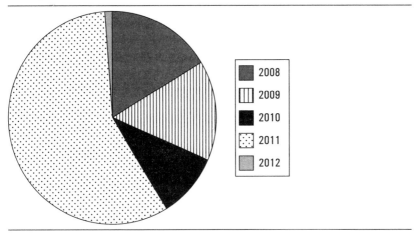

■	2008
⊞	2009
■	2010
⠂	2011
▨	2012

Source: Author.
Note: Accessed in February, 2012.

The analysis in the supplementary appendix of Spears (2012a) approached this question in two complementary ways, constructing two datasets. Constructing the first dataset started with randomly drawing a sample of villages from the 2001 Census. This sample was drawn from among villages with populations within 100 people of the discontinuities. Four hundred and sixty of these were able to be matched to TSC data, based on the village name. The advantages of this data are that its sample is focused on the discontinuity; it uses real 2001 Census population data; and it is from all states. The disadvantages are that that the dataset is very small; almost no controls are available; and there is no reason to believe that matchability of village names is ignorably "random."

The second dataset was constructed by matching the TSC construction data to the TSC's own baseline survey for 50 districts. Entire blocks (subdistrict units) were randomly selected, to be representative of the 280 districts used in the district-level analysis. Unfortunately, the TSC's baseline survey recorded the count of households, not populations, so each village's population is estimated by multiplying the count of households in each village by the average household size for that district in the 2001 Census. This estimation would be expected to attenuate the estimated effect of the incentive (some villages will be placed on the wrong side of the discontinuity).

With either dataset, the key econometric test is to regress village-level TSC intensity—that is, latrine construction per capita—on that village's

NGP incentive per capita, with controls for population and other village-level characteristics. In both cases, a higher NGP incentive appears to have encouraged village-level latrine construction. Extrapolating linearly, a 100-rupee increase in the NGP incentive per capita would be associated with an about 20 percentage point increase in household sanitation coverage, although this figure should not be taken literally.

The credibility of interpreting this effect causally depends on the plausibility that villages with similar populations on either side of the NGP cut points are also similar in other, unobserved ways, on average. Unfortunately, the data are not nearly complete enough to compute a technical regression discontinuity. However, the most densely populated discontinuity in the prize is around 1,000 people. Among the 79 randomly selected villages with populations estimated to be between 1,000 and 1,200, 7 percent (or 9 percent) of them won the "open defecation free" prize; among the 64 villages with populations from 800 to 1,000, none of them did.

4.2.2. COULD THE PRIZE EVER BE TOO HIGH? Based on these results, should the NGP reward amount be increased to encourage more village chairmen to attempt to win prize? Perhaps so, but there is a countervailing consideration: limited government monitoring and evaluation capacity.

R. Lamba and Spears (2012) study the NGP incentive game theoretically, as a mechanism design problem in which the government aims to incentivize *pradhans* to implement sanitation, *pradhans* try to maximize their income and minimize their costs, and only limited resources are devoted to verifying NGP applications. In this situation, increasing the prize amount will increase sanitation and effort to win the prize legitimately, but it will also increase fake applications from *pradhans* with relatively high costs of achieving open defecation free status but relatively low administrative costs of submitting the application.

What happens next depends on the resources devoted to evaluating NGP applications. If evaluations are accurate, then *pradhans* will learn not to submit false applications. However, if monitoring resources are limited so that some false applications win the prize, then as word of this gets out, even more *pradhans* will submit false applications. This will further overwhelm limited monitoring resources, further blunting the incentive, leading to even more false applications, and so on as the incentive unravels.

To avoid this possibility, it is important that as the NGP incentive is increased, the quality of monitoring and of evaluating prize applications be increased as well. At any particular, limited level of monitoring quality, the incentive can be too high.[4] However, sufficiently increasing both the incentive and monitoring quality is likely to improve sanitation outcomes.

Policy Lesson 5. Incentives to local leaders for outcomes are useful and should be strengthened by both increasing the monetary incentive and devoting resources to ensure accurate evaluation and adjudication.

5. Reaching the Rest

Econometric methods are good at identifying averages. The research in Section 3, for example, has answered the question: "What has been the average effect of the TSC so far?" However, the policy question now is how much to invest in expanding sanitation coverage to the many places where it has not yet reached. To answer this question, one would like to know not the average effect of the TSC so far but the marginal effect: What would be the benefits of the *next* TSC latrines? Would these benefits be worth the further cost?

This section pursues answers to these policy questions about marginal effects. Determining how much more the Indian government should invest in completing sanitation coverage will require a combination of statistical evidence and basic theory of public economics, and will not be able to provide the precise answers of Section 4. First, I will compare the effects of the TSC across different states. Then I will consider whether sanitation coverage so far appears to have responded to social costs and benefits—as economic theory would recommend—or to private costs and benefits—which would indicate a continuing need for government action. The results indicate that the TSC should be intensified to reach the remaining rural population.

5.1. Heterogeneous Effects

The effect of the TSC on infant mortality described in Section 3.2.1 averaged over all of rural India, using the DLHS-3. This section presents results from estimating the same regression on the same data, but restricting the data to each large enough state in turn. This produces an estimate of the effect of TSC latrines in each state.

This analysis by state is important for policy because it helps answer the question of whether to continue to pursue TSC coverage in states where

4. I thank Diane Coffey for suggesting another mechanism by which this generically could happen: with a higher prize, a *pradhan* can better afford to bribe corrupt monitors and still have enough prize money left over to make submitting a false application worth the costs.

coverage remains low. If, for example, the places where latrines have already been built are the only places where they have been helpful, it might suggest careful thinking before attempting to build more latrines in places where the latrines that have been built have not helped. On the other hand, if in places with few latrines, the ones that have been built have been very helpful, this suggests that there are still high marginal returns to sanitation coverage in these places where coverage is low.

Importantly, these will not be estimates of the total effect of the TSC in each state. This is because each state has implemented the TSC with a different intensity. Here, the question is not "how many latrines haven been built in each state," but "of the latrines that have been built in each state, what has their average effect been?" So, we are asking not about the total effect of the TSC by state, nor about heterogeneity on the *extensive* margin (how many villages have been nominally reached, for example), but about heterogeneity on the *intensive* margin: in each place, what has the average reported TSC latrine accomplished?

Figure 6 presents the results: there is a range of variation across states in the effectiveness of reported TSC activity on the intensive margin.[5] It is natural to want to make comparisons: it may be unsurprising that TSC latrines have been effective in Gujarat and Maharashtra, on average, and not in Jharkhand or Uttar Pradesh. However, there needs to be an important caveat: although they are not included in the graph, the standard errors of these estimates would be large because each comes from a small sample. Therefore, precise comparisons between states are probably inappropriate. Instead, what might be helpful would be to consider patterns of effectiveness: with what do differences in effectiveness across states correlate?

Additionally, it is not necessarily clear what exactly these differences in effectiveness imply. The independent variable here is *reported* TSC latrine construction. There are at least two ways in which reported latrines could have a low effect on infant mortality. First, they could be made but made badly: perhaps given to the wrong people, or not accompanied by motivation to use them. Second, they could be not made at all, and merely reported; in this case reported latrines would surely be expected to have a low effect.

A first question is whether TSC latrines have been more effective on the intensive margin in states with better or worse sanitation coverage.

---

5. For clarity and comparability, the regression coefficients (estimated as effects of moving from 0 to 1 latrine per capita) from each state were multiplied by the all-India average TSC intensity. This figure does not necessarily claim, for example, that IMR in Gujarat decreased by eight deaths per 1,000 due to the TSC.

FIGURE 6. Effectiveness of TSC Latrines on the Intensive Margin by State

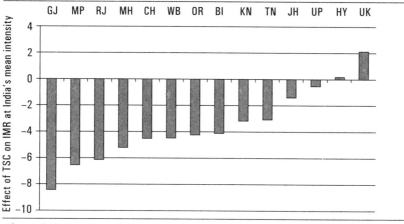

Source: Author.

Figure 7 suggests an answer; note that a more negative effect is a better effect, as it represents a larger decline in infant mortality. The negative slope suggests that the greater open defecation was before the program, the more effective the marginal TSC latrine has been, although the result is only marginally statistically significant (one-sided $p = 0.07$).

FIGURE 7. TSC Effectiveness and Baseline (2001) Open Defecation

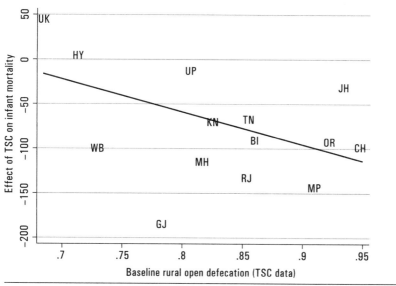

Source: Author.

If this correlation is credible, it suggests that effective programs can occur even in places where things are going wrong. From a policy perspective, this result is consistent with economists' law of diminishing marginal returns. Given this law, it may be unsurprising that additional latrines have been more helpful in places where there were fewer of them, and that in Haryana and Uttarakhand, where open defecation was relatively low to begin with, TSC latrines have not caused much of an improvement.

In contrast, as Figure 8 shows, there is essentially no correlation between the effect of TSC latrines on infant mortality and levels of open defecation in the 2011 Census, after the period studied in this paper. The district-level correlation is similarly flat, with a t-statistic of -0.02. It is difficult to draw any conclusion from such a null result, but one implication may be that there is no evidence here that TSC latrines will be particularly ineffective in the places where more are still needed.

FIGURE 8. TSC Effectiveness and Current (2011 Census) Open Defecation

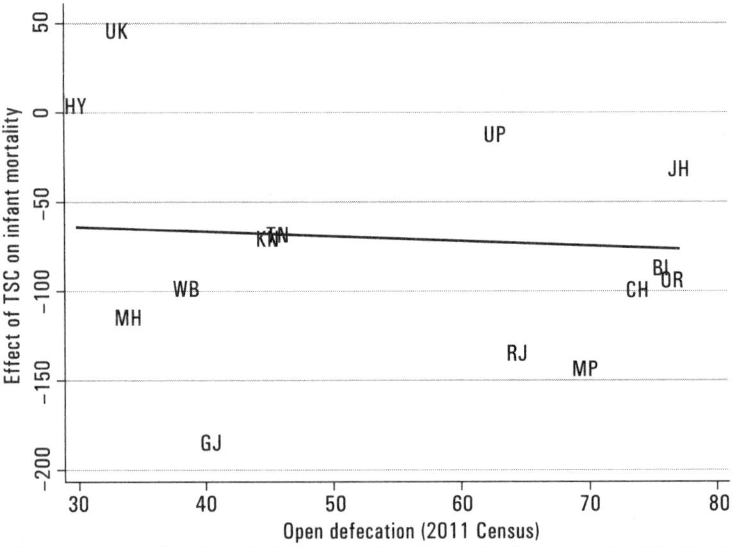

Source: Author.

Finally, the TSC administrative data includes a "goal" sanitation coverage that was articulated by the program for each state. Figure 9 compares the effectiveness of TSC latrines with the percentage of its goal that each state met. Perhaps surprisingly, the upward slope suggests that TSC latrines were less effective, on average, in states that more nearly met their goal. One possibility is that some states artificially inflated their latrine construction figures more than others, resulting both in appearing to reach their goals and in ineffective "reported" latrines. However, with a t-statistic of 1.02, no real inference of any slope can be made.

FIGURE 9. TSC Effectiveness and Percent of State "Goal" Achieved

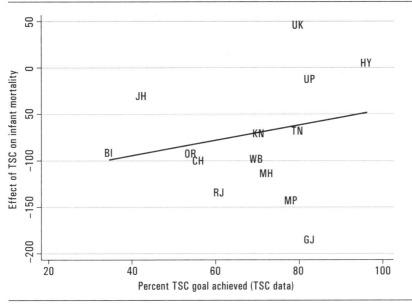

Source: Author.

5.2. Optimal Diligence: Marginal Social Costs and Benefits

Although Figure 9 suggests that many states report reaching around 80 percent of their TSC goals, Figure 8 shows that the 2011 Indian Census finds over half of Indian households still openly defecating. How much effort should the Indian government put into continuing to expand TSC coverage?

According to economic theory, private actors—such as households and village politicians—will improve sanitation coverage to the level where their private marginal benefits equal their private marginal costs. The government should extend sanitation coverage to the point where its social marginal benefit equals the social marginal cost. Because of the negative externalities of open defecation, the private and social marginal benefits are very different. Therefore, one approach to assessing how much more effort the government should put into the TSC is to ask whether coverage so far appears to have responded to private or social marginal costs and benefits. Is sanitation take-up explained by private or public incentives?

We have seen several pieces of evidence that TSC coverage so far has responded to private incentives. A discontinuity in the NGP incentive that has nothing to do with underlying sanitation requirements predicts village leaders' motivation to pursue sanitation. Random assignment of village governance to members of socially excluded groups decreases the chances of a village being certified as open defecation free, even though the caste of the *pradhan* is irrelevant to the social marginal benefit of latrine construction.

In contrast, a range of evidence suggests that the marginal social benefits of sanitation coverage still exceed the marginal social costs. First, the marginal benefits are high relative to the costs: properly used sanitation is a cheap and effective way to save infant lives and build human capital. Second, state level evidence suggests that economists' law of diminishing marginal returns applies to sanitation, yet open defecation remains widespread. Finally, it does not appear to be the case that, for example, the TSC has been implemented more thoroughly in districts with higher population density; coverage does not appear to be determined by the social threat of disease.

Policy Lesson 6. The additional benefit of extending effective TSC implementation to remaining Indian children would probably substantially exceed the additional cost.

6. Conclusion

6.1. How Might the TSC Have Partially Succeeded Where Other Programs Have Failed?

Although earlier sanitation programs in India and elsewhere that focused on latrine construction have failed (Black and Fawcett 2008), this paper has presented evidence that, on average, the TSC improved children's health and human capital. Why might the TSC have succeeded—at least, in those places where it has been well implemented—given the failure of earlier attempts? One answer suggested by Spears (2012a) may be that in its focus on village-level incentives, the TSC was getting its economics right and getting its sociology right.

The TSC is getting its economics right by offering an ex post incentive for achieving the necessary outcome: villages becoming open defecation free. As Holmstrom and Milgrom (1991) describe, incentivizing an agent for performance on one input toward a complex goal could worsen the final product; this is sometimes called the "teaching to the test" problem. Indeed, Glewwe et al. (2003) find that a program that rewarded teachers in Kenya based on students' test scores caused an increase in short-term exam preparation sessions, with little further effect. However, the TSC does not merely reward latrine construction or other inputs, it reward villages where everybody uses latrines.

The program is getting its sociology right by offering this incentive to village leaders, and thereby making use of existing village social hierarchy and knowledge. Strictly speaking, in government documents, the NGP funds are supposed to be used for village improvement projects. However, there is ample evidence from other programs that money being fungible, local elites can privately capture such funds. Far from a problem, however, this may be exactly why the NGP is helpful: it gives local leaders an incentive to ensure compliance. These local leaders may know more than outside planners how exactly to best promote sanitation in their village. Moreover, village chairmen draw freely on traditional social values in achieving their goal: I have seen villages where the *pradhan* is trying to win the prize, and has had painted on village walls "do not let your daughters and daughters in law go outside; make a latrine in your house."

However, as R. Lamba and Spears (2012) model and Section 4.2.2 discussed, there could be an important limit to what the incentive could accomplish if accurate monitoring and enforcement of the incentive conditionality is not maintained. A large incentive without accurate verification is a recipe for corruption. Policy-makers should carefully expand and strengthen the NGP incentive. More research is needed about the quantitative response to possible incentive amounts, about how incentive verification is conducted in practice, and about the motivations and activities of village leaders attempting to win the prize.

6.2. Better Data Could Promote Better Policy

Effective governance requires information, especially for a country as large and diverse as India. As evidence of the lack of information about what is occurring in rural villages, in discussions about the research in this paper, district and top central government officials as well as NGO staff and international funding agencies have all reported wanting to learn *from me* what was going with the TSC on the ground. Achieving an open defecation free India will require more and better data—both administrative data about the implementation of the TSC and survey data for research. It is difficult but necessary to have useful information about hundreds of districts, hundreds of thousands of villages, and a 600 million people's open defecation. There is attainable room for improvement.

First, the attention that the TSC itself has devoted to collecting and making available its own administrative data has been admirable. These monitoring systems should be given the support and resources necessary to improve data quality and preserve what has been achieved.

Already, as Figure 5 displayed, the village-level data is largely out of date, whatever the quality of the initial data submissions. It will be important to maintain the quality of the district-level data. Imbert and Papp (2011) study the quality of government administrative data about the National Rural Employment Guarantee Scheme, available from a similar online database. They find substantial inflation of workdays relative to household surveys. Part of the explanation may be that officials wish to appear that they are meeting demand for work, in order to fulfill legal requirements. It is important that TSC "goals" do not corrupt administrative data. One solution may be providing resources for record-keepers, perhaps even at relatively local levels, who will be independent of any incentives for good performance.

Beyond the administrative data, sanitation research faces sharp data constraints. No large household survey dataset with health data has been collected since the 2008 DLHS, four years ago.[6] Existing datasets sometimes are crucially incomplete. The DLHS did not measure children's height, which reflects long-term health, but only weight, which reflects shorter-term health and nutrition. The 2005 NFHS-3, the third round of India's DHS survey, does not include district identifiers, not only making a matching exercise such as the one done here impossible, but further preventing even district fixed effects (or replicating the state-level analysis of Section 2.1 at the district level). Apparently, this may be due to confidentiality concerns, despite the fact that average Indian districts are larger than many whole countries where DHS surveys have been conducted. Frequently collected high-quality, multipurpose datasets, independent of any particular program's or official's bureaucratic interests, are a relatively low-cost investment in a public good that is critical for policy-making in such a large country.

Policy Lesson 7. Achieving total sanitation coverage will require both safeguarding the quality of TSC administrative data—perhaps by providing resources for data sources that bypass bureaucratic interests—and investing in large datasets about health outcomes.

---

6. NCAER is currently collecting a new round of the India Human Development Survey, which will be especially useful as a longitudinal panel. However, even with its 40,000 households it may be difficult to reliably detect effects on low-probability events such as infant mortality.

6.3. From TSC to NBA: Opportunities, but Still Much to Do

Widespread open defecation in India is not only a critical public health concern; it also limits human capital accumulation, and therefore economic potential. Adequately constructed and used pit latrines are well-known to be a safe method of excreta disposal. The data reviewed here suggest that the TSC and NGP can motivate villages to construct and use latrines.

However, coverage is still quite incomplete, and more of the same may not be enough. Increasing and publicizing the prize may be good first steps, but better monitoring of prize applicants will be crucial, especially if a larger prize makes submitting a false application more attractive. If it is true that sanitation is implemented at the village level, then policy-makers in Delhi and state capitals have no alternative but to focus on the details of what motivates local politics and policy. This may require developing alternative channels of information that bypass bureaucratic, financial, and political interests. The difficult part of creating a useful administrative data system is not establishing a modern, online, computerized database; it is ensuring that the people collecting and entering the underlying data have an interest in meaningful and accurate information. The challenge is considerable, but given the deep costs of open defecation and the negative externalities that make latrines a social and government concern, meeting the challenge must be a top priority.

As we meet at the India Policy Forum, the government is in the process of converting the TSC into the NBA. The government, Minister Jairam Ramesh, and everyone contributing to this reinvigorated commitment deserve wide applause for this important investment in making India open defecation free.

Increasing the government's investment in sanitation promises important opportunities, but there will be risks as well—risks that more money will attract unwanted attention, and that the so-far successful incentives behind the TSC could be undermined. These risks can be minimized—and the promise of the NBA ensured—by emphasizing those principles that contributed to the successes that the TSC did achieve. Before the TSC, the Central Rural Sanitation Program (CRSP) emphasized subsidies and latrine construction: incentives for building latrines that nobody will use. If the NBA returns to these principles, it will probably miss this opportunity to end open defecation. If, instead, the NBA strengthens monitoring systems and incentives for latrine *use*, we can hope for healthier children who become more productive adults.

Appendix

T A B L E A . Recent Papers Reviewed in This Article

Citation	Approach	Findings
Spears (2012a)	Econometric evaluation of impact of TSC (2001–11) on health using large surveys and census data	The TSC reduced infant mortality, on average, by 4 deaths per 1,000 and increased height for age by 0.2.
Spears and Lamba (2012)	Econometric evaluation of impact of TSC (2001–03) on cognitive skills, using ASER data	Children exposed to more TSC latrines in early life recognized more letters and numbers at age six.
Spears (2012b)	International comparisons of sanitation coverage and height, using 140 DHS surveys	Country-years with less open defecation have taller children, a result that is not cause by fixed differences among countries or regions.
Spears (2012c)	Correlation of child height and cognitive achievement using IHDS and HDPI data from NCAER	Taller children score higher on learning tests in India with a much steeper association than in the US; early life sanitation and hygiene matters.
Kishore and Spears (2012)	Modeling village sanitation coverage as a coordination game; comparing open defecation at the village level	Open defecation varies at the village level: in many villages either all or none of the DLHS respondents openly defecate.
S. Lamba and Spears (2012)	Comparison of TSC outcomes with randomized local governance reservations in Rajasthan	Villages in which the chairman's office has been reserved for a member of a low-ranking caste are less likely to win the clean village prize.
R. Lamba and Spears (2012)	Theoretical model of the clean village prize, given corrupt village leaders and limited state capacity	If monitoring resources are limited, increasing the prize amount could perversely worsen compliance, by encouraging false applications that overwhelm the monitoring system.

Source: Author.

References

Accountability Initiative. 2011. "Total Sanitation Campaign GOI, 2011–12." *Budget Briefs*, Centre for Policy Research.

Ahuja, Amrita, Michael Kremer, and Alix Peterson Zwane. 2010. "Providing Safe Water: Evidence from Randomized Evaluations," *Annual Review of Resource Economics*, 2: 237–56.

Almond, Douglas and Janet Currie. 2011. "Chapter 15: Human Capital Development before Age Five," *Handbook of Labor Economics*, 4 (b): 1315–486.

Alok, Kumar. 2010. *Squatting with Dignity: Lessons from India*. New Delhi: SAGE Publications.

Banerjee, Abhijit and Esther Duflo. 2011. *Poor Economics*. Public Affairs, New York. Available at http://www.amazon.com/Poor-Economics-Radical-Rethinking-Poverty/dp/1610390938

Barham, Tania. 2012. "Enhancing Cognitive Functioning: Medium-Term Effects of a Health and Family Planning Program in Matlab," *American Economic Journal: Applied Economics*, 4 (1): 245–73.

Bhandari, Nita, Rajiv Bahl, Sunita Taneja, Mercedes de Onis, and Maharaj K. Bhan. 2002. "Growth Performance of Affluent Indian Children is Similar to that in Developed Countries," *Bulletin of the WHO*, 80: 189–95.

Black, Maggie and Ben Fawcett. 2008. *The Last Taboo: Opening the Door on the Global Sanitation Crisis*. London: Earthscan.

Case, Anne and Christina Paxson. 2010. "Causes and Consequences of Early-life Health," *Demography*, 47: S65–S85.

Chattopadhyay, Raghabendra and Esther Duflo. 2004. "Women as Policy Makers: Evidence from a Randomized Policy Experiment in India," *Econometrica*, 72 (5): 1409–43.

Coffey, Diane. 2011. "Limits to Experimental Evaluation and Student Attendance in Rural Indian Schools: A Field Experiment." Paper presented at annual meeting session 89, Population Association of America, Washington.

———. 2012. "Early-Life Mortality, Income, and Adult Height in India." RICE working paper. Available at www.riceinstitute.org

Cunha, Flavio, James Heckman, and Susanne Schennach. 2010. "Estimating the Technology of Cognitive and Noncognitive Skill Formation," *Econometrica*, 78 (3): 883–931.

Das, Jishnu, Jeffrey Hammer, and Carolina Sánchez-Paramo. 2012. "The Impact of Recall Periods on Reported Morbidity and Health Seeking Behavior," *Journal of Development Economics*, 98 (1): 76–88.

Deaton, Angus. 2007. "Height, Health, and Development," *PNAS*, 104: 13232–37.

Dhaliwal, Iqbal, Esther Duflo, Rachel Glennerster, and Caitlin Tulloch. 2011. "Comparative Cost-Effectiveness Analysis to Inform Policy in Developing Countries: A General Framework with Applications for Education." Abdul Latif Jameel Poverty Action Lab (J-PAL), MIT.

Duflo, Esther, Rachel Glennerster, and Michael Kremer. 2007. "Chapter 61: Using Randomization in Development Economics Research: A Toolkit," *Handbook of Development Economics*, 4: 3895–3962.

Franceys, R., J. Pickford, and R. Reed. 1992. *A Guide to the Development of On-site Sanitation*. Geneva: World Health Organization.

Galiani, Sebastian, Paul Gertler, and Ernesto Schargrodsky. 2005. "Water for Life: The Impact of the Privatization of Water Services on Child Mortality," *Journal of Political Economy*, 113 (1): 83–120.

George, Benny. 2010. "Total Sanitation Campaign: A Review," in Alok Kumar and B. S. Bisht (eds), *Sanitation and Health in Rural India: Problems and Management Options*. National Institute of Administrative Research.

Glewwe, Paul, Nauman Ilias, and Michael Kremer. 2003. "Teacher Incentives." Working paper 9671, National Bureau of Economic Research (NBER).

Hammer, Jeffrey S. 1997. "Economic Analysis for Health Projects," *World Bank Research Observer*, 12 (1): 47–71.

Hanushek, Eric A. and Ludger Woessmann. 2008. "The Role of Cognitive Skills in Economic Development," *Journal of Economic Literature*, 46 (3): 607–68.

Holmstrom, Bengt and Paul Milgrom. 1991. "Multitask Principal-Agent Analyses: Incentive Contracts, Asset Ownership, and Job Design," *Journal of Law, Economics, & Organization*, 7 (special issue): 24–52.

Humphrey, Jean H. 2009. "Child Undernutrition, Tropical Enteropathy, Toilets, and Handwashing," *Lancet*, 374: 1032–35.

Imbert, Clément and John Papp. 2011. "Estimating Leakages in India's Employment Guarantee," in Reetika Khera (ed.), *The Battle for Employment Guarantee*. Oxford.

Kishore, Avinash and Dean Spears. 2012. "Improved Rural Sanitation as a Village-level Coordination Game." RICE working paper. Available at www.riceinstitute. org

Kremer, Michael, Jessica Leino, Edward Miguel, and Alix Peterson Zwane. 2011. "Spring Cleaning: Rural Water Impacts, Valuation, and Property Rights Institutions," *Quarterly Journal of Economics*, 126 (1): 145–205.

Lamba, Rohit and Dean Spears. 2012. "Policy Incentives amidst Low State Capacity and Corruption: India's Clean Village Prize as a Mechanism Design Problem." RICE working paper. Available at www.riceinstitute.org

Lamba, Sneha and Dean Spears. 2012. "Effects of Caste Reservation of Village Governance on Sanitation Implementation in Rajasthan." RICE working paper. Available at www.riceinstitute.org

Miguel, Edward and Michael Kremer. 2004. "Worms: Identifying Impacts on Education and Health in the Presence of Treatment Externalities," *Econometrica*, 72 (1): 159–217.

Mondal, Dinesh, Juliana Minak, Masud Alam, Yue Liu, Jing Dai, Poonum Korpe, Lei Liu, Rashidul Haque, and William A. Petri, Jr. 2011. "Contribution of Enteric Infection, Altered Intestinal Barrier Function, and Maternal Malnutrition to Infant Malnutrition in Bangladesh," *Clinical Infectious Diseases*.

Nordhaus, William. 2007. "Critical Assumptions in the Stern Review on Climate Change," *Science*, 317 (13 July): 201–02.

Olken, Benjamin A. 2007. "Monitoring Corruption: Evidence from a Field Experiment in Indonesia," *Journal of Political Economy*, 115 (2): 200–49.

Ravallion, Martin. 2012. "Fighting Poverty One Experiment at a Time: A Review of Abhijit Banerjee and Esther Duflo's Poor Economics: A Radical Rethinking of the Way to Fight Global Poverty," *Journal of Economic Literature*, 50 (1): 103–14.

Schmidt, Wolf-Peter, Benjamin F. Arnold, Sophie Boisson, Bernd Genser, Stephen P. Luby, Mauricio L. Barreto, Thomas Clasen, and Sandy Cairncross. 2011. "Epidemiological Methods in Diarrhea Studies: An Update," *International Journal of Epidemiology*, 40 (6): 1678–92.

Spears, Dean. 2012a. "Effects of Rural Sanitation on Infant Mortality and Human Capital: Evidence from a Local Governance Incentive in India." RICE working paper. Available at www.riceinstitute.org

———. 2012b. "Sanitation and Open Defecation Explain International Variation in Children's Height: Evidence from 140 Nationally Representative Household Surveys." RICE working paper. Available at www.riceinstitute.org

———. 2012c. "Height and Cognitive Achievement among Indian Children," *Economics and Human Biology*, 10: 210–19.

Spears, Dean and Sneha Lamba. 2012. "Effects of Early-Life Exposure to Rural Sanitation on Childhood Cognitive Skills: Evidence from India's Total Sanitation Campaign." RICE working paper. Available at www.riceinstitute.org

Steckel, Richard H. 2009. "Heights and Human Welfare: Recent Developments and New Directions," *Explorations in Economic History*, 46: 1–23.

Zwane, Alix Peterson, Jonathan Zinman, Eric Van Dusen, William Pariente, Clair Null, Edward Miguel, Michael Kremer, Dean S. Karlan, Richard Hornbeck, Xavier Giné, Esther Duflo, Florencia Devoto, Bruno Crepon, and Abhijit Banerjee. 2011. "Being Surveyed Can Change Later Behavior and Related Parameter Estimates," *PNAS*, 108 (5): 1821–26.

Comments and Discussions

Rohini Somanathan
Delhi School of Economics

This paper uses several data sets and alternative empirical approaches to estimate the effects of increases in sanitation coverage through the Total Sanitation Campaign (TSC) on child health in India. There are three measures of health used: anthropometric data on child heights, scores from cognitive tests and infant mortality rates. The principal data sets used are the third round of the National Family Health Survey (NFHS) and administrative data from the TSC.

The paper begins with suggestive correlations of the heights of children below 3 and the prevalence of open defecation using cross-country and cross-state data. Children are shorter in areas where the fraction of the population using toilets is lower. Village data from the NFHS also shows that average heights of children in villages where a large fraction of households have toilets are higher even if these children are in households without toilets.

Estimates of the impact of the TSC on infant mortality rates are obtained using two different empirical strategies. The first uses the NFHS-3 and asks whether mortality rates were lower for those children that were born in districts and in years when more toilets were built. The second uses district data on infant mortality and the number of toilets built between 2001 and 2011. The claim is that at the end of this 10 year period, the TSC resulted in a decline of 4 infant deaths per 1,000 live births. There is also some limited evidence on the cognitive effects of improved child health resulting from the sanitation campaign and districts with more latrines per capita also have more children who recognize numbers at the age of 6.

In terms of mechanisms, the paper argues that incentives at the local level matter for the success of the scheme. Under the TSC, villages that have eliminated open defecation receive the Nirmal Gram Puruskar (NGP), a cash prize that varies by the population size of the village. The paper examines toilet construction rates in villages with sizes on either side of the threshold at which the cash prize jumps up, and finds that those just above the threshold undertake construction much more energetically.

The models based on district level data are carefully done, yet identification does remain problematic. While these models include time and district effects, it is not possible to control for other government programs that are associated with improved health. These could include piped water schemes, immunization programs, improved health centers or successful information campaigns that encourage hygienic behavior. Bureaucrats or local political representatives that are energetic in the TSC are also likely to be more effective in these other dimensions. If this is indeed the case, then the estimates obtained will be too high because they reflect the combined effect of these programs. The heterogeneous effects by state that are found in the paper may also partly reflect this problem of missing information on other government schemes and on administrative capacity in general. One worrying pattern in the paper is the extremely high current rates of open defecation in spite of 10 years of the program and evidence that many of the toilets constructed are used only as storage areas.

The discontinuity in payoffs implicit in the NGP prizes can help isolate the effects of sanitation relative to these other schemes. There is no infant mortality data matched to these villages in the paper, but this is a relatively clean identification strategy and could be successfully pursued in future work if data on health could be obtained at the village level for a sample of villages.

Louis Boorstin
Gates Foundation

By the initial standard I guess I am qualified as I have definitely practiced open defecation before, although I haven't done it in India. I lived in the Wyoming woods for a month once, which called for that sort of behavior. I am also perhaps qualified because I have been involved in this field for the last seven years, having founded the Water Sanitation and Hygiene Programme at the Bill & Melinda Gates Foundation. I am, however, profoundly unqualified to sit in a room of PhD economists and social scientists and focus strictly on the economic issues.

With that as background, my first comment is that it is great to see sanitation on the agenda at this conference. Sanitation is a critical issue for Indian policy-makers and it needs a sustained interest. It cannot be a one-time event. It is also very heartening to see the type of rigorous research that Dean has undertaken here. If you look at the research out there, not just in India but across the world, his work is seminal and critical in establishing that rural sanitation saves lives and is cost-effective. I would also say that my reading of this paper has been formed by our experience here in India. For the last six years we have supporting the government through different grantees to implement rural sanitation in several different states.

Dean's paper raises two fundamental policy issues: The first is whether rural sanitation is a worthwhile investment. And the second is, if it is worthwhile, how do you implement it most effectively? I am not going to speak to the "whether" question, the first question, because the paper does a very good job of that (and my colleagues who are well qualified in this area were very pleased with it on that basis). So let me focus on the second question, how best to achieve improved sanitation in India which, as Dean said, is critical because there are 600 million practicing open defecation here.

Let us start with the three core strengths of the rural sanitation program in India. The first is the *focus on outcomes*, which Dean mentioned. Since 2003, with the advent of the NGP program, the focus has been rightly on achieving open-defecation-free communities, which can only be done if there is sustained and consistent use of latrines as opposed to just counting whether toilets have been installed.

The second point which is crucial to understand, particularly if you are not a sanitation policy wonk or practitioner, is that this is not a matter of giving away latrines. The most effective sanitation programs have been about *behavior change*—about working with communities to decide that they want to become open defecation free. Once that decision is made, it has a profound effect on what the community does. Note that this approach can work without a subsidy, and India is unusual in being able to provide subsidies on such a large scale, which many countries cannot do. In that sense this is very much a demand-led approach.

The third strength is the importance of *incentives* to achieving the desired sanitation outcomes. As we say in the US, "You get what you pay for," and so if you simply pay for latrines you typically get latrines but they are not often used. If you really want to achieve open-defecation-free status, and you have reliable reporting about that, then that is what you should reward through programs such as the NGP.

Having said that there are strengths to the program here, there are also several challenges, and it is worthwhile noting that the government has become fairly candid about these. I was here about a year and a half ago and attended the first conference of State Ministers in charge of sanitation. At that conference, I was surprised at how willing they were to stand up and talk about the fact that there were challenges in implementation as well as in reporting. So the first challenge is the *large degree of variability in how the programs have been implemented*. Some areas have truly achieved

100 percent open defecation free status. Others have not, and there are more that haven't than have.

The second challenge is *sustaining the use of latrines* over time. It is one thing to get people to want to use latrines and it is another to make sure that the latrines continue to be used over time. This can be especially difficult if you are very good at convincing villagers to install latrines, but then they build such poor quality latrines that they can't survive the next rainy season. Finally, as Dean mentioned, in a number of cases *communities have received ex post incentives inappropriately*, which is to say when they have not actually achieved 100 percent open defecation free status. Figuring out how to deal with that problem is quite important.

Using that as the context, and being sort of a policy wonk on sanitation, I am going to amplify on a few points that Dean made. The first is a aspect that Professor Somanathan highlighted: Dean's research has just looked at the *average* implementation of TSC. If you are noticeably saving lives on a cost-effective basis with just the average implementation, then what happens if we actually get good at it? Can you actually get much better results? I believe you can. A lot of the grants we have funded here in India and elsewhere are about trying to find out how to do that.

The second point is that it is clear from Dean's research, as well as from other work, that the outcome-based payments are critical. This is important because the initial data coming out of this new NBA program is that the focus is once again will be more on paying for latrines. Instead, one should look at the history of the outcome-based award here and consider putting more funding into that.

A third point relates to subsidizing the construction of latrines. There is clearly a desire to do that here, and there are situations where it makes sense because you want people to put in attractive, durable latrines that will actually be used and last over time. So the money can be helpful. But what you need to do is to minimize the use of that subsidy, make sure it is just what it is needed for the materials, and then sequence the provision of those funds. Careful sequencing of hardware subsidies means that in each one of these villages you start the demand led process by going in, working with that community, getting them to make the decision that they want to put in sanitation. Only then do you make the hardware subsidies available. If you do it the other way around or you only come in with the money, the experience in the 1990s here in India as well as in most other countries is you will fail miserably.

Finally to the last point that Dean made. Accurate reporting is absolutely essential here. You want this data to be credible, you want it to be transparent and, you want people to know that when a village has been declared open defecation free, there is a good likelihood that it actually *is* open defecation free.

General Discussion

The general discussion focused on the emphasis of the paper on demand-side incentives as opposed to supply-side subsidies for latrine use. Most participants were complementary in applauding the finding that the outcome-based incentive programs were effective; but there were concerns about verification of village performance and questions about the extent that the gains would continue after termination of the payments to village elders. Also, there was strong approval of the randomized design of the program.

K. Muralidharan focused on the evidence of health gains and thought there might be important nonlinearities in the relationship; perhaps the health gains would substantially larger once the sanitation program had achieved a high level of coverage. He also thought it would be important to be able to separate and measure the effects of the supply and demand-side elements of the program. Others agreed that the evidence of improvements in health were striking, but expresses some concern about its significance.

Ashok Lahiri and Abhijit Banerjee raised concerns about the importance of water availability. There should be an effort to test the differences in outcomes between latrines with access to water and dry latrines. Banerjee thought that dry latrines may be more practical in many parts of the country but wondered about their effect on usage rates. Lahiri thought similar issues might arise with respect to the availability of electricity.

Rinku Murgai thought the paper was an important counterpoint to a general perception that the sanitation program was not accomplishing much. She wondered about the sustainability of the gains in future years when the incentives end. She also pointed to government arguments that the supply-side subsidy was too small and a belief that the benefit of the demand-side incentives was conditional on ensuring that more latrines were built—expansion of the subsidy. She echoed Spears concerns that the revised program would place to little emphasis on the demand-side incentives.

Some questions were also asked about the applicability of the program to different locations, such as urban versus rural.

SHEKHAR AIYAR
International Monetary Fund

ASHOKA MODY
Princeton University

The Demographic Dividend: Evidence from the Indian States*

ABSTRACT   Large cohorts of young adults are poised to add to the working-age population of developing economies. Despite much interest in the consequent growth dividend, the size and circumstances of the potential gains remain under-explored. This study makes progress by focusing on India, which will be the largest individual contributor to the global demographic transition ahead. It exploits the variation in the age structure of the population across Indian states to identify the demographic dividend. The main finding is that there is a large and significant growth impact of both the level and growth rate of the working-age ratio. This result is robust to a variety of empirical strategies, including a correction for interstate migration. The results imply that a substantial fraction of the growth acceleration that India has experienced since the 1980s—sometimes ascribed exclusively to economic reforms—is attributable to changes in the country's age structure. Moreover, relative to the age structure at the turn of the millennium, the demographic dividend could add about 2 percentage points per annum to India's per-capita Gross Domestic Product (GDP) growth over the next two decades. With the future expansion of the working-age ratio concentrated in some of India's poorest states, income convergence may well speed up, a theme likely to recur on the global stage.

Keywords: *Demographic Dividend, Indian States, Age-structure, Migration, Convergence*

JEL Classification: *O47, O15, O53, J11*

* *saiyar@imf.org; ashokamody@gmail.com*   The views expressed here are those of the authors and should not be attributed to the International Monetary Fund or its Board of Executive Directors. We are grateful to our discussants Pranab Bardhan and Sonalde Desai for their thoughtful comments and suggestions and to Arvind Panagariya for his guidance in finalizing the paper. Participants at the IPF, including Surjit Bhalla, Dilip Mookherjee, T. N. Srinivasan, and John Williamson, also provided helpful comments, as did Ejaz Ghani, Kalpana Kochhar, Anusha Nath, Franziska Ohnsorge, Venugopal Reddy, and Arvind Subramanian.

1. Introduction

In the next 40 years, the world's population will increase by about 2.4 billion people, with almost all of the increase occurring in developing countries (Figure 1). More importantly, the numbers of those between the ages of 15 and 64—the so-called working-age population—will swell. This boost in potential workers is the outcome of the "demographic transition": declining infant mortality rates that are being followed by falling fertility rates. Thus, with children more likely to survive into productive adulthood and fewer children being produced, the share of working-age populations will increase. For the least developed countries, this share will continue to increase through 2050; for other less developed countries, the share has been steadily increasing and will peak in the coming two decades.[1]

An increase in the working-age ratio can raise the rate of economic growth, and hence confer a "demographic dividend." This can occur through several channels. First, there is the labor-input effect, whereby a greater proportion of workers in a fixed population produces more output per capita. Second, in general, workers save while dependants do not, and even if the correspondence between savers and the working-age population is not exact, the overlap is likely to be considerable. Therefore a bulge in the working-age ratio contributes to higher savings rates, increasing the domestic resources available for productive investment. Finally, the fertility decline that is the source of the changed age structure may induce higher productivity through associated attention to primary education and health, and may also encourage greater female labor supply (Bailey 2006).

While there is a sizeable literature on demographic trends and their economic ramifications, the econometric evidence for the growth impact of the working-age ratio is more limited. Bloom and Canning (2004) is a landmark contribution. For a panel of countries from 1965 to 1995, the authors find a sizeable impact of the working-age ratio on economic growth but only if the economy is "open." Thus, they conclude that the potential for a dividend exists but that it is realized mainly when incentives are in place to exploit that potential. Several papers find that national savings rates are strongly connected to demographic structure (Fry and Mason [1982], Higgins [1998], and Kelley and Schmidt [1996]). Other papers focus on particular countries

---

1. While the proximate cause of the bulge in working-age populations is the sequence of falling infant mortality rates followed by declining fertility rates, there is much debate about ultimate causes, especially with respect to fertility patterns. See Galor (2011) for a comprehensive review of the theoretical and empirical literature.

FIGURE 1. The Demographic Transition

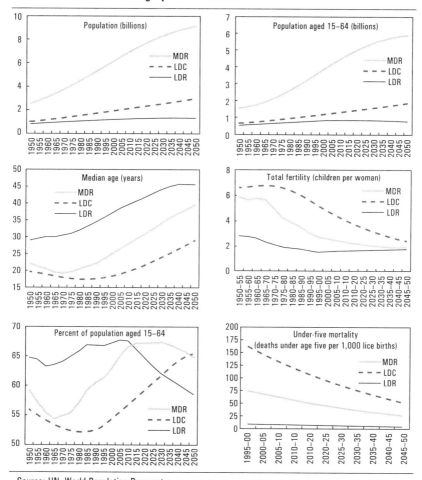

Source: UN, World Population Prospects.
MDR = More developed regions
LDC = Least developed countries
LDR = Less developed regions, excluding least developed countries

or regions. Persson (2002) and Feyrer (2007) document the relationship in the US between demographic structure and, respectively, output and productivity. Bloom, Canning, and Malaney (2000) and Mason (2001) conclude that East Asia's "economic miracle" was associated with a major transition in age structure, while Bloom, Canning, and Sevilla (2002) find that much of Africa's relatively poor economic performance can be accounted for by the lack of such a transition.

Given the importance of the demographic transition, this paper seeks to deepen our understanding of the size and circumstances of the demographic dividend. In doing so, we focus on India. This focus is motivated by several factors. First, India is in the midst of a major demographic transition that started about 40 years ago and will likely last another 30 years. As a simple quantitative matter, about a quarter of the projected increase in the global population aged 15–64 years between 2010 and 2040 will occur in India.[2] The working-age ratio in the country is set to rise from about 64 percent currently to 69 percent in 2040, reflecting the addition of just over 300 million working-age adults. This would make India—by an order of magnitude—the largest single positive contributor to the global workforce over the next three decades.

Second, recent research on economic growth emphasizes the difficulties of controlling for widely differing economic and noneconomic conditions across countries. An advantage of focusing on India is that we can exploit the variations across Indian states, which are more homogenous than the typical cross section of countries. For our purpose, Indian states have historically exhibited large differences in age structure, both in the level and growth rate of the working-age ratio. And the correlation between states' demographic trends and economic performance appears striking. The paper provides a more careful estimate of the impact of the working-age ratio on economic growth.

Third, for those engaged in the sport of India–China comparisons, the demographic dividend offers the single biggest hope for India to catch up (Kelkar 2004). China saw its population pyramid shift from the bottom-heavy distribution typical of a young and growing population in the early 1980s to a mature population structure by 2000. Over the coming decades, as the working-age population of China declines, that of India will rise rapidly.

In this paper, we describe how a standard conditional convergence framework can be adapted to derive a panel specification in which both the level and the growth rate of the working-age ratio help determine economic growth. The framework is applied to data on the Indian states. In principle, the specification captures all the channels through which a rise in the working-age ratio confers a growth dividend. Thus, this exercise may be viewed as an effort to quantify the aggregate economic impact of India's evolving age structure.

We reach three principal conclusions. First, the demographic dividend in the Indian context has been substantial. This result is robust to adjustments

2. United Nations (2009).

for interstate migration that may be stimulated by growth differentials and to a two-stage procedure in which lagged fertility decisions are used to instrument the growth in working-age population. Our econometric estimates imply that relative to the age structure in 1960, between 40 to 50 percent of the per capita income growth over the next four decades was attributable to the ongoing demographic dividend. While policy reforms had an important role to play in the growth acceleration starting in the 1980s, the results caution that their contribution was less than commonly perceived once the concurrent rise in working-age ratios is taken into account. Second, unlike Bloom and Canning (2004), we do not find the demographic dividend to be conditional on specific policies or social environments. We read the evidence to say that the very features that lead to a demographic transition— mortality decreases followed by fertility decline—also reflect broader health and educational achievements that are conducive to the exploitation of the demographic dividend. Finally, going forward, it is the poorest Indian states that stand to gain the most from the forthcoming demographic transition, since they are the ones that have so far lagged behind in both the transition and in income growth. The prospect of such gains is a source of hope beyond India, where the potential benefits of the demographic dividend are also most on tap for the least developed economies.

The rest of this paper is organized as follows. Section 2 reports on state-specific trends in the age structure of the population and its correlations with income growth. Section 3 describes an econometric framework that is used in Sections 4 and 5 to estimate the demographic dividend, paying attention to various robustness considerations. In Section 6, we use the regression coefficients to quantify the contribution of the demographic dividend in the past four decades and in the decades beyond. The final section offers some concluding remarks.

2. Data and Summary Statistics

We create a database of the age distribution of population, per capita income, and numerous social and economic indicators across Indian states by decade. Data on the age distribution are from successive rounds of the Census of India (COI).[3] Unfortunately, the age groups reported in successive COIs are not uniform. Hence, instead of defining the working-age ratio as the share

---

3. The Indian census is conducted every 10 years and published in the first year of the decade; thus the ones used in this study are for the years 1961, 1971, 1981, 1991, and 2001.

of population aged 15–64 years, as is conventional, we define it instead as the share of population aged 15–59 years, a group for which we do have a consistent panel.

Two adjustments are made to the population data to account for the creation of new states during the sample period. First, the 2001 data is adjusted to take account of the creation of Jharkhand, Chhattisgarh, and Uttaranchal. These states were carved out of the existing territory of the states of Bihar, Madhya Pradesh, and Uttar Pradesh in 2000. The COI 2001 reports age distributions for these states separately. Since we have the complete age distribution for both the new states as well as the rest of the old states, we consolidate Bihar with Jharkhand, Madhya Pradesh with Chhattisgarh, and Uttar Pradesh with Uttaranchal so that the time series for each state remains consistent with the old geographical divisions. Second, a more complicated adjustment is made to account for the creation of Haryana from the territory of Punjab in 1966.[4]

Real per capita net state domestic product (NSDP) is sourced from the Central Statistical Organization (CSO).[5] With that, for income and age distribution, we have a largely balanced panel of 22 states, with data at 10-year intervals from 1961 to 2001.[6] Data sources for the other variables used will be described as they are introduced, in Sections 4 and 5.

4. The 1966 redesignation also created the Union Territory of Chandigarh, originally a city in Punjab, to serve as the joint capital of Punjab and Haryana. From the COI 1971, we calculate Punjab's population as a ratio of the combined population of Punjab, Haryana and Chandigarh. We do this separately for each age group. We then apply this ratio to the COI 1961 population data on (the old) Punjab, to get a time series that is consistent with the new geographical area. We repeat the procedure for Haryana.

5. The data we actually employ is the Economic and Political Weekly Research Foundation (EPWFR) panel of NSDP (from 1961 through 2004), available on CD-ROM, and sourced from the CSO and Directorates of Economics and Statistics of respective state governments. The data for 1961–71, however, covers only four states. Hence for that decade, we use data from Indiastat (http://www.indiastat.com), a Web site that agglomerates Indian national and state-level data from diverse sources. The CSO data series on real per-capita NSDP have been periodically rebased. To construct a consistent constant price time series we use the base year 1993–94. For any of the previous years, we employ growth rates from differently based series to back out levels corresponding to the 1993–94 base year. For example, growth rates from 1981–82 to 1992–93 are taken from the CSO's base 1980–81 series, and the levels backed out from the fixed point of the per-capita real NSDP in 1993–94.

6. The states are: Andhra Pradesh, Arunachal Pradesh, Assam, Bihar, Gujarat, Haryana, Himachal Pradesh, Jammu and Kashmir, Kerala, Karnataka, Maharashtra, Manipur, Madhya Pradesh, Meghalaya, Nagaland, Orissa, Punjab, Rajasthan, Tamil Nadu, Tripura, Uttar Pradesh, and West Bengal. Data are missing on income and age distribution for Arunachal Pradesh 1961; income data are missing for Nagaland 1961, Meghalaya 1971 and Nagaland 1971; and age distribution data are unavailable for Assam 1981 and Jammu and Kashmir 1991. Age

Table 1 reports summary statistics for the key variables of interest: the growth in per capita income, the working-age ratio, and the growth rate of the working-age ratio. The first three rows show summary statistics treating each state-time period combination as a separate observation, while the next three rows show summary statistics across states (averaged over time). Both panels attest to the enormous diversity across Indian states.

TABLE 1. Summary Statistics

		Mean	S.D.	Minimum	Maximum
Across states and time periods	Per capita income growth (percent)	2.13	1.67	−1.83 Rajasthan (1971–81)	6.26 Tripura (1991–2001)
	Working age ratio (percent)	54.93	3.37	47.98 Haryana (1971)	64.4 Tamil Nadu (2001)
	Working age ratio growth (percent)	0.22	0.38	−0.68 Madhya Pradesh (1961–71)	0.85 Tripura (1971–81)
Across states	Per capita income growth (percent)	2.18	0.79	0.87 Madhya Pradesh	3.8 Arunachal Pradesh
	Working age ratio (percent)	54.9	1.89	52.2 Bihar	59.7 Tamil Nadu
	Working age ratio growth (percent)	0.21	0.19	−0.09 Jammu & Kashmir	0.55 Haryana

Source: Census of India; CSO; and authors' calculations.

Table 2 reports the evolution of our variables of interest for six selected states. The states have been chosen as representative of two groups: "Leaders" or high-growth states, typically from the south and west of the country, and "Laggards" or low-growth states, largely concentrated in a broad swath of territory running across central and northern India where Hindi and associated dialects are spoken (hence the term "Hindi Heartland"). The divergence in per capita income growth between Leaders and Laggards is well known, with the divergence being highest for the most recent period 1991–2001. What may be less well known is that these trends in income growth are mirrored in the demographic data. A large and widening gap has opened up between the working-age ratios in Leaders and Laggards over the 40-year period. In the decade 1991–2001, the gap reached 8.6 percentage points or 2.6 standard deviations (across state-time observations).

distribution data for Jammu and Kashmir in 1991 are unavailable because there was no census carried out in Jammu and Kashmir in that year.

TABLE 2. Demographic Evolution and Income Growth in Selected States

		1961	1971	1981	1991	2001
	Leaders (South and West)					
	Tamil Nadu	56.8	56.5	58.6	62.4	64.4
	Karnataka	52.1	51.5	53.9	57.8	60.4
	Gujarat	52.2	51.7	55.3	58.8	60.3
Working Age	*Simple Average*	*53.7*	*53.2*	*55.9*	*59.7*	*61.7*
Ratio	Laggards (Heartland)					
	Bihar	52.1	51.5	51.5	53.6	52.1
	Madhya Pradesh	54.0	50.5	52.3	55.3	54.8
	Uttar Pradesh	53.2	51.4	51.5	53.7	52.3
	Simple Average	*53.1*	*51.1*	*51.8*	*54.2*	*53.1*

		1961–71	1971–81	1981–91	1991–2001
	Leaders (South and West)				
	Tamil Nadu	−0.06	0.36	0.64	0.31
	Karnataka	−0.13	0.45	0.71	0.44
Working Age	Gujarat	−0.10	0.67	0.61	0.26
Ratio Average	*Simple Average*	*−0.09*	*0.50*	*0.65*	*0.34*
Annual Growth	Laggards (Heartland)				
Rate (%)	Bihar	−0.11	0.00	0.40	−0.29
	Madhya Pradesh	−0.68	0.35	0.54	−0.09
	Uttar Pradesh	−0.35	0.02	0.41	−0.26
	Simple Average	*−0.38*	*0.13*	*0.45*	*−0.21*

		1961–71	1971–81	1981–91	1991–2001
	Leaders (South and West)				
	Tamil Nadu	0.4	0.1	4.1	5.1
	Karnataka	2.0	0.7	3.0	6.0
Per Capita	Gujarat	1.9	0.9	3.1	3.6
Income Average	*Simple Average*	*1.4*	*0.5*	*3.4*	*4.9*
Annual Growth	Laggards (Heartland)				
Rate (%)	Bihar	0.3	0.6	2.7	−0.1
	Madhya Pradesh	−0.5	0.6	2.2	1.1
	Uttar Pradesh	0.7	0.7	2.6	0.8
	Simple Average	*0.2*	*0.6*	*2.5*	*0.6*

Source: Census of India; Central Statistical Organization; and authors' calculations.

3. Estimation

Following Bloom and Canning (2004), we use a standard conditional convergence equation to derive a relationship between per capita income growth and demographic trends.

$$g_z = \lambda(z^* - z_0)$$

The equation above is a staple of the growth literature, derived and extensively discussed in Barro and Sala-i-Martin (1995). Log income per worker is denoted by z, and growth in income per worker by g_z. The equation states that, over any given time period, growth in per worker income is related to the gap between the steady state level of income per worker and the level of income per worker at the beginning of the period. λ parameterizes the speed of adjustment to the steady state. In turn, the steady state income per worker is a function of several variables that impact potential labor productivity. These include measures of health and education, which determine the quality of the labor stock, or time-invariant factors such as climate, geography, and culture. Denoting these determinants of labor productivity by the vector X and the associated vector of parameters by β, the equation can be rewritten as:

$$g_z = \lambda(X\beta - z_0) \tag{1}$$

To relate this to demographic variables, consider the following simple identity:

$$\frac{Y}{N} = \frac{Y}{L}\frac{L}{WA}\frac{WA}{N}$$

where N denotes population, L the labor force and WA the working-age population. The identity states that income per capita equals labor productivity times the participation rate times the working-age ratio. Let lowercase letters represent the log of these ratios,

$$y = \ln(\frac{Y}{N}); z = \ln(\frac{Y}{L}); p = \ln(\frac{L}{WA}); w = \ln(\frac{WA}{N})$$

It follows that:

$$z = y - p - w \tag{2}$$

And, assuming that participation rates remain constant within each state,

$$g_y = g_z + g_w \tag{3}$$

where g_y is the growth in income per capita and g_w the growth in the working-age ratio. Substituting (2) and (3) into (1) yields:

$$g_y = \lambda(X\beta + p + w_0 - y_0) + g_w \tag{4}$$

Equation (4) is the basis for our empirical estimation. It says that over a given time period, both the initial working-age ratio and the growth rate of the working-age ratio should be positively related to per capita income growth. This is in addition to the impact of any other factors that may affect steady state labor productivity. Note that the vector X could also contain time-invariant variables.

Equation (4) imposes strict parameter restrictions on the coefficients for the working-age ratio and the growth rate of the working-age ratio. But the restrictions will not be valid if behavior changes in response to the changes in the working-age population ratio. As argued by a large literature, this is unlikely to be the case. The life cycle hypothesis posits that workers have positive savings while the young and the old consume more than they earn. Thus an expansion in the working-age ratio—the converse of the dependency ratio—is likely to be associated with increased aggregate savings and hence the potential stock of capital. Being born into a large cohort—so called "generational crowding"—could also impact behavior, influencing individual labor supply and relative wages (Easterlin 1980; Bloom, Korenman, and Freeman 1987; Korenman and Neumark 2000). Changes in the working-age ratio could also influence fertility decisions and participation rates. Moreover, to the extent that workers are healthier than the old, an expansion in the working-age ratio could also be accompanied by improvement in the stock of human capital stock, which may not be captured by "input" indicators of health. For these reasons, no restrictions are imposed on the coefficients of demographic variables, allowing the data to speak to their effect.

We estimate various specifications of the form:

$$g\_y_{i,t} = \rho \ln y_{i,t} + \beta_1 \ln w_{i,t} + \beta_2 g\_w_{i,t} + \gamma' X_{i,t} + f_i + \eta_t + \varepsilon_{i,t} \quad (5)$$

where the dependant variable $g\_y_{i,t}$ is the annual average growth rate of per capita income in state i over the decade beginning in year t. The main regressors are the log of initial per capita income, the log of the initial working-age ratio, and the average annual growth rate of the working-age ratio over the decade. $X_{i,t}$ is a vector of explanatory variables that might impact steady state labor productivity. f_i is a time-invariant fixed effect, capturing state-specific effects, while η_t is a time dummy, capturing effects unique to the decade beginning in year t (in our case, the national policy environment and international growth impulses). Thus the framework comprises a standard application of the within estimator.

All regressions are estimated with heteroskedasticity-robust standard errors. All control variables are measured at time t, and, like the initial working-age ratio, should be predetermined with respect to income growth over the following decade. The growth rate of the working-age population, being contemporaneous with the dependant variable, is potentially more problematic. The main determinant of this growth rate should be fertility decisions in the previous decade or earlier. However, other contemporaneous influences on the growth rate of the working-age population may include feedback effects from income growth. This endogeneity concern is taken up at some length in the next section.[7]

4. The Demographic Dividend

Column 1 in Table 3 presents the results from a regression using our two demographic variables—initial working-age ratio and the growth rate thereof—together with state-specific fixed effects and time period dummies. Both variables have the expected sign and are significant. Moreover, their magnitude is large, implying a very substantial impact on income growth. An increase of 0.01 in the log of the initial working-age ratio (i.e., a 1 percent increase in the working-age ratio) is associated with a 0.2 percentage points

---

7. The specification in equation (5) is technically equivalent to a dynamic panel with a lagged dependent variable, raising the usual issue of upward bias in the lagged dependant variable, in this case the log of initial per-capita income. It has become customary to address this bias using one of two variants of GMM, the difference estimator and the system estimator (Arellano and Bond [1991], Blundell and Bond [1998]). We do not follow this approach here. The difference and system estimators suffer from econometric issues of their own, which in this application are larger than the problems with the within estimator. The difference estimator uses lagged levels to instrument for a specification in first differences; this has the effect of magnifying gaps in unbalanced panels like ours and reducing the number of usable observations. In our case, using the difference estimator reduces the sample size to 38 observations, which we judge insufficient given that we must estimate 27 parameters (fixed effects for each state, plus time dummies, plus coefficients on the lagged dependant variable and demographic variables). The system estimator, on the other hand leads to a proliferation of instruments. In our case, 29 instruments are generated, relative to only 22 groups (panels). Such overfitting can result in biased estimates. Moreover, since the number of elements in the estimated variance matrix of moments is quadratic in the instrument count, it is quartic in T. In our case, with a relatively small sample size, the matrix becomes singular for both estimators, forcing the use of a generalized inverse. This distances the estimates from the asymptotic case and weakens the Sargan-Hansen test (Anderson and Sorensen [1996], Bowsher [2002]). Having said this, the estimates of the impact of demographic variables obtained from the difference and system estimators are qualitatively similar to those obtained by the within estimator (but not so for the lagged dependent variable).

increase in annual average per capita income growth over the succeeding decade. Since the standard deviation of ln $w_{i,t}$ across states is 0.03, a one standard deviation increase in the working-age ratio is associated with an increase of about 0.6 percentage points in per capita income growth. Also, a one standard deviation increase in the growth rate of the working-age ratio is 0.19, which would increase per capita income growth by about 0.5 percentage points.

TABLE 3. The Impact of Demography on Per-capita Growth Controlling for Migration[a]

	Dependent variable: Annual per capita income growth			
	(1)	(2)	(3)	(4)
Log initial income per capita	−0.088***	−0.101***	−0.090***	−0.101***
	0.0175	0.013	0.0167	0.014
Log initial working age ratio	0.188**	0.234***	0.201**	0.235***
	0.077	0.081	0.074	0.076
Growth rate of working age ratio	2.478**		2.548**	
	1.026		0.982	
Adjusted growth rate of working age ratio[b]		1.57***		1.56***
		0.50		0.49
Labor participation rate			−0.016	0.029
			0.032	0.025
R-sqaured	0.73	0.69	0.73	0.74
Observations	76	72	75	72
Groups	22	22	22	22

Source: Authors.

Notes: [a] All regressions employ the within estimator with robust standard errors.

[b] It is assumed that all migrants are of working age. Accordingly, for each decade a counterfactual growth rate of the working age ratio is constructed by deducting the number of net inward migrants over the decade from both the end-of-decade population and the end-of-decade working age population.

*, **, and *** denote significance at the 10%, 5%, and 1% levels, respectively.

As noted in the previous section, the initial working-age ratio should be predetermined with respect to per capita income growth. However, there is one obvious channel through which per capita income growth could have a contemporaneous impact on the growth rate of the working-age ratio: interstate migration. Although it is widely held that interstate migration is considerable and should therefore be associated with growth patterns, there has been little effort to quantitatively assess this possibility. Cashin and Sahay (1996) studied migration between the Indian states, and found scant evidence that interstate population flows responded to income differentials.[8]

8. They write (p. 162): "...while the [inward] migration rate for the states of India is positively related to initial per-capita income, it is not statistically different from zero. In that

They pointed to strong barriers to the mobility of labor, such as local labor unions that resist competition from migrants, lack of urban housing in migrant destinations, and most importantly, linguistic and cultural impediments to cross-border labor substitutability. In fact, most migration tends to be within-state female migration caused by newly married wives relocating to their husband's village (Datta 1985; Skeldon 1986).

Nonetheless, we attempt to control for the impact of migration on our contemporaneous regressor, using interstate migration data from the COI.[9] For each decade, we construct a counterfactual growth rate of the working-age ratio, i.e., that growth rate which would have prevailed in the absence of inward or outward migration. Lacking data on the age distribution of migrants, we assume that all migrants are of working age. For each decade and state, we subtract the number of (net inward) migrants from both the end-of-decade total population and the end-of-decade working-age population. This yields a migration-adjusted end-of-decade working-age ratio, which is compared to the initial working-age ratio to calculate an adjusted growth rate. Note that our assumption that all migrants are of working age maximizes the possible impact of migration on the growth rate of the working-age ratio. If we had assumed that migrants had the same age distribution as the initial age distribution of the existing population, this would lead to a much smaller adjustment for migration.

Column 2 in Table 3 shows the results from a specification with the growth rate of the working-age population adjusted for migration in this manner. Both the initial level of the working-age ratio and its growth rate remain significant. While the point estimate of the coefficient on the adjusted growth rate of the working-age ratio falls slightly, it is statistically indistinguishable from the non-adjusted coefficient, and is more tightly estimated. These results provide confidence that migration flows in response to per capita income growth are not the main story; instead, causation does seem to run from the demographic variables to income growth.

sense, the income elasticity of migration across the states of India more closely resembles the relatively weak responsiveness of population movements to differentials in the regions of Europe than the relatively stronger responsiveness to differentials in the states of the USA or the prefectures of Japan."

9. We are grateful to Cashin and Sahay for making their dataset on immigration available to us, which fills some omissions in the census data with calculations from vital statistics. Their dataset, however, only contains net migration data for the 1960s, 1970s, and 1980s. For the period 1991–2001 we use our own calculations. For each state, the net inward migration rate is given by $g_N - (b_r - d_r)$, where g_N is the annual growth rate of the population (in percentage terms), and b_r and d_r are the crude birth and death rate per 100 persons, respectively.

Columns 3 and 4 in Table 3 include the labor participation rate, constructed from census data.[10] In principle, a higher labor participation rate should also have a positive impact on economic growth, through the labor-input channel. However, the data do not indicate a significant relationship. While this topic deserves serious research in its own right, we can point to at least a couple of reasons why this might be the case. The average labor force participation rate across states fell precipitously from 83.5 percent in 1961 to 66.4 percent in 1971; it decreased further to 63.4 percent in 1981; and then rose to 67.4 percent in 1991 before falling again to 56.1 percent in 2001. This pattern—or rather, this absence of a pattern—suggests that some significant part of these variations reflect changing census definitions over time, as detailed in footnote 10. Moreover, participation rates—unlike structural variables such as the working-age ratio—are likely to vary with the business cycle. Since state-wise participation rates are measured in a single (pre-census) year, they are likely to incorporate business cycle effects and therefore poorly predict economic growth over the next decade. For the remainder of this paper, we omit participation rates from the specifications.

Table 4 provides an alternative approach to identify the impact of growth in the working-age ratio on income growth. Column 1 reports again the result from the baseline specification. Columns 2 and 3 are IV specifications to reduce the potential bias arising from endogeneity, or from omitted or mismeasured variables. In column 2, the lagged birth rate is used as an instrument.[11] That is, the birth rate in 1961 is used as an instrument for the

10. From 1981 onward, the Census of India reports state level data on two categories of workers: "Main Workers" and "Marginal Workers." Main workers are those who worked for major part of year preceding enumeration (for 183 or more days in the year). Marginal workers are those who worked any time at all in preceding year, but for less than 183 days. Participation rates are defined as the ratio of Main Workers to the working-age population. Unfortunately the censuses of 1971 and 1961 follow a different convention, reporting only a single category: "Worker." For these two decades the participation rate is defined as the ratio of Workers to the working-age population. The 1961 Census defines workers as (*a*) those engaged in seasonal tasks and who worked for more than one hour a day through the greater part of the working season and (*b*) those in regular employment in any trade, profession, service, business, or commerce who were employed during any of the 15 days before enumeration (or absent due to illness or other good cause). The 1971 Census changes the definition of "Worker," bringing it closer to the "Main Worker" of 1981; thus the 1981 Census notes, "It was expected that the Main Worker of 1981 would correspond to the worker of 1971, and the Main Worker and Marginal Worker together of 1981 would correspond to the worker of 1961."

11. State-wise data on birth and death rates in India have several gaps. Moreover, because their source is the Sample Registration System (initiated in 1964–65), and various fertility surveys (initiated in 1972), no direct estimates are available for 1961. For that year we use

TABLE 4.   The Impact of Demography on Per-capita Growth Instrumental
Variables

	Dependent variable: Annual per capita income growth		
	(1)	(2)	(3)
Log initial income per capita	−0.088***	−0.076***	−0.080***
	0.0175	0.025	0.025
Log initial working age ratio	0.188**	0.36***	0.38***
	0.077	0.12	0.093
Growth rate of working age ratio	2.478**	4.13*	4.98**
	1.026	2.34	1.98
Instruments			
Lagged birth rate		Y	Y
Lagged working age ratio		N	Y
R-sqaured	0.73		
Observations	76	48	47
Groups	22	18	18
First stage F-statistic		10.7	8.3
Overidentifying restrictions (H0: Instruments uncorrelated with error process)			
Sargan-Hansen statistic			0.23
p-value			0.63
Exogeneity of instrumented explanatory variable (H0: Variable is exogenous)			
Difference in Sargan statistic		0.032	0.067
p-value		0.86	0.79

Source: Authors.
Notes: *, **, and *** denote significance at the 10%, 5%, and 1% levels, respectively.

average annual growth rate of the working-age ratio between 1971 and 81, and so on. And the presumption is that fertility decisions lagged by a decade are exogenous with respect to current income growth. With one instrument for one endogenous variable, standard tests of overidentifying restrictions are not possible, so column 3 uses the lagged working-age ratio as an additional instrument, with almost identical results.

There are two ways of interpreting these results with past birth rates as an instrument for working-age population growth. A purely statistical approach is based on the argument that lagged fertility is a valid instrument if: (*a*) it is strongly correlated with the regressor that is likely endogenous, and (*b*) it also does not itself belong in the regression, that is, it satisfies the exclusion restriction. Fertility is statistically significant in the first stage equation that explains the growth in working-age population. The F-statistic is greater

---

intracensal 1961–71 estimates from Bhat et al. (1984). Bhat et al. estimate 1961–71 birth and death rates using both forward and reverse survival analysis; we take the mean of these two techniques.

than 10, assuaging concerns about instrument strength (Staiger and Stock 1997). Moreover, the Sargan-Hansen statistic implies that fertility does not necessarily belong directly in the growth equation, that is, we cannot reject the null hypothesis of zero correlation between the instruments and the error process of the structural equation.

The broader question of interest is whether the validity of fertility as an instrument gives us further insights into the process that generates the demographic dividend. In the first stage regression, the coefficient on fertility has a negative sign. In other words, a decline in fertility is associated, all else equal, with a rise in the growth rate of the working-age population. As Sah noted in 1991, empirical studies had a clear consensus that fertility declined in response to lower child mortality. More recent studies have robustly confirmed that a dominant component of fertility decline is due to the decline in mortality rates, especially child mortality rates (see World Bank 2010; especially Angeles 2010 and Herzery et al. 2011). As is well-known, fertility falls at a slower speed than the decline in child mortality, such that the "net fertility rate," or the fertility net of survival of children, rises for some decades. It is this process that generates the demographic bulge, which leads to the growth in the working-age population. The lags in this process are complex and are not precisely pinned down. In using fertility lagged by a decade, we believe we are capturing a summary statistic of this transition at a relevant moment.

Thus, the first stage regression provides *prima facie* evidence that the growth in the working-age population is primarily driven by the classic demographic transition. In turn, this transition is aided by a variety of public health interventions, primarily improved sanitation to reduce child and maternal mortality, as well as greater access to contraception (Van De Walle 1992) and family planning services (Robinson and Ross 2001), along with the associated rise in the age of first union (Bongaarts 1982). It is possible that some of these as also other social and economic determinants of demographic transition (e.g., urbanization) affect future income growth not only through the working-age ratio but also directly. If so, that would undermine the validity of the instrument. Indeed, Herzery et al. (2011) find that reduced fertility is associated with higher growth. Our interpretation of the post-estimation statistics, which suggest that the exclusion restriction is satisfied, is that the component of fertility decline associated with the demographic transition works primarily through the growth in the working-age population to spur growth.

In the absence of a natural experiment there is no perfect instrumentation scheme. As such, the plausibility of our results rests on the slow-moving nature of age distribution variables, the restriction of changes in the working-age ratio to those changes induced by fertility decisions from a decade ago or earlier (which, in turn, are induced by prior infant mortality trends), and the post-estimation tests supporting the exclusion restriction.

Although columns 2 and 3 verify the important impact of our demographic variables on income growth, the IV procedure suggests an even stronger impact of demographic variables on income growth (although the error bands of point estimates in columns 2 and 3 encompass the point estimate in column 1). This may imply that higher growth, rather than stimulating an increase in the working-age population through inducing inward migration, has the contemporary effect of lowering the working-age population, possibly by increasing the demand for children. The result could also reflect differences in the sample. The IV procedure necessitates a significantly smaller sample: our data on birth rates begins in 1961, so the observations in the structural equation are limited to the period 1971–2001.

Finally, a large enough quantitative difference between the baseline and IV estimates could indicate that the growth rate of the working-age ratio is not, in fact, exogenous in the structural equation. To assuage this concern, a formal test of exogeneity is provided by the Difference-in-Sargan statistic. This is constructed as the difference of two Sargan-Hansen statistics, one in which the suspect regressor is treated as endogenous, and the other in which it is treated as exogenous. Under the null hypothesis that the regressor is actually exogenous, the statistic is distributed as chi-squared with one degree of freedom.[12] In our case, the null cannot be rejected at conventional levels of significance under either IV specification. Given this result, and given the much larger sample available, the basic fixed-effects framework and its greater efficiency relative to IV, we use the standard within estimator in the rest of this paper. While the remaining results are presented using non-adjusted growth rate for the working-age ratio, all specifications with the adjustment for net migration described in Table 3 lead to qualitatively identical and quantitatively very similar results.

5. Allowing for Other Growth Influences

Are the demographic variables reflecting other growth influences? In this section, we consider a variety of other correlates of growth to assess the

---

12. The test is a heteroskedasticity-robust variant of a Hausman test, to which it is numerically equivalent under homoskedastic errors. See Hayashi (2000).

robustness of our estimates of the demographic dividend. Table 5 introduces three "core" variables to control for human capital and social development.[13] These include the literacy rate, the number of hospital beds per 1,000 residents, and the sex ratio. Of course, there are numerous alternative indicators of education and health. Hospital beds, in particular, are an "input" measure of health rather than the kind of "output" measure that would be more desirable in principle. But in the context of the Indian states, these variables have the best data availability in long time series.[14]

TABLE 5. Introducing Core Control Variables

	Dependent variable: Annual per capita income growth			
	(1)	(2)	(3)	(4)
Log initial income per capita	−0.096***	−0.09***	−0.092***	−0.103***
	0.0133	0.017	0.016	0.013
Log initial working age ratio	0.226***	0.177**	0.147*	0.169***
	0.056	0.084	0.076	0.059
Growth rate of working age ratio	2.375**	2.52**	2.22**	2.214**
	0.917	1.019	1.04	0.928
Core controls				
Literacy rate	0.03			0.031
	0.019			0.02
Hospital beds per 1,000 residents		0.003		0.006
		0.005		0.007
Sex ratio (females/males)			0.133**	0.123***
			0.053	0.042
R-sqaured	0.74	0.75	0.75	0.76
Observations	76	76	76	76
Groups	22	22	22	22

Source: Authors.
Notes: *, **, and *** denote significance at the 10%, 5%, and 1% levels, respectively.

The sex ratio captures gender bias. Sen (1992) and others have argued that the phenomenon of "missing women" reflects the cumulative effect of gender discrimination against all cohorts of females alive today. Gender bias

13. Several studies have used educational attainment to measure the stock of human capital in an accounting framework, such as Klenow and Rodriguez-Clare (1997), Hall and Jones (1999), Aiyar and Dalgaard (2002), and Caselli (2005). Cross-country panel studies have found that education has a significant impact on income growth (Barro and Lee 1994; Islam 1995; and Caselli, Esquivel, and Lefort 1996). Indicators of health—often proxied by life expectancy—are almost as ubiquitous in the development accounting and empirical growth literatures. Examples include Barro and Lee (1994), Caselli, Esquivel, and Lefort (1996), Shastri and Weil (2003) and Weil (2007). Aiyar (2001) and Purfield (2006) have used both variables to proxy for human capital in cross-state growth regressions for India.

14. For example data on infant mortality rates—a frequently used "output" measure of health—is only widely available on a state-specific basis since the 1980s.

could impact economic growth through higher child mortality, increased fertility rates, and greater malnutrition (Abu-Ghaida and Klasens 2004). Gender bias also acts to reduce the current average level of human capital (Knowles et al. 2002), while limiting the educational gains of the next generation. More generally, increased bargaining power for women within the household is associated with a range of positive development outcomes (World Bank 2001). As such, gender bias acts as a proxy indicator for social development more generally.

Because data on these variables is complete, introducing them into the baseline specification leads to no reduction in observations, an important consideration given our limited sample size. We subsequently report results with additional variables of policy relevance, but that entails substantial attenuation of the sample size.

Columns 1 to 3 of Table 5 introduce each of these variables separately, and column 4 introduces them in tandem. The sex ratio is highly significant: more women relative to men is not only good social policy but is associated with higher economic growth. The other two human capital indicators, though bearing the right signs, are not statistically significant. Importantly, the working-age ratio variables remain strongly robust to the introduction of these additional explanatory variables.

Much effort has been devoted to identifying various growth-enhancing policies in the Indian context (as surveyed by Purfield 2006). Besley and Burgess (2000) examine the impact of land reforms and labor legislation on agricultural and manufacturing growth. Banerjee and Iyer (2005) find differences in agricultural productivity between districts that assigned proprietary land rights to cultivators rather than landlords. Kocchar et al. (2006) find that states with weaker institutions and infrastructure suffer lower GDP and industrial growth.

In many cases, the time dimension or cross section dimension (or both) of the data is severely limited. For example, the measure of transport infrastructure (used, for example, in Purfield 2006) would reduce the number of observations from 76 to 29. We, therefore limit attention to variables whose introduction does not reduce the sample size to below 50 observations.[15] The variables studied are:

- *Social and economic expenditure per capita:* The Indian census reports data on capital expenditure by state governments on social

15. We are grateful to Catriona Purfield for sharing the policy variables' data used in Purfield (2006).

infrastructure (categories such as education, water supply, sanitation and medical, and public health), and on economic infrastructure (expenditures on transportation, power and electricity, telecommunications, and irrigation projects). Taken together, these expenditures comprise "development expenditure." Aiyar (2001) found evidence that these expenditures, measured on a per-capita basis, promoted human capital development and private investment, thus contributing indirectly to economic growth.

- *Scheduled commercial bank credit per capita:* While there are no state-level data available on investment rates or other direct measures of capital accumulation, some studies have used credit extended by scheduled commercial banks as a proxy. The measure should also proxy for financial deepening. Aiyar (2001) and Purfield (2006) found a significant impact of this variable on income growth. Data are sourced from several issues of the Reserve Bank of India's *Statistical Tables Relating to Banking.*

- *Land concentration:* This variable measures inequality in agricultural land holdings. It is only partially a measure of policy, since it is also likely to reflect initial conditions. A priori land inequality could have a positive or negative impact on income growth, with different theories yielding different relationships. Data are taken from the Besley and Burgess (2000) database, which are originally sourced from various rounds on the National Sample Survey (NSS).

- *Cumulative land reform index:* This variable directly measures and aggregates different categories of legislative reforms undertaken at the state level. Besley and Burgess (2000) classify land reforms into four categories: tenancy reforms, abolishing intermediaries, establishing land ceilings, and consolidation of disparate landholdings. Their paper finds no impact of land reform legislation on state per-capita income; a positive impact of land consolidation legislation on agricultural income, and a negative impact of tenancy reform on agricultural income.

- *Cumulative labor reforms index:* Besley and Burgess (2004) examine state amendments to the Industrial Disputes Act of 1947, and code all amendments as being pro-worker, pro-employer, or neutral. The index rises in the degree to which cumulative legislation has been pro-worker.[16] They find that labor reforms are uncorrelated with per-capita

---

16. The method classifies Andhra Pradesh, Karnataka, Kerala, Madhya Pradesh, Rajasthan, and Tamil Nadu as pro-employer states. Gujarat, Maharashtra, Orissa, and West Bengal are

income, but negatively related to manufacturing output (i.e., they find that pro-labor reform is bad for manufacturing growth). Their data is extended to include amendments implemented post-1992 reported in Malik (2003).

Tables 6 and 7 report the results of introducing these policy variables. There is some evidence that development expenditure—particularly economic expenditure—by state governments can spur growth. And land reforms appear to be negatively related to per-capita growth. Of relevance, however, is the robustness of the demographic variables to the introduction of these diverse control variables. The point estimate of the coefficient on

TABLE 6. Controlling for Core and Policy Variables (Part 1)

	Dependent variable: Annual per capita income growth			
	(1)	*(2)*	*(3)*	*(4)*
Log initial income per capita	-0.104***	-0.121***	-0.13***	-0.084***
	0.018	0.0131	0.018	0.025
Log initial working age ratio	0.246**	0.196**	0.243***	0.188*
	0.114	0.075	0.07	0.105
Growth rate of working age ratio	2.281	2.549***	2.925***	3.14**
	1.51	0.841	0.878	1.426
Core controls				
Log literacy rate	-0.007	-0.029	-0.017	0.047
	0.032	0.033	0.033	0.034
Log hospital beds per 1,000 residents	-0.002	-0.002	-0.002	0.009
	0.011	0.009	0.011	0.007
Log sex ratio (females/males)	0.094	0.073*	0.057	0.451***
	0.086	0.039	0.044	0.146
Policy controls				
Log social expenditure per capita	0.001			
	0.019			
Log economic expenditure per capita		0.029**		
		0.014		
Log development expenditure per capita			0.035*	
			0.017	
Log scheduled commercial bank credit per capita				-0.004
				0.006
R-squared	0.76	0.82	0.80	0.81
Observations	58	58	58	57
Groups	16	16	16	21

Source: Authors.
Notes: *, **, and *** denote significance at the 10%, 5%, and 1% levels, respectively.

pro-worker states. India's six other large states did not implement any amendments to the Industrial Disputes Act over the period. For critiques of the Besley–Burgess methodology, see Bhattacharjea (2006) and Gupta, Hasan, and Kumar (2008).

TABLE 7. Controlling for Core and Policy Variables (Part 2)

	Dependent variable: Annual per capita income growth		
	(1)	(2)	(3)
Log initial income per capita	-0.113***	-0.121***	-0.104***
	0.0196	0.009	0.016
Log initial working age ratio	0.241***	0.304***	0.24***
	0.072	0.068	0.0809
Growth rate of working age ratio	2.945**	2.928***	2.272*
	1.124	0.88	1.187
Core controls			
Log literacy rate	0.025	-0.034	-0.007
	0.047	0.036	0.032
Log hospital beds per 1,000 residents	0.004	-0.007	-0.002
	0.013	0.008	0.01
Log sex ratio (females/males)	0.132*	0.184**	0.101*
	0.076	0.078	0.059
Policy controls			
Log land gini co-efficient	0.092		
	0.074		
Cumulative land reforms index		-0.003*	
		0.001	
Cumulative labor reforms index			-0.001
			0.003
R-squared	0.78	0.82	0.76
Observations	55	58	58
Groups	15	16	16

Source: Authors.
Notes: *, **, and *** denote significance at the 10%, 5%, and 1% levels, respectively.

the initial working-age ratio is significant in every specification and quantitatively fairly stable. The growth rate of the working-age ratio is significant in six out of seven specifications, and falls within a narrow numerical range.

We also tried various specifications with age-structure variables interacted with the control variables (see Bloom and Canning 2004). Significant interaction terms would suggest, for example, that the impact of demographic change is enhanced by the presence of a well-educated and healthy labor force, or by a lack of gender bias. But, surprisingly, no significant role for such interactions was found. While this result should be regarded as tentative, the implication is that the health and educational preconditions that make the demographic dividend possible are also sufficient conditions for the exploitation of the dividend.

This explanation, however, is less likely to account for the lack of significant interaction terms with policy variables. Here it seems more plausible that the variables examined in this paper do not adequately capture the kinds of institutions and policies that are complementary to demographic change.

For example, three of the key elements of the economic reforms of the 1980s and 1990s were the dismantling of industrial licensing, trade policy reforms, and greater exchange rate flexibility. All these reforms were applied at an all-India level. The absence of state-level variation may be one reason why there is no evidence of interacting effects. However, in principle, reforms at the all-India level could have a differential impact by state if one state's industrial base contains many more deregulated industries than another, or if it engages in more international trade than another. Such policy complementarities constitute a worthwhile future research agenda, and could possibly provide the counterpart to the interaction between economic openness and the demographic dividend found in cross-country panels. Similarly, a case could be made that considerable social change in the Southern and Western states accompanied the demographic transition and together these had an important impact on the totality of opportunities and policy environment. Where the demographic transition is occurring faster than social change, the gains from that transition may be more difficult to realize.[17]

6. Extra Growth from Demographic Change: Some Simulations

We now apply the point estimates from our regression to assess the past and likely future magnitude of the growth dividend. Let $t = 0$ for some base year. In any period $t > 0$, per-capita income growth *inclusive* of changes in age structure between period t and period $t+1$ is defined by equation (5) from Section 3:

$$g\_y_{i,t} = \rho \ln y_{i,t} + \beta_1 \ln w_{i,t} + \beta_2 g\_w_{i,t} + \gamma' X_{i,t} + f_i + \eta_t + \varepsilon_{i,t} \quad (5)$$

Now consider a counterfactual in which the working-age ratio remains fixed at the level of the base year, that is, there is no change in the age structure between period 0 and period t. In this case, $w_{i,t} = w_{i,0}$ and $g\_w_{i,t} = 0$. It follows that:

$$g\_y_{i,t} = \rho \ln y_{i,t} + \beta_1 \ln w_{i,0} + \gamma' X_{i,t} + f_i + \eta_t + \varepsilon_{i,t} \quad (6)$$

The demographic dividend, DD_t, is the difference between (5) and (6):

---

17. We are grateful to Dr Venugopal Reddy for this thought. The specific social change that he refers to in personal communication to us is the upliftment of backward classes in the Southern and Western states.

$$DD_t = \beta_1(\ln w_t - \ln w_0) + \beta_2 g\_w_{i,t} \qquad (7)$$

Thus DD_t represents the average annual increment in per-capita income growth over the decade starting in year t that can be attributed to changes in the age structure from period zero onwards. It consists of two terms, which have an intuitive interpretation. The first term represents the boost to income growth from the increase in the working-age ratio that has already occurred (relative to the base year). The second term represents the boost to income growth from the growth in the working-age ratio that will occur over the ongoing decade.

6.1. The Dividend thus Far

Applying this formula to historical working-age ratios, Table 8 shows calculations of the dividend by decade, against a counterfactual of no demographic change since 1961. We use the point estimates from the baseline specification in column 1, Table 4 ($\beta_1 = 0.188$; $\beta_2 = 2.478$).

TABLE 8. India's Past Age Distribution and Demographic Dividend[a]

(in percent)

Age group	1961	1971	1981	1991	2001
0–14	41.0	42.0	39.6	37.3	35.4
15–59	53.3	52.0	53.9	56.7	57.1
60+	5.6	6.0	6.5	6.0	7.5
	1960s	*1970s*	*1980s*	*1990s*	
Demographic dividend	−0.61	0.42	1.46	1.34	
Per capita income growth[b]	1.24	0.91	3.16	3.44	
Net of demographic dividend	1.85	0.49	1.70	2.10	

Source: Census of India; CSO; and authors' calculations.

Notes: [a] Demographic dividend calculated as the increment to annual per capita income growth relative to a counterfactual in which the working age ratio stays fixed at the 1961 level.

[b] Growth in per capita net domestic product in constant 1993–94 prices.

India's working-age ratio rose—from a very low level—after 1971, with the share of children in the population falling more rapidly than the rise in the share of the old. Moreover, the working-age population accelerated in the 1980s. The demographic dividend mirrored these trends in the age distribution. From small and negative in the 1960s and small and positive in the 1970s, the dividend became substantial in the 1980s and 1990s.

Thus, a considerable fraction of India's growth acceleration from the 1980s to the new millennium may be attributed to the shift in the structure of the country's age distribution. This vital contributor to growth has been missed even in comprehensive accounts for India's growth (e.g., Rodrik and Subramanian 2005). Thus, the dramatic increase in per-capita income growth dating from the 1980s is less dramatic—although still substantial—after netting out the demographic dividend. Indeed, the most striking characteristic of the demography-adjusted per-capita income growth series is that the 1970s appear to be a "lost decade," surrounded on either side by much higher growth regimes.[18]

6.2. The State-wise Distribution of the Dividend

We revisit the experience of the selected states examined in Section 2, to highlight the role played by the demographic dividend. Table 9 illustrates the pivotal role played by the evolution of the age distribution in the economic performance of leaders and laggards among Indian states. Tamil Nadu, Karnataka, and Gujarat, among the best-performing Indian states in recent times, have also reaped an enormous demographic dividend: in the 1980s the increment to per-capita income growth generated by the age distribution was 2.4 percent per annum, rising to 3 percent in the 1990s. Meanwhile, the laggards of the Hindi Heartland reaped a meager dividend, averaging only 0.6 percent in the 1980s and zero in the 1990s. This discrepancy explains a substantial part of the divergence between leaders and laggards from 1981–2001, as illustrated by the bottom panel containing growth rates net of the demographic dividend.

6.3. What May the Future Hold?

Finally, we calculate the demographic dividend for the previous and next four decades, relative to a counterfactual in which the working-age ratio stays at its 2001 level. Table 10 shows a range of projections for India's age distribution.[19] The Census of India 2001 provides projections through 2026,

18. The 1970s were a turbulent decade, encompassing a war with Pakistan in 1971 and the imposition of emergency rule by Prime Minister Indira Gandhi from 1975–77 (see Guha 2007). Even before netting out the demographic dividend, the lower rate of growth in this decade stands in stark contrast to the 1960s and 1980s.

19. The standard method for projecting forward the age distribution is the cohort-component method (the US Census Bureau 2010 has a useful summary). This tracks cohorts of individuals belonging to the same age- and sex-group through their lifetimes. Typically five-year age groups are used. An initial or base year population, disaggregated by age and sex, is exposed to estimated age- and sex-specific chances of dying as determined by estimated and projected mortality levels and age patterns. Once deaths are estimated, they are subtracted from each age, yielding the next older age in the subsequent time period. Fertility rates are projected and applied to the female population of childbearing age to estimate the number of births every

TABLE 9. Demographic Dividend: Selected States

		1960s	1970s	1980s	1990s
	Leaders (South and West)				
	Tamil Nadu	−0.1	0.8	2.2	2.7
	Karnataka	−0.3	0.9	2.4	3.2
	Gujarat	−0.2	1.5	2.6	3.0
Demographic	*Simple Average*	−0.2	1.0	2.4	3.0
dividend	Laggards (Heartland)				
	Bihar	−0.3	−0.2	0.8	0.0
	Madhya Pradesh	−1.7	−0.4	0.7	0.3
	Uttar Pradesh	−0.9	−0.6	0.4	−0.4
	Simple Average	−0.9	−0.4	0.6	0.0
	Leaders (South and West)				
	Tamil Nadu	0.4	0.1	4.1	5.1
	Karnataka	2.0	0.7	3.0	6.0
Per capita	Gujarat	1.9	0.9	3.1	3.6
income growth	*Simple Average*				
rate	Laggards (Heartland)	1.4	0.5	3.4	4.9
	Bihar	0.3	0.6	2.7	−0.1
	Madhya Pradesh	−0.5	0.6	2.2	1.1
	Uttar Pradesh	0.7	0.7	2.6	0.8
	Simple Average	0.2	0.6	2.5	0.6
	Leaders (South and West)				
	Tamil Nadu	0.5	−0.7	1.9	2.4
Per capita	Karnataka	2.3	−0.2	0.6	2.8
income growth	Gujarat	2.1	−0.6	0.5	0.6
rate net of	*Simple Average*	1.7	−0.5	1.0	1.9
demographic	Laggards (Heartland)				
dividend	Bihar	0.6	0.8	1.9	−0.1
	Madhya Pradesh	1.2	1.0	1.5	0.8
	Uttar Pradesh	1.6	1.3	2.2	1.2
	Simple Average	1.1	1.0	1.9	0.6

Source: Census of India; Central Statistical Organization; and authors' calculations.

while the United Nations Population Division (UNPD) and the International Data Base (IDB) of the US Census Bureau provide projections through 2050. Differences in projections arise because of different assumptions about age-specific fertility and mortality, which are themselves based on patterns estimated from past data and international comparisons.[20]

---

year. Each cohort of children born is also followed through time and survivors are calculated after exposure to mortality.

20. The UNPD projections, for example, have eight variants corresponding to parametric assumptions: low fertility; medium fertility; high fertility; constant-fertility; instant-replacement-fertility; constant-mortality; no change (constant-fertility and constant-mortality); and zero-migration. Here we show the medium fertility variant, highlighted in United Nations (2009).

TABLE 10.   Demographic Projections for India[a]

Age group	Census of India			
	2001	2011	2021	2026
0–14	35.5	29	25.1	23.4
15–59	57.8	62.7	64.0	64.3
60+	6.9	8.2	10.7	12.5

Age group	United Nations Population Division[b]					
	2001	2010	2020	2030	2040	2050
0–14	35.5	30.8	26.7	22.8	19.7	18.2
15–59	57.8	61.6	63.5	64.8	64.6	62.2
60+	6.9	7.5	9.8	12.4	15.6	19.6

Age group	IDB, US Census Bureau[b]					
	2001	2010	2020	2030	2040	2050
0–14	35.5	30.1	26.3	23.5	21.4	19.8
15–59	57.8	61.7	63.5	63.3	61.9	60.1
60+	6.9	8.2	10.2	13.2	16.7	20.1

Source: Census of India; United Nations Population Division; and US Census Bureau.
Notes: [a] All numbers are in percent of total population.
[b] Estimates for 2001 are from the Census of India.

All projections show rapid growth in India's working-age ratio from 2001 through 2021, as the reduction in the country's population of children outstrips the increase in the ranks of the old. The Census of India shows a further (albeit decelerating) increase in the working-age ratio through 2026, and the UNPD through 2030. The IDB projects the working-age ratio as leveling off in 2030. The UNPD projects a leveling-off of the ratio by 2040 and then a decline in the decade leading to 2050.

Table 11 reports the calculations. These suggest that over the previous decade, the increment to per-capita income growth from demographic change has been between 1.5 and 2 percent points per annum. Over the next two decades, the demographic dividend (relative to the age structure in 2001) is projected to peak—adding about 2 percentage points to annual per-capita income growth. Subsequently the dividend should begin to decrease gradually (while remaining positive) based on the UNPD projections, and decrease rapidly according to the IDB projections.

We are unaware of any state-wise projections of the evolution of the age-distribution over the next few decades. However, it is possible to speculate about the likely direction of future changes. The states in the south and west of India have already undergone a major part of their demographic transition, while the laggards have not. Since the average 2001 working-age ratio among the leaders was 62.1 percent versus 53.4 percent in the

TABLE 11. India's Coming Demographic Dividend by Decade[a]

(in percent)

	2000s	2010s	2020s[b]	2030s	2040s
Using projections from					
Census of India 2001	2.02	2.04	2.16		
United Nations Population Division	1.60	1.95	2.27	2.10	1.17
US Census Bureau	1.62	1.93	1.69	1.15	0.57
Average	1.74	1.98	2.04	1.62	0.87

Source: Census of India; United Nations Population Division; US Census Bureau; and authors' calculations.
Notes: [a] Calculates the increment to annual per capita income growth relative to a counterfactual in which the working age ratio stays fixed at the 2001 level.
[b] 2021–2026 for projections from the Census of India.

laggards, it seems likely that the bulk of the projected large increments to India's working-age ratio will come from the laggards. A sustained growth acceleration in India's poorest states may now be feasible.

Indeed, the process may already have started. Consider Bihar, the worst of the laggard states. From 2001 through 2009, Bihar's per-capita income grew at an average rate of 6.2 percent per annum, representing a tremendous acceleration from about zero in the previous decade, and well above the median growth rate in our sample for this period.[21] This impressive economic performance has been attributed, especially in the later part of the decade, to the good governance and developmental focus of state's administration.[22] While the reforms implemented have undoubtedly been instrumental in Bihar's turnaround, it is also likely that Bihar's working-age ratio has risen from the very low level of 52.5 percent in 2001 and hence contributed to the growth acceleration. The Census of 2011—whose results are being released in a piecemeal fashion—will reveal the extent of such an increase. The age distribution of the population by state in 2011 would allow the calculation of the growth rate of the working-age ratio from 2001 to 2011, and help assess the contribution of the demographic dividend and its state-wise distribution during the past decade.

21. Among the four big Hindi heartland states, Rajasthan also registered above-median growth of 6.1 percent per annum, while Uttar Pradesh and Madhya Pradesh registered much lower average growth rates of 3.2 percent and 2.7 percent respectively. The median growth rate was 5.7 percent.

22. Chief Minister Nitish Kumar's efforts to improve the law and order in the state, combined with efforts to build infrastructure and expand health and education services, have been viewed as critical to recent improvements in growth performance.

7. Conclusion

The level and the growth rate of the working-age ratio have been robustly associated with India's economic growth. Indeed, a substantial part of India's growth acceleration since the 1980s can be attributed to demographic change. At the very least, to the extent that economic reforms unlocked India's growth potential, demography was fortuitously supportive. That said, the evidence in this paper is, somewhat surprisingly, more favorable to a view that the age structure was an independent source of growth. We find little empirical evidence of complementarities between demographic variables and various facets of social development or the policy environment.

It is possible that the social preconditions for the demographic transition also generate the ability to benefit from the resulting increase in the share of the working-age population. In particular, the demographic transition requires public health and associated social innovations, which, our results imply, work their way to improved growth outcomes through a larger working-age population. It is also possible that the economic policies and reforms most complementary to demographic change were those applied at the national level. We do control for such national influences, although only imperfectly, through time dummies. Research into such complementarities could shed further light on the likely trajectory of economic growth in India and in other countries with the potential to exploit the demographic dividend over the next few decades.

If past relationships hold over the next two decades, India's continuing demographic transition relative to the age structure at the turn of the millennium could yield a further growth dividend of about 2 percent per annum. More interestingly, while the largest expansions in the working-age ratio to date have occurred in southern and western states that have led India in terms of recent economic growth, the bulk of the remaining demographic transition will be concentrated in lagging states, thus raising the prospect of substantial income convergence between rich and poor states.

References

Abu-Ghaida, D. and S. Klasen. 2004. "The Costs of Missing the Millennium Development Goals on Gender Equity," *World Development*, 37 (2): 1075–07.

Aiyar, S. 2001. "Growth Theory and Convergence across Indian States," in T. Callen, P. Reynolds, and C. Towe, eds., *India at the Crossroads: Sustaining Growth and Reducing Poverty*, Indian Monetary Fund.

Aiyar, S. and C-J. Dalgaard. 2005. "Total Factor Productivity Revisited: A Dual Approach to Development Accounting," *IMF Staff Papers*, 52 (1): 82–102, Indian Monetary Fund.

Anderson, T. and B. Sorensen. 1996. "GMM Estimation of a Stochastic Volatility Model: A Monte Carlo Study," *Journal of Business and Economic Statistics*, 14 (3): 328–52.

Angeles, L. 2010. "Demographic Transitions: Analyzing the Effects of Mortality on Fertility," *Journal of Population Economics*, 23: 99–120.

Arellano, M. and S. Bond. 1991. "Some Tests of Specification for Panel Data: Monte Carlo Estimations and an Application to Employment Equations," *Review of Economic Studies*, 58.

Bailey, M. 2006. "More Power to the Pill: The Impact of Contraceptive Freedom on Women's Labor Supply," *Quarterly Journal of Economics*, 121 (1): 289–320.

Banerjee, A. and L. Iyer. 2005. "History, Institutions, and Economic Performance: The Legacy of Colonial Land Tenure Systems in India," *American Economic Review*, Vol. 95, No. 4.

Barro R. and J-W. Lee. 1994. "Sources of Economic Growth," Carnegie-Rochester Conference Series on Public Policy 40.

Barro, R. and X. Sala-i-Martin. 1995. *Economic Growth*. New York: McGraw-Hill.

Besley, T. and R. Burgess. 2000. "Land Reform, Poverty Reduction and Growth: Evidence from India," *Quarterly Journal of Economics*, 115 (2): 389–430.

———. 2004. "Can Labor Reform Hinder Economic Performance? Evidence from India," *Quarterly Journal of Economics*, 119 (1): 91–131.

Bhat, P.N.M., S. Preston, and T. Dyson. 1984. "Vital Rates in India, 1961–1981," Report No. 24, Committee on Population and Demography, National Academy Press, Washington, D.C.

Bhattacharjea, A. 2006. "Labour Market Regulation and Industrial Performance in India: A Critical Review of the Empirical Evidence," *The Indian Journal of Labour Economics*, 49 (2): 211–32.

Bloom, D. and D. Canning. 2004. "Global Demographic Change: Dimensions and Economic Significance," NBER Working Paper 10817, National Bureau of Economic Research.

Bloom, D., D. Canning, G. Fink, and J. Finlay. 2007. "Does Age Structure Forecast Economic Growth?" International *Journal of Forecasting*, 23 (4): 569–85.

Bloom, D., D. Canning and P. Malaney. 2000. "Demographic Change and Economic Growth in Asia," *Population and Development Review*, 26.

Bloom, D., D. Canning, and J. Sevilla. 2002. *The Demographic Dividend: A New Perspective on the Economic Consequences of Population Change*. Santa Monica, California: RAND, MR–1274.

Bloom, D., S. Korenman and R. Freeman. 1987. "The Labor Market Consequences of Generational Crowding," *European Journal of Population*, 3: 131–76.

Blundell, R. and S. Bond. 1998. "Initial Conditions and Moment Restrictions in Dynamic Panel Models," *Journal of Econometrics*, 87 (1): 115–43.

Bongaarts, J. 1982. "The Fertility-Inhibiting Effects of Intermediate Fertility Variables," *Studies in Family Planning*, 13 (6/7): 179–89.

Bowsher, C. 2002. "On Testing Overidentifying Restrictions in Dynamic Panel Data Models," *Economics Letters*, 77 (2): 211–20.

Caselli, F. 2005. "Accounting for Cross-Country Income Differences," in A. Philippe and D. Steven (eds), *Handbook of Economic Growth*, 1 (1): 679–741.

Caselli, F., G. Esquivel, and F. Lefort. 1996. "Reopening the Convergence Debate: A New Look at Cross-Country Growth Empirics," *Journal of Economic Growth*, 1 (3): 363–89.

Cashin, P. and R. Sahay. 1996. "Internal Migration, Center-State Grants and Economic Growth in the States of India," IMF Staff Papers Vol. 43, No. 1, Indian Monetary Fund.

Cleland, J. 2001. "The Effects of Improved Survival on Fertility: A Reassessment," *Population and Development Review*, 27: 60–92.

Datta, P. 1985. "Inter-State Migration in India," *Margin*, 18 (1): 69–82.

Easterlin, R. 1980. *Population and Economic Change in Developing Countries* (ed), Chicago: University of Chicago Press for NBER.

Feng, W. and A. Mason. 2005. "Demographic Dividend and Prospects for Economic Development in China," paper prepared for *UN Expert Group Meeting on Social and Economic Implications of Changing Population Age Structures*, Mexico City.

Feyrer, J. 2007 "Demographics and Productivity," *The Review of Economics and Statistics*, MIT Press, 89 (1): 100–09.

Fry, M. and A. Mason. 1982. "The Variable Rate of Growth Effect in the Life-Cycle Model," *Economic Enquiry*, 20: 426–42.

Galor, O. 2011. "The Demographic Transition: Causes and Consequences," *NBER Working Paper 17057*.

Guha, R. 2007. *India after Gandhi*. New York: HarperCollins Publishers.

Gupta, P., R. Hasan, and U. Kumar. 2008. "Big Reforms but Small Payoffs: Explaining the Weak Record of Growth in Indian Manufacturing," *India Policy Forum*, Brookings Institution, 5 (1): 59–123.

Hall, R. and C. Jones. 1999. "Why Do Some Countries Produce So Much More Output than Others?" *Quarterly Journal of Economics*, 114 (1): 83–116.

Hayashi, F. 2000. *Econometrics*. Princeton University Press.

Herzery, D., H. Strulik, and S. Vollmer. 2010. "The Long-run Determinants of Fertility: One Century of Demographic Change 1900–1999," *PGDA Working Papers 6310*, Program on the Global Demography of Aging.

Higgins, M. 1998. "Demography, National Savings, and International Capital Flows," *International Economic Review*, 39: 343–69.

Islam, N. 1995. "Growth Empirics: A Panel Data Approach," *Quarterly Journal of Economics*, 110 (4): 1127–70.

Joshi, S. and P. Schultz. 2004. "Family Planning as an Investment in Development: Evaluation of a Program's Consequences in Matlab, Bangladesh," Mimeo, Yale University.

Kelkar, V. 2004. "India: On the Growth Turnpike," Narayanan Oration, Speech delivered at the Australian National University, Canberra.

Kelley, A. and R. Schmidt. 1996. "Saving, Dependency, and Development," *Journal of Population Economics*, 9 (4): 365–86.

Klenow, P. and A. Rodriguez-Clare. 1997. "The Neoclassical Revival in Growth Economics: Has It Gone Too Far?" *NBER Macroeconomics Annual*, 12.

Knowles, S., P. K. Lorgelly and P. D. Owen. 2002. "Are Educational Gender Gaps a Brake on Economic Development? Some Cross-Country Empirical Evidence," *Oxford Economic Papers*, 54 (1): 118–49.

Kocchar, K., U. Kumar, R. Rajan, A. Subramanian, and I. Tokatlidis. 2006. "India's Pattern of Development: What Happened, What Follows?" *Journal of Monetary Economics*, 53 (5): 981–1019.

Korenman, S. and D. Neumark. 2000. "Cohort Crowding and Youth Labor Markets (A Cross-National Analysis)," in *Youth Employment and Joblessness in Advanced Countries*, NBER Chapters, pp. 57–106, National Bureau of Economic Research.

Malik, P. 2003. *Industrial Law*. Lucknow: Eastern Book Company.

Mason, A., ed. 2001. *Population Change and Economic Development in East Asia: Challenges Met, Opportunities Seized*. California: Stanford University Press.

Persson, Joakim. 2002. "Demographics, Human Capital, and Economic Growth: A Study of U.S. States 1930–2000," *FIEF Working Paper*.

Purfield, C. 2006. "Mind the Gap: Is Income Growth in India Leaving Some States Behind?" *IMF Working Paper* 06/103.

Robinson, W. and J. Ross. 2007. *The Global Family Planning Revolution: Three Decades of Population Policies and Programs*. Washington, D.C.: The World Bank.

Rodrik, D., ed. 2003. *In Search of Prosperity: Analytical Narratives on Economic Growth*. Princeton, New Jersey: Princeton University Press.

Rodrik, D. and A. Subramanian. 2005. "From 'Hindu Growth' to Productivity Surge: The Mystery of the Indian Growth Transition," *IMF Staff Papers*, 52 (2): 193–228.

Sah, R. 1991. "The Effects of Child Mortality Changes on Fertility Choice and Parental Welfare," *Journal of Political Economy*, 99 (3): 582–606.

Sen, A. 1992. "Missing Women," *British Medical Journal*, Vol. 304.

Shastri, G. and D. Weil. 2003. "How Much of Cross-Country Income Variation is Explained by Health?" *Journal of the European Economic Association*, 1 (2–3): 387–96.

Skeldon, R. 1986. "On Migration Patterns in India During the 1970s," *Population and Development Review*, 12 (4): 759–79.

Staiger, D. and J. Stock. 1997. "Instrumental Variables Regression with Weak Instruments," *Econometrica*, 65 (3): 557–86.

United Nations. 2009. "World Population Prospects: The 2008 Revision," Department of Economic and Social Affairs, Population Division, New York. Available at http://esa.un.org/unpd/wpp2008/index.htm

US Census Bureau. June 2010. "International Data Base: Population Estimates and Projections Methodology." Available at http://www.census.gov/ipc/www/idb/

Van De Walle, E. 1992. "Fertility Transition, Conscious Choice and Numeracy," *Demography*, 29 (4): 487–502.

Weil, D. 2007. "Accounting for the Effect of Health on Economic Growth," *Quarterly Journal of Economics*, 122 (3): 1265–306.

World Bank. 2001. *Engendering Development*, Washington, D.C.: The World Bank.

———. 2010. "Determinants and Consequences of High Fertility: A Synopsis of the Evidence," *ESW Report*.

Comments and Discussions

Sonalde Desai
National Council of Applied Economic Research and University of Maryland College Park

As a demographer, I find it somewhat ironic that after decades of claiming that demographic growth is "neutral" to economic growth, increasing attention is being directed toward positive impacts of demographically driven age structure on economic growth. While I hate to look a gift horse in the mouth, we have not fully understood how demographic dividend operates and whether it has a long term transformative impact on the economy or whether it is simply a deposit that current generation of workers make, to be withdrawn when they get older. Unfortunately the paper by Aiyar and Mody does little to help us address this issue.

Research on the link between population growth and economic growth appears to have come a full circle. The 1960s and 1970s were dominated by studies that suggested that population growth depressed capital/labor ratio and reduced growth (Coale and Hoover 1958; Meadows, Meadows, Randers, and Breherns 1972), in contrast the literature in 1980s and 1990s focused on medium and long term benefits of larger population to be contrasted with short term costs (Cassen 1994; Johnson and Lee 1986). It is only since mid-1990s that following the East Asian economic growth, the attention has shifted to the positive impact of lower dependency ratio during the twilight when past high fertility allows for a large working age population while recent fertility decline results in fewer dependent children. It would be great to accept this optimism; certainly it bodes well for India's future. However, until we understand why and under what conditions we expect this lower dependency ratio to convert into higher economic growth, it would be difficult to bank on this dividend.

As Figure 1 indicates, increase in GDP per capita can be divided into three components: increase in per-capita income is a function of working age population, productivity per worker and work participation rate. Aiyar and Mody summarize these three components nicely. The first component is based on working-age population as a proportion of population, frequently called support ratio. This component, called first demographic dividend by Ronald Lee in a seminal paper (Lee 2003) is more or less mechanical. More workers mean more production. This first demographic dividend is more of a deposit. Fertility decline results in a demographic bulge that leads to higher production while the bulge generation is of working and will lead to higher consumption when it grows older. Lee estimates the size of this first demographic dividend for India to be about 0.5 percent per year—remarkably similar to Aiyar and Mody's estimate of 0.6 percent.

FIGURE 1.   Components of Demographic Dividend

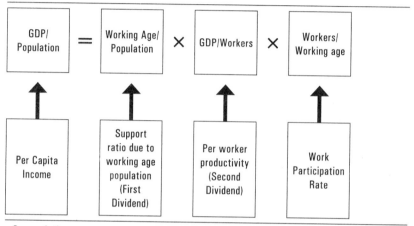

Source: Author.

But greed for demographic dividend goes beyond this first dividend—often called a one-time bonus. It is also expected that as dependency burden declines, society will be able to increase savings and improve education, thereby increasing productivity. However, the extent to which India is able to realize this second demographic dividend remains an open question. The very small difference between estimates of Ron Lee's first demographic dividend (about 0.5 percent per year) and Aiyar and Mody's estimates of combined effect of first and second demographic dividend (about 0.6 percent per year) suggests that size of the second demographic dividend in India may well be quite modest. If we reflect on why we expect the second demographic dividend to be important, it is easy to see why its size may not be large for India. Cross-national regressions show that economic growth is far more sensitive to child population size than adult population size (Heady and Hodge 2009), perhaps because decline in child dependency ratio allows for great savings. But decline in total investment in children in India is counterbalanced with growing enrollment and rising privatization of education. While this investment in children may lead to higher productivity in the next generation, poor quality of Indian education, documented by Karthik Muralidharan in this volume may dampen this impact. Comparison of private educational expenditure with children's skill acquisition across states suggests little benefit of additional spending in terms of educational quality.

Moreover, lack of non-manufacturing job opportunities along with very slow agricultural productivity growth has meant that an increasing proportion of Indian labor force is been crowded into agriculture whose weight in the economy is rapidly diminishing. Without increasing labor absorption in nonagricultural employment, size of the second demographic dividend is likely to stay small.

It is the third component, work participation rate, which deserves the greatest attention when engaging in cross-national or interstate comparisons. Here demography is swamped by differences in female labor force participation rates. Female labor force participation rates differ substantially across countries and across states. Indian female labor force participation rate is about half that of China. Thus, any advantage India is likely to have with increasing size of working age population is washed away when we compare proportion of workers in the population and in terms of dependency ratio, India actually is going to remain far behind China for at least until 2030.

One might argue that both development and declining fertility will lead to higher female labor force participation but this is not an automatic relationship. Boserup argued that there is a U-shaped curve of female labor force participation rate with development (Boserup 1970), with female employment falling in initial stages of development and rising in the later stages. This is consistent with the Indian experience where we have seen a 6-percentage point decline in female workforce participation rate between 2004–05 and 2009–10 as per NSS data. Nor is low fertility automatically associated with high female labor force participation. Spain and Italy have very low female labor force participation rates and extremely low fertility whereas Sweden has much higher fertility and higher rates of women's employment. Social institutions such as child care systems, cultural norms and work opportunities shape this relationship or lack thereof. In India, women who have more children also seem to be working more, partly because they are rural, and partly because they come from poorer households.

As we start disentangling different aspects of demographic dividend and explore the pathways through which demography may affect economic growth, four aspects of Aiyar and Mody paper deserve greater attention:

1. *First vs Second Dividend*: First demographic dividend is more or less automatic. Additional workers should add to GDP. However, the size

of the dividend depends on changes in per worker productivity. Thus, it would be helpful if the dependent variable for Aiyar and Mody's analysis were GNP per worker in addition to GNP per capita. This is a particular concern because unless there is a long-term systemic change due to the demographic bonus of having extra workers, added workers of today are simply added dependents of tomorrow. As discussed above, it is possible that per worker productivity growth in India may be may be modest at best.

2. *Focus on Workers Rather than Working-age Population*: Independent variable for this analysis should be worker/population ratio rather than working age/population ratio. This is particularly important in comparing across states. Demographic laggards have considerably lower female work participation rates than the leaders. For example, 41 percent of the women in rural Tamil Nadu work compared to 7 percent in rural Bihar (National Sample Survey Office 2011). Hence, any future predication regarding demographic dividend in laggard states are likely to be overestimates.

3. *Spillover Effects across States*: Aiyar and Mody do a very nice job of examining spillover effects via migration. However, it is important to analyze which pathway for increasing worker productivity is most important in Indian conditions and to see if this may involve spillovers across states. For example, if demographic dividend is obtained via higher savings rates and higher worker to capital ratios, do savings get invested within the same state or are they invested in other states? The paper pays more attention to the mechanical aspects of age composition and less to theory underlying economic changes. Unfortunately when it comes to speculations regarding future impacts of demographic change, greater attention to theory and potential pathways through which demography may affect economy are required.

4. *Endogeneity of Fertility*: Aiyar and Mody assume that main determinants of fertility are socio-cultural norms and public health and not income. However, this assumption runs contrary to substantial accumulated evidence on development as the best contraception. While there are many on-going debates within demography on the role of development vs. ideational change in fertility decline, there is a need to at least consider the potential that fertility may be endogenous (Bloom, Canning, and Sevilla, 2003). Even the data presented in Aiyar and Mody's paper hints at this. Demographic leaders, net of dividend, experienced growth rate of 1.9 percent compared to 0.6 percent for the laggards.

Given these conceptual and empirical concerns, Aiyar and Mody's optimism that demographic changes will help ameliorate spatial inequalities may be closer to wishful thinking.

Pranab Bardhan
University of California, Berkeley

The paper is on an important topic. It shows a large role of demographic dividend in explaining the rise in growth rate since the 1980s. This is in line with several papers, like that of Bloom and Williamson (1997) which shows that the demographic transition explained as much as one-third of the East Asian "miracle" growth.

A hopeful aspect of the results in the paper is that for some of the poorer states in the next two decades demographic transition is going to increase the growth rate (already apparent in the last decade's high growth in Bihar, Orissa, and Chhattisgarh).

Four sets of comments:

1. Two mechanisms through which demographic dividend works are not emphasized in the paper:

   (i) Increase in female participation in labor force (since general labor participation is found statistically insignificant in a regression quite early in the paper, it is dropped from further discussion).

   (ii) The effect of saving on the growth rate is not considered in the model of the paper. The age-groups relevant to increasing productivity (through a younger work force) and those for increasing the saving rate are not the same. So, looking to the future, the effect of saving on the growth rate will peak later than the peak in the working age population.

2. A conspicuous absentee in the "other correlates of growth" that the authors consider is sectoral reallocation of labor (from agriculture to other sectors). Census data are available on this.

   In fact in the original Bloom and Canning (2004) paper, on which the regression equation (5) is based, the labor productivity variable is a weighted average of the sectoral labor productivities.

This is important, because if the working age population increase remains trapped in low-productivity agriculture and other informal activities, growth effect will be small
Here policy reform may be quite relevant.

3. In the discussion on State-wise distribution of the demographic dividend, the authors discuss the cases of the leading states (Tamil Nadu, Karnataka, Gujarat) and laggard states (Bihar, MP, UP).

    But one state I'd like more discussion of is Kerala, where the demographic transition and the health and educational improvements came first in India. Yet over the decades considered in this paper Kerala's growth performance has not been spectacular. So more analysis is needed. Two special things to note about Kerala:

    (i) it's partly a remittance economy (which is not captured directly in SDP); and (ii) Kerala has not been an enthusiastic adopter of economic reforms.

4. Some comments on the statistical exercise:

    Is the exclusion restriction satisfied for the instrument variable? A lagged birth rate, through fewer children, may lead to a rise in female participation for the same working age group, which may have a direct effect on the growth rate. The power of the Sargan test (based on asymptotic approximation) is not strong enough, particularly in cases of limited observations, to rule out this likely economic effect.

The "policy control variables" in Table 6 may be endogenous. There may be reverse causality, as growth may affect the variable scheduled commercial bank credit per capita, or social and economic expenditure per capita (through generating more tax resources). An exogenous variable like average distance to ports may capture effects of trade liberalization and other aspects of the policy environment

In general, policies that are complementary to demographic change are not adequately captured, as the paper admits.

In the "core" variables some obvious growth correlates are not considered because data limitations reduce the number of observations for the whole period. One variable, on which Census data should be available for the whole period, is the percentage of villages that are sparsely populated, reflecting problems of rural infrastructure and geographic barriers.

General Discussion

The Chair, Surjit Bhalla, opened the discussion. He stated that the paper made much of the acceleration in GDP growth that took place starting in the mid-1980s when Indian GDP growth went up to about 5.5 percent. One hypothesis is that the drop in the share of agriculture in the GDP explains that acceleration. You now offer the alternative hypothesis that demographic transition is behind that acceleration. Bhalla said that his own view was that the authors' calculations attribute too high a proportion of the acceleration to the demographic transition. It basically left no role, practically zero role, for any contribution to growth of capital formation. He thought that updating the analysis to the 2000s will radically change the results because all the laggard states are now going faster. So then one will need to explain how come this happened in just this decade and not the decade before and the decade before that.

The first speaker from the floor stated that it would be nice to know more about the relationship between these demographic changes and the saving rate. It is inside the model doesn't quite become explicit. At the aggregate level, we know that in the last decade, the national saving rate is gone up hugely but that is not because of household savings have gone up. The increase in savings rate is all due to corporate savings going up.

T. N. Srinivasan said that he was still trying to absorb the paper. One thing that he didn't quite understand is that the authors start from growth equation and then do the counterfactual exercise to get the demographic dividend. But then they later on add policy controls to that equation that were not part of the original theory that led to the growth equation. So what is being estimated later seems an exercise devoid of any theory.

Sheetal Sekhri said that it appeared from the results that there is some degree of heterogeneity to the dividend. So for example, it has increased over the years and you do not see it in Kerala. So maybe it does not pay off in vacuum. Maybe institutions are relevant to whether you will see a demographic dividend or not. It would be worthwhile to look at some sort of heterogeneity in terms of when and where this type of dividend pays off.

Dilip Mukherjee said that he was surprised to hear Sonalde Desai say that economists think that demographics is unimportant. In development economics we think that it's fundamental. The Solow model initially dominated growth theory. We then had the convergence literature à la Mankiw, Romer, and Weil. Capital was very important in this literature. You start with the production function, then the output per capita is a function of the total factor productivity and the capital labor ratio and then if you want to look at changes, then savings and population growth come in naturally. Look at all the Mankiw, Romer, and Weil calculations; the population growth rate number is very negative and significant. Demographics are certainly very important. But if we take that as a departure, which seems to be well received part of macro tradition, then it would seem that it would be natural to extend Mankiw, Romer, and Weil kind of decomposition and so you would have savings rates, population growth rates, but then you'd add labor force participation and you'd add age structure. But the present paper is not decomposing growth in that way; it just has the initial per-capita income and then it's only the working age ratio. So the working age ratio is obviously correlated with everything else, with the savings rate, with labor force participation rates, with population growth rates and so on. So what we've got is a reduced form, but the problem is to interpret the reduced form. It would be much preferred if the authors had written down a production function with savings rates, with population growth rates, labor force participation rates and age structure which would naturally arise if you took the age structure seriously in writing down the economy's production function. Then you would have a direct effect of changes in the age structure, but the age structure would also affect the savings rate and the population growth rates. So then hopefully, if all of this can be done, you could decompose the direct and the indirect effects, which will help us interpret what really is going on here. Mukherjee said he felt a bit suspicious of all the controls because, for instance, one of the authors' controls that seemed to be significant was the sex ratio. Now, do we have any theory on how the sex ratio affects growth rates, and one would suspect that the control is really serving as a proxy for health improvements and so on. This goes back to what Srinivasan said that it would be much preferable to write down the theory upfront and then use that to estimate the whole way through, so that we can properly interpret what's happening.

In response, Ashoka Mody opened by stating that it is always tempting to start a paper with a China–India comparison, because it perks up people's interest, as it indeed did. In a way, this comes at an odd time when Indian growth rates are slowing down and the idea that India is embarking on a transition to overtake China seems a little bit less likely than when the paper was initially drafted. What this brings out is that just because China is ageing doesn't mean that China will not continue to benefit from some positive demographic forces. Here it is helpful to go back to the literature. The literature says everything else equal if the share of the working age population goes up, your growth rate per capita may or may not go up. The answer to why it may not can be found in the Arab literature under the rubric Youth Bulge. If you produce a lot of people who are in the working age group and you don't have productive opportunities for them you are actually going to make things worse than if you have a lot of people who are in the working age group and are employed productively. So we are asking the sample question whether more people in the working-age group translate into a higher per-capita income. There is a separate question about the mechanism through which the increase happens. Mody pointed out that one of the early comments they got on the paper related to the Bloom and Canning paper, which says that there is a demographic dividend provided economies are open. The interpretation of that conclusion is that if there is some degree of competitiveness in the economy, some pressures to deploy people productively then having more people in the work force will lead to greater growth and not otherwise.

Turning to the issue of mechanism, Mody noted that this is a question the paper has not addressed. Savings is an important way to address it but it is unlikely that the available state-level data will allow it. Referring to similar mechanism issues raised by Bhalla and Bardhan, Mody said that he saw the issue as one of the nature of deployment of the additional work force that demographic transition makes possible. One possibility was that the gains came from the reallocation out of agriculture into other activities. Another possibility is that the gains came from increased savings. Whatever the mechanism that the gains came through is an interesting and legitimate question and one worthy of further research.

Mody concluded by retuning to China. He noted that just because China was ageing, it was not inevitable that it would slow down. As Bardhan pointed out, it may take a while for the savings rate to decline. Another possibility is that the labor force participation may rise. The demographic dividend as narrowly defined in the paper did not include the labor force participation. Countries like Japan, China, and others, which are ageing, are countering it by changing the labor force participation rates.

Shekhar Aiyar provided additional responses. He said that this paper could be seen as opening the door to a much richer literature. There's plenty more that can be done. Just to go forward with what Mody had said, if one were to take the results seriously, then there is a rich agenda in terms of figuring out the exact mechanisms whereby this increase in the working age ratio is actually translated into growth. You could have a series of papers examining things like savings rates, sectoral reallocation, and all the other mechanisms by which this might operate. Related, many commentators talked about the female participation rate but state-level data going back in a time on this variable could not be found. Exclusion of female participation may bias the estimates in the paper if it is correlated with the working age ratios. If female participation tends to be higher in those States which have either higher working age ratio or those States in which the working age ratio is growing faster, the estimate of the demographic dividend would be higher than what is reported in the paper.

Turning to interactions with policy variables, Aiyar said that he and Mody had carried out a number of tests but found no significant effects but further investigation along the lines suggested by Bardhan was possible. One could investigate whether the reforms in 1991, carried out at the central level, could have differential effects across states depending on state-level policies relating to, say, restrictiveness of labor laws. So, the same federal intervention could actually have differential impacts by State and it would be worthwhile research agenda to look at whether those different effective state interventions interact with the demographic dividend.

Mody rejoined the discussion by commenting on Kerala. He said that there were two points to be made with respect to that state. One, for several decades, it seemed that Kerala was not growing very rapidly. But according to Arvind Panagariya, Kerala has actually done better than most people believe. But one could still persist that that is a more recent and we still need to explain the prior decades. That leads to the second point, which is that is there was extensive migration from Kerala and this is not just a Gulf phenomenon but much older. So the one State that did have a demographic dividend in the sense defined in the paper gave it away to the world through migration.

The Chair concluded by thanking the authors for an excellent paper and other participants for very interesting discussion. He noted that demographic dividend was now an important stylized facts in the development literature, second only the catch up. He felt, however, that the estimates offered by the authors were far too high.

References

Bloom, David and Canning, David. 2004. "Global Demographic Change: Dimensions and Economic Significance," NBER Working Paper 10817, NBER.

Bloom, David, Canning, David, and Sevilla, Jaypee. 2003. *The Demographic Dividend: A New Perspective on the Economic Consequences of Population Change*. Santa Monica: The RAND Corporation.

Bloom, David and Williamson, J.G. 1997. "Demographic Transitions and Economic Miracles in Emerging Asia," NBER Working Paper 6268, NBER.

Boserup, Esther. 1970. *Woman's Role in Economic Development*. London: George Allen and Unwin.

Cassen, Robert. 1994. *Population and Development: Old Debates, New Conclusions*. Washington, D.C.: Overseas Development Council.

Coale, Ansley J. and Edger M. Hoover. 1958. *Population Growth and Economic Development in Low Income Countries*. Princeton: Princeton University Press.

Heady, Derek and Andrew Hodge. 2009. "The Effect of Population Growth on Economic Growth: A Meta-Regression Analysis of the Macroeconomic Literature," *Population and Development Review*, 352 (2): 221–48.

Johnson, D. Gale and Ronald D. Lee. 1986. *Population Growth and Economic Development: Policy Questions*. Washington, D.C.: National Academy Press.

Lee, Ronald. 2003. "The Demographic Transition: Three Centuries of Fundamental Change," *The Journal of Economic Perspectives*, 17 (4): 167–90.

Meadows, Donella, Dennis Meadows, Jorgen Randers, and William H. Breherns. 1972. *Limits to Growth*. New York: Universe Books.

National Sample Survey Office. 2011. *Employment and Unemployment Situation in India 2009–2010*, Vol. 537. New Delhi: National Statistical Organisation, Government of India.

SHEETAL SEKHRI
University of Virginia

Sustaining Groundwater: Role of Policy Reforms in Promoting Conservation in India*

ABSTRACT   Groundwater depletion has become an increasingly important policy concern in many countries around the world, especially in India, which is the largest user of groundwater for irrigation. Groundwater is contended to have ushered Green Revolution in the country. However, a downside to this pattern of development is that it is not sustainable. As in other countries, the stocks of groundwater are rapidly depleting in India. Against this backdrop, it is important to understand what policies can help conserve this vital resource. This study uses data from observation and monitoring wells of the country to identify depletion hot spots and evaluate the impact of two policies—rainwater harvesting mandates and delaying of paddy transplanting time—on water tables. Rainwater harvesting mandates did not have beneficial effects on water tables in the short run and delayed transplanting of paddy resulted in increased use of groundwater.

Keywords: *Groundwater Conservation, Sustainable Development*

JEL Classification: *O13, O38, Q15, Q25*

1. Introduction

India is the largest user of groundwater for irrigation in the world. The amount of groundwater drawn is estimated to be 230 billion cubic meters per year (in 2004) compared to 101 billion cubic meters in China and 108 billion cubic meters in US in 2005 (Food and Agriculture Organization, Aquastat dataset). Indian agriculture is sustained by groundwater. According to the 2005–06 Agricultural Census of the country, 60.4 percent of the net irrigated area is irrigated using groundwater. Agriculture is the source of livelihood for majority of Indian population. In 2009–10, agriculture

* *ssekhri@virginia.edu*   I wish to thank the Central Groundwater Board of India for providing the groundwater data. Daniel Muldoon provided excellent research assistance.

employed 52.9 percent of the working population (National Sample Survey Office, 2011). In addition, around 80 percent of the rural population relies on groundwater for meeting their drinking water needs.

Groundwater is contended to have ushered Green Revolution in the country (Repetto 1994; Shah et al. 2007). Groundwater irrigation has ensured food security in times of deficit rainfall and facilitated a manifold increase in agricultural productivity. The country has become a net exporter of food grains. However, this pattern of development is not sustainable. As in other countries, the stocks of groundwater are rapidly depleting in India. According to the central groundwater board, 15 percent of the administrative blocks are overexploited (more water is extracted than is replenished each year) and are growing at a rate of 5.5 percent per annum.

India's legal framework allows for unchecked open access to groundwater. Riparian rights govern extraction of groundwater. Any person who owns land can extract groundwater free of cost. In addition to this, most states provide huge electricity subsidies to the farm sector. In large agricultural states such as Punjab and Tamil Nadu, farmers get free electricity. In other states, electricity is not metered but provided at a flat rate based on horse power of the pumps used for groundwater extraction. The central governments assured minimum support pricing policy distorts the prices of food grains such as wheat, and more importantly, paddy incentivizing growing paddy in areas not conducive for it. These factors compound the depletion problem.

Against this backdrop, it is important to understand what policies can help conserve this vital resource. There are more than 27 million private tube wells in the country (Shankar et al. 2011). Pervasive usage of individual wells makes monitoring and enforcement extremely difficult, and hence impedes conventional policy design to check overextraction. Therefore, public policy focus has mostly been on supply side interventions. This study uses data from observation and monitoring wells to evaluate the impact of two policies—rainwater harvesting mandates and delaying of paddy transplanting time—on water tables.

This paper has three objectives. First, the paper highlights the depletion hot spots and trends in water table decline in these hot spots. Second, the paper summarizes the literature to establish the expected welfare costs of groundwater depletion. Third, the paper presents detailed evaluation of three policies targeted toward reversing water table decline in various parts of the country. The paper is organized as follows: Section 2 discusses current groundwater situation and trends in groundwater decline in the entire country. Section 3 discusses potential welfare implications of declining groundwater levels. In section 4, I provide detailed discussion of the three policies being evaluated in this paper. Section 5 provides concluding remarks including comments on the characteristics of policies that can effectively address the issue of declining groundwater levels.

2. Current Groundwater Scenario and Depletion Trends

In this section, I highlight the spatial distribution of the current groundwater situation in the country and the trends in the depletion rates. For the purposes of this assessment, I use the monitoring wells (observation wells) level data for each well from 1980 onwards and the spatial boundaries of Indian districts from Census of India 2001. Monitoring wells data contains 4 quarterly observations on level of groundwater in meters below ground level (mbgl). Annual averages are constructed for each district for each year using this data.

Figure 1 shows the changes in the stock of groundwater over a period of 30 years between 1980 and 2010 (negative numbers indicate rises in the water level). The most substantial decline in groundwater level is observed in northwestern India. In parts of Gujarat and Rajasthan, groundwater level fell more than 16 meters over this period. In central Punjab and Haryana, the groundwater level declined between 12 and 16 meters. Other pockets of Punjab, Haryana, Rajasthan, Gujarat, Western Uttar Pradesh, and New Delhi also experienced noticeable declines between 8 and 12 meters. A few districts in coastal Gujarat, central Rajasthan, Madhya Pradesh, Uttar Pradesh, West Bengal, Karnataka, and Tamil Nadu saw a decline of 4 to 8 meters. In addition, a 1 to 4 meters' decline over this period was widespread, extending to many other states. Figure 2 panels A, B, and C show the patterns of decline by decade. Groundwater depletion had already commenced between 1980 and 1990. But in the following decades, there was a sharp downward trend in the northwestern region of the country. Trends in groundwater level for states in the top quartile of absolute water table decline and top quartile of percentage change are shown in Figure 3, panels A and B. Punjab, Gujarat, and Delhi experienced the largest quantum of change. Figure 4 shows the area within states that experienced different degrees of decline. Delhi has the largest area experiencing the worst decline, followed by Punjab.

The cost of extracting groundwater depends on the depth of water table. There is a sharp rise in the fixed cost of extracting groundwater at around 8 meters. At 8 meters, surface pumps become infeasible to extract water and farmers have to invest in more expensive technologies such as submersible

FIGURE 1. Changes in India District Groundwater Depth, 1980–2010

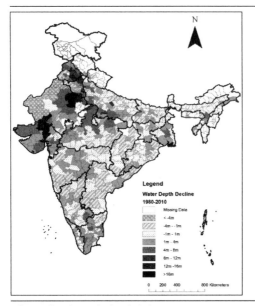

Source: Based on author's calculations.

FIGURE 2. Decadal Changes in Indian District Groundwater Depth

Panel A: Changes in Indian District Groundwater Depth, 1980–1990

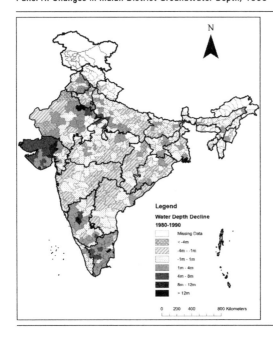

Panel B: Changes in Indian District Groundwater Depth, 1990-2000

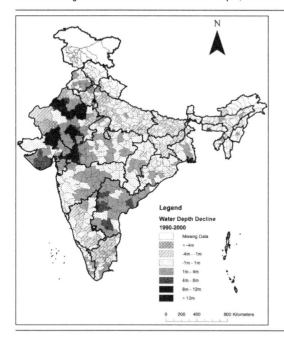

Panel C: Changes in Indian District Groundwater Depth, 2000-2010

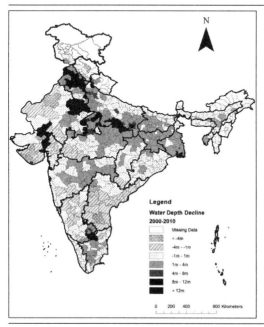

Source: Based on author's calculations.

FIGURE 3.   District Groundwater Depth in Selected States, 1980–2010

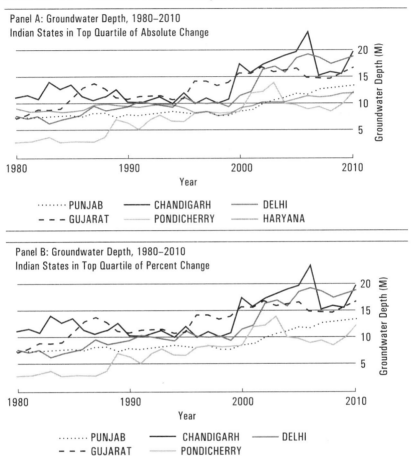

Panel A: Groundwater Depth, 1980–2010
Indian States in Top Quartile of Absolute Change

PUNJAB ········   CHANDIGARH ——   DELHI ——
GUJARAT – – –   PONDICHERRY ——   HARYANA ——

Panel B: Groundwater Depth, 1980–2010
Indian States in Top Quartile of Percent Change

PUNJAB ········   CHANDIGARH ——   DELHI ——
GUJARAT – – –   PONDICHERRY ——

Source: Based on author's calculations.

pumps to extract groundwater.[1] From social and economic perspective, it becomes important to determine the extent of depletion where water tables fall from over 8 meters to below 8 meters. Figure 5 shows the proportion of districts in selected states where the water table has fallen below 8 meters between 1980 and 2010. Most districts in Punjab have experienced such patterns of decline. Other states including Haryana, New Delhi, Gujarat, Rajasthan, Madhya Pradesh, Maharashtra, Uttar Pradesh, Bihar, Jharkhand, West Bengal, Andhra Pradesh, Pondicherry, Kerala, and Tamil Nadu also

1. Surface pumps use atmospheric pressure to draw water. Atmospheric pressure can practically support the weight of a column of water of height 8 meters.

FIGURE 4. Distric Groundwater Depth Changes Selected States, 1980–2010

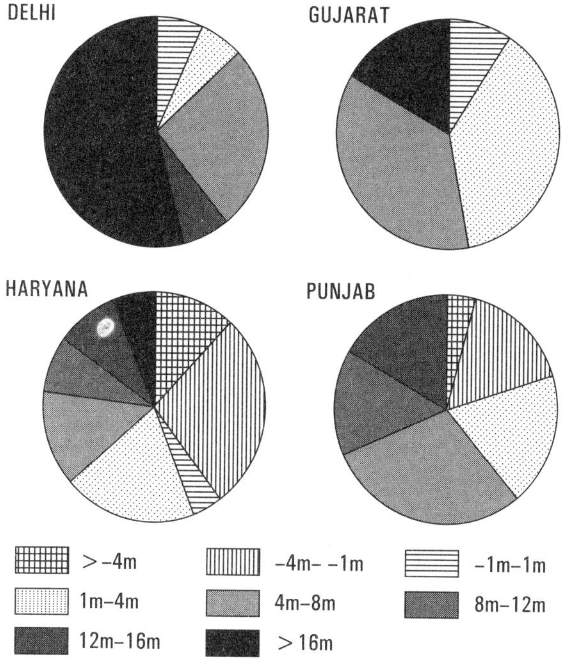

DELHI GUJARAT

HARYANA PUNJAB

▦ > -4m	▥ -4m- -1m	▤ -1m-1m
▨ 1m-4m	▨ 4m-8m	■ 8m-12m
■ 12m-16m	■ > 16m	

Source: Based on author's calculations.

have pockets where declines of water table are costly to the farmers. Figure 6 shows the trends over time in the top five states—Punjab, Gujarat, Delhi, Pondicherry, and Madhya Pradesh—where average groundwater depth went from above 8 meters to below 8 meters. Figure 7 shows the area of the states that experienced decline from above 8 to below 8 meters. Punjab had the largest area experiencing such decline, followed by Pondicherry, Madhya Pradesh, Haryana, New Delhi, and Gujarat.

Three important facts emerge from these figures. One, the decline in water tables in India is spatially heterogeneous with northwestern region affected the most.[2] Two, the bread basket states, including Punjab and Haryana with endowments of thick aquifers, are experiencing significant declines in water tables. These states are the role models of Green Revolution. Three, the decline has accelerated over time.

---

2. This is consistent with other findings using recent satellite based data. Data from NASA's GRACE satellites shows significant depletion of groundwater levels in Northern India. Non-renewable aquifers are being mined over large areas (NASA 2009).

FIGURE 5. Costly Changes in Indian District Groundwater Depth, 1980–2010

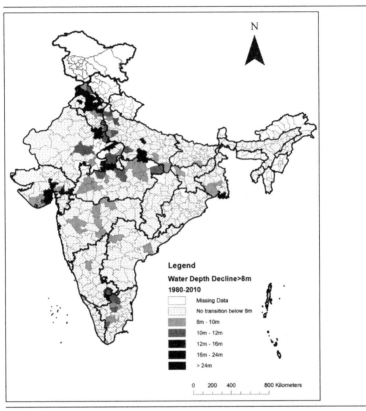

Source: Based on author's calculations.

FIGURE 6. Groundwater Depth, 1980–2010

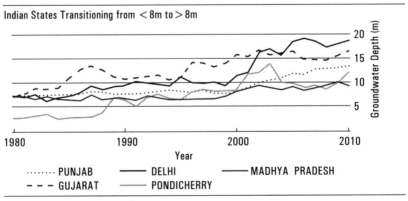

Source: Based on author's calculations.

FIGURE 7. Costly Changes in Indian State Groundwater Depth, 1980–2010

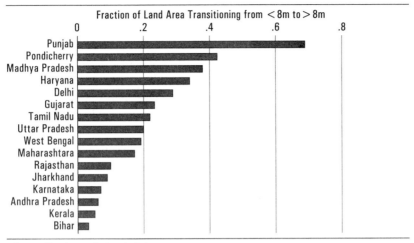

Source: Based on author's calculations.

3. Why Is Conservation Vital? Poverty and Other Implications

From welfare perspective, rapid decline in water tables can result in significant social cost. Case studies have documented that access to groundwater
can reduce poverty and ensure food security (Moench 2001; Moench 2003;
Mukherji 2008). Sekhri (2011a) uses groundwater data in conjunction with
annual agricultural output data at the district level to show that a 1-meter
decline in groundwater from its long-term mean can reduce food grain
production by around 8 percent. Controlling for district fixed effects, year
fixed effects, and district-specific trends, this paper uses the plausibly exogenous fluctuations in groundwater depth from long-term means to estimate
the effect of groundwater scarcity on food grain production. A 1-meter
decline of groundwater depth results in very large reduction in food grain
production. Given that groundwater irrigation is the main stay of irrigation
in India, this is not unexpected. Consistent with previous field studies, this
paper shows that groundwater depletion can have significant effect on food
security in the country.

Sekhri (2012) identifies the causal impact of groundwater scarcity on
poverty. Using village-level data from Uttar Pradesh, and exploiting the
fact that there is a nonlinearity in cost required to access groundwater at 8
meters, this study shows that poverty rate increases by around 11 percent as
groundwater depth falls below 8 meters. The full sample estimation controls

for other village characteristics that may be correlated with poverty rate and hence, generate omitted variable bias. These include geographical controls like rainfall and temperature; geological controls like elevation and slope; demographic characteristics like population, literacy rate, total female population; infrastructure including availability of schools, medical facilities, access to electricity, distance to nearest town, village council expenditure on public goods, banking facility and bus service. This study uses a regression discontinuity design for identification. Both parametric and nonparametric techniques have been used to show that the results do not depend on the estimation method. The study provides a variety of tests to substantiate the findings. This study also shows that self-reported conflict over irrigation water increases substantially near the cutoff. The findings echo the results of field studies. Groundwater scarcity increases poverty. On the flip side, uncontrolled access can lead to very rapid depletion. Therefore, sustainable access to groundwater is required to curb poverty in rural areas of the country. One limitation of this study is that is provides a static estimate. How poverty dynamically evolves with groundwater depletion is not well-understood. More work is required to understand and estimate the optimal level of depletion in the long term.

In Gujarat, where the water tables are falling almost at a rate of 3 meters a year, Narula et al. (2011) estimate that water savings of 30 percent can free up 2.7 billion units of electricity for nonagricultural use. Department of Drinking Water Supply, Government of India, estimates that in 2010, approximately 15 percent of the total habitations in the country went from full coverage of drinking water to partial coverage due to drying up of sources. These findings indicate that the welfare costs of groundwater depletion are very large in magnitude, and thus groundwater depletion warrants an appropriate policy response.

4. Policy Response

State governments have introduced policies with the objective to reverse these trends of rapidly falling groundwater. One of the first policies that has been introduced across many states is mandated rainwater harvesting. States opted into selecting various measures for mandating rainwater harvesting. These measures included construction of rainwater harvesting structures on the roofs of buildings which met specific size criterion. Delhi was the first to pass this mandate in 2001. The other states that mandated rainwater harvesting include Andhra Pradesh, Tamil Nadu, Kerala, Madhya Pradesh,

Rajasthan, Bihar, and West Bengal. Table 1 provides details of the mandates along with the dates on which the mandates were passed. In this paper, I conduct a district-level analysis to examine whether such mandates have had any short-run impact on water table decline.

TABLE 1. **Rainwater Harvesting Mandates**

State	Year passed	Description
Delhi	2001	RWH mandatory for all new buildings with more than 100 sq m roof area and all newly developed plots of land larger than 1,000 sq m. Also,mandated RWH by March 31, 2002 for all institutions and residential colonies in notified areas (south and southwest Delhi, and adjoining areas) and all buildings in notified areas that have tubewells
Andhra Pradesh	2002	Andhra Pradesh Water, Land and Tree Act, 2002 stipulates mandatory provision to construct RWH structures at new and existing constructions for all residential, commercial and other premises and open space having area of not less than 200 sq m in the stipulated period, failing which the authority construct such RWH structures and recover the cost incurred along a prescribed penalty
Tamil Nadu	2003	Vide Ordinance No. 4 of 2003 dated July 2003 mandates RWH facilities for all existing and new buildings. Like Andhra Pradesh, the state may construct RWH facilities and recover the cost incurred by means of property taxes
Kerala	2004	Roof top RWH is mandatory for all new buildings as per Kerala Municipality Building (Amendment) Rules, 2004
Madhya Pradesh	2006	The State Govt. vide Gazette notification dated 26.8.2006, has made roof top RWH mandatory for all buildings with plot size larger than 140 sq.m. Also there is a 6 percent rebate in property tax to individuals for the year in which the individual installs roof top RWH structures
Rajasthan	2006	Roof Top RWH is mandatory in state-owned buildings and all buildings with plots larger than 500 sq m in urban areas
Bihar	2007	The Bihar Groundwater Act, enacted in 2007, mandates privions of RWH structures for buildings with plots larger than 1000 sq m
West Bengal	2007	Vide Rule 171 of the West Bengal Municipal (Building) Rules, 2007, mandates installation of RWH system on new and existing buildings

Sources: http://www.rainwaterharvesting.org/Policy/Legislation.htm#
State profiles at http://cgwb.gov.in/gw_profiles/st_ap.htm
http://www.cseindia.org/content/legislation-rainwater-harvesting.

I also examine the impact of a policy pursued by the Gujarat government that promoted decentralized rainwater harvesting. Concentrated efforts to recharge groundwater began in the Saurashtra region of Gujarat after the drought of 1987 (Mehta 2006). Initial efforts to divert run-off to groundwater wells led to widespread adoption of the practice by farmers throughout Saurashtra without government intervention. Over time, farmers experimented with new technologies and farmers began constructing check dams in streams and rivers to reduce water speed and to allow the river water to seep into the ground and replenish the groundwater supply (Mehta 2006). Farmers continued constructing check dams through the 1990s with assistance from nongovernmental organizations (NGOs) who bore some of the costs.

In January 2000, Gujarat government introduced the Sardar Patel Participatory Water Conservation Project in response to the work of farmers and NGOs in the Saurashtra, Kachchh, Ahmedabad, and Sabar Kantha regions (Government of Gujarat 2012b). The first phase of the program ran from January 17, 2000 to February 20, 2001, and 10,257 check dams were constructed by September 1, 2000. The program initially funded 60 percent of the estimated cost of new check dams, and beneficiaries/NGOs financed the remaining 40 percent. By early 2004, almost 24,500 check dams had been constructed, of which roughly 18,700 were in the Saurashtra region (Pandya 2004). In 2005, the government increased its financing to 80 percent of the estimated cost, and the pace of construction increased outside of the Saurashtra region. According to statistics from the Gujarat government, 70,719 check dams had been constructed in total under the project by the end of March, 2012. Of these, 26,799 (38 percent) are in the Saurashtra region, and 22,257 (31 percent) are in Kachchh or North Gujarat (Government of Gujarat 2012a). Figure 8 shows the geographic distribution of check dams constructed under the Sardar Patel Participatory Water Conservation Project.

As discussed above, Punjab and Haryana are experiencing very rapid decline in water tables (see Figure 8). This can threaten future food security in the country. Punjab did not mandate rainwater harvesting. One of the key initiatives undertaken in Punjab to decelerate water table decline is mandated delay of paddy transplanting. In 2006, the state government influenced the date of paddy transplanting by changing the date on which free electricity is diverted to the farm sector for operating mechanized tube wells for groundwater extraction. The date was pushed to June 10, thereby reducing the amount of intensive watering that the crop can receive during its production cycle (Tribune News Service 2006). The delayed date was mandated in 2008 via an ordinance. This was later turned into a law: The Punjab Preservation of Sub-Soil Water Act, 2009. The main purpose of the law is to preserve groundwater by prohibiting sowing paddy before May 10 and transplanting paddy before June 10. In addition, the law creates the

FIGURE 8. **SPPWC Check Dams in Gujarat, March 2012**

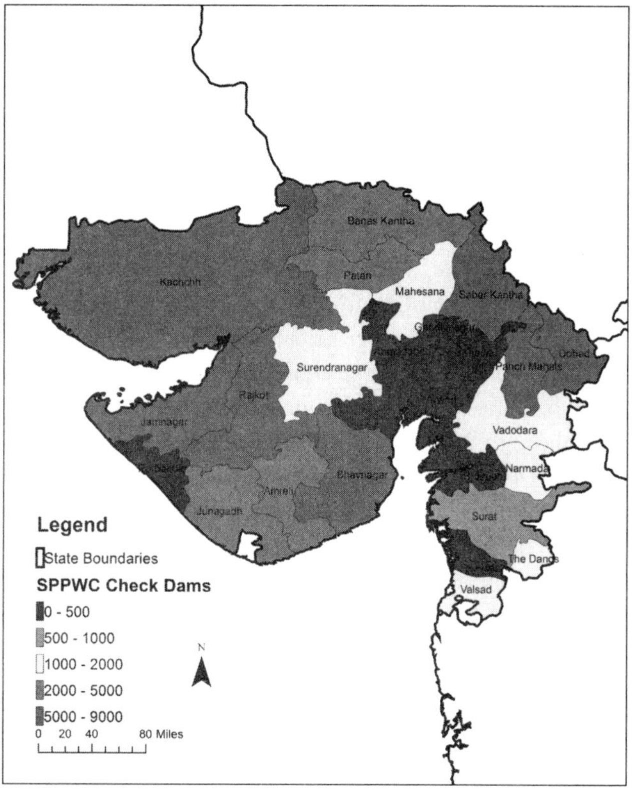

Source: Based on author's calculations.

authority to destroy, at the farmer's expense, paddy sowed or transplanted early, and the law assesses a penalty of ₹10,000 per month, per hectare of land in violation of the law (Government of Punjab 2009).

Haryana followed suit and mandated delay in paddy transplanting in 2009. Haryana passed its Preservation of Sub-Soil Water Act in March 2009, and it is very similar to the Punjab act. Its main provisions prohibit sowing paddy before May 15 and transplanting paddy before June 15. The law also contains punitive provisions similar to Punjab. These include destruction of paddy sowed or transplanted early and a penalty of ₹10,000 per month, per hectare of land in violation of the law (Government of Haryana 2009). The law took immediate effect for the 2009 paddy season.[3] In this paper, I make

3. Singh (2009) provides more details.

use of the timing of the introduction of this policy in Punjab and Haryana to isolate the causal effect of the policy on water tables. Because of the de facto prohibition of transplanting paddy before June 10 in Punjab, I treat 2006 as the effective year for Punjab's policy rather than 2008.

4.1. Data

Data from several sources have been combined to analyze the trends in Indian groundwater levels since 1980, and to evaluate the impact of various policies on water table decline. The groundwater level data are from the Indian Central Groundwater Board. Individual monitoring well data has been used to construct measures of district groundwater depth from 1980 through 2010. The precipitation data from the University of Delaware Center for Climactic Research have been used to calculate district annual average monthly precipitation through 2008. The district precipitation data from the India Meteorological Department has been used for the years 2009 to 2010. In addition, district demographic and socioeconomic characteristics are from the 2001 Census of India. Area under various crops by districts is from the Directorate of Economics and Statistics, Department of Agriculture and Cooperation, Ministry of Agriculture. This has been used to classify districts as high rice growing districts as explained later.

4.1.1. GROUNDWATER DATA The Indian CGWB measures groundwater depth throughout each year at approximately 16,000 monitoring wells across India. In this paper, I use observations from 1980 to 2010 to construct district-level measures of groundwater depth. Groundwater depth is typically measured in January, May, August, and November although some wells have more or fewer observations within a given year. The number of wells in the sample increased greatly over the years. There were 3,305 wells in 1980; 11,063 in 1990; 15,782 in 2000; and 13,683 in 2010. The density of wells in states increased to cover more geographical area and more states started coverage. In the policy analysis conducted later, I use observations from year 2000 to 2010. During this time, the number of wells was, by and large, stable. The monitoring wells are spread over the entire country and not concentrated in any particular area. Wells have not been located in places where the groundwater has been depleting the most. For these reasons, endogenous well placement will not be a concern in the policy analysis.

In addition to groundwater depth, the data include latitude and longitude for each well, and I use this information to match each well to the spatial boundaries of the Indian districts in 2001 and construct a district-level panel of monthly and annual groundwater depth. These district-level measures of groundwater levels are the primary outcomes studied in this paper.

4.1.2. PRECIPITATION DATA   I use precipitation data from the University of Delaware and the India Meteorological Department to control for annual variation in precipitation which greatly affects groundwater depth. The Center for Climactic Research at the University of Delaware compiled monthly weather station data from 1900 to 2008 from several sources.[4] From this data, all grid points within India's administrative boundaries were extracted to construct district-level annual average and monthly precipitation in each year. Since the Center for Climactic Research's data only cover years through 2008, I use data from the India Meteorological Department for 2009 to 2010. The India Meteorological Department collects monthly rainfall data for all Indian districts and publishes tables for each district containing monthly rainfall for the past five years (India Meteorological Department 2012). For 2009 to 2010, district-level annual average and monthly precipitation was calculated from these tables.

4.1.3. DEMOGRAPHIC DATA   The 2001 Indian census data has been used to control for district demographic and socioeconomic characteristics. Specifically, district population, percentage of the district population with at least some college education, district literacy rate, district employment rate, and the percentage of the district population that is female have been controlled. Because these variables have not been observed in intercensal years, these have been interacted with indicators for each year in the sample to control for these characteristics non-parametrically in regression analysis.

4.1.4. CROP PRODUCTION DATA   Data on area under various crops by district has been used to construct high rice production and low rice production district groups in the analysis of Punjab's and Haryana's policies to delay paddy transplanting before the middle of June. Specifically, the fraction of

---

4. These sources include the Global Historical Climatology Network, the Atmospheric Environment Service/Environment Canada, the Hydrometeorological Institute in St Petersburg, Russia, GC-Net, the Automatic Weather Station Project, the National Center for Atmospheric Research, Sharon Nicholson's archive of African precipitation data, Webber and Willmott's (1998) South American monthly precipitation station records, and the Global Surface Summary of Day. After combining data from various sources, the Center for Climactic Research used various spatial interpolation and cross-validation methods to construct a global 0.5 degree by 0.5 degree latitude/longitude grid of monthly precipitation data from 1900 to 2008 (Matsuura and Wilmott 2009).

cultivated area under rice for each district in Punjab and Haryana has been calculated. I then classify districts in Punjab and Haryana above the median as "high rice growing districts."

4.2. Conceptual Framework

The change in the depth of groundwater is a function of demand side variables, supply side variables, and natural recharge rate.

The change in depth can be modeled as:

$$W_t - W_{t-1} = R_t - D_t + S_t + E_t$$

where R_t is the rate of recharge. This would be influenced by the geology of the place including soil characteristics, slope, elevation, and such features. These features are time invariant. The recharge will also be affected by precipitation. D_t represents the demand side variables which may include population, type of industry or sector that is dominant in the district, crops grown, area under various crops, number of pumps being used, availability of alternate form of irrigation, prices of crops, and inputs such as electricity and diesel. The supply side variables S_t include management policies and prevalent institutions. E_t represents an error term. Most of the policies that have been designed change the factors in the set S_t. In what follows, I examine a subset.

A few comments on relating this model to the policy analysis conducted are in order. I use panel data and the methodologies used control for time invariant characteristics of districts. I also control for rainfall and temperature in every regression to account for the recharge. I do not have data on very comprehensive set of variables that can affect the demand for groundwater. I do control for a set of demographic and economic variables. But to the extent that these variables have not influenced policy choices or implementation logistics differentially in treated and control areas, the estimation yields unbiased results.

The following analysis is carried out at the level of districts. Districts are administrative units under states. Most program allocations and monitoring of government programs are delegated to districts. Hence, they are a natural choice for unit of analysis. One concern may be that the underlying aquifers are interconnected. The lateral velocity of groundwater is very low (Todd 1980). Hence, over this time frame spatial externalities may not have arisen. I address this more specifically in the analysis, where I allow spatial correlation between standard errors.

4.3. Identification Strategy

Rainwater harvesting mandates the states selected into mandating rainwater harvesting. Hence, comparing the outcomes in the states that mandated rainwater harvesting with the ones that did not, will result in biased estimates. Therefore, I compare groundwater levels in districts in the states that passed the mandates earlier to the states that passed them later in order to circumvent selection concerns. The identifying assumption is that the timing of such mandates is plausibly exogenous.

The empirical model is as follows:

$$Y_{ist} = \alpha_0 + \alpha_1\, T_t + \alpha_2 d_{is} + \alpha_3 Post * d_{is} + \alpha_4 X_{ist} + \varepsilon_{ist} \tag{1}$$

where Y_{ist} is the groundwater level in district i in state s at time t, T_t are the year fixed effects, d_{is} is the treatment indicator which takes the value 1 if the district is in a treated state, and X_{ist} is a vector of time varying district specific controls. *Post* is an indicator variable that switches to 1 after the rainwater harvesting mandates were passed in the states. The coefficient α_3 is the parameter of interest. ε_{ist} is the error term. Robust standard errors are clustered at the level of states. Year specific common shocks to all districts are absorbed by the time fixed effects. Time invariant district specific omitted variables that affect the likelihood of treatment are controlled for by including the treatment indicator. The interaction *Post* * d_{is} yields the effect of the treatment on the treated post treatment where the treatment is passing of rainwater harvesting mandates.

4.3.1. DECENTRALIZED RAINWATER HARVESTING: SARDAR PATEL PARTICIPATORY WATER CONSERVATION PROJECT
I compare the groundwater levels of districts in the regions that received the subsidy program earlier in January 2000 (treatment regions: Saurashtra, Kachchh, Ahmedabad, and Sabar Kantha regions) to the districts that received the program later in 2005 when it expanded (control regions).[5] Figure 9 plots the average groundwater level in the treated and the control districts from 1990 to 2011. The pretreatment groundwater levels prior to 2000 are similar across these districts and the two groups do not exhibit differential trends. The following empirical model is estimated using the data from 1990 to 2011:

---

5. Districts in treated group include Rajkot, Junagadh, Bhavnagar, Porbandar, Jamnagar, Amreli, Surendranagar, Ahmedabad, Kachchh, and Sabar Kantha. Control group includes Banas Kantha, Patan, Mahesana, Gandhinagar, Kheda, Anand, Panch Mahals, Dahod, Valdora, Narmada, Bharuch, Surat, Navsari, the Dangs, and Valsad.

FIGURE 9. Groundwater Depth in Gujarat Treatment and Control Districts, 1990–2011

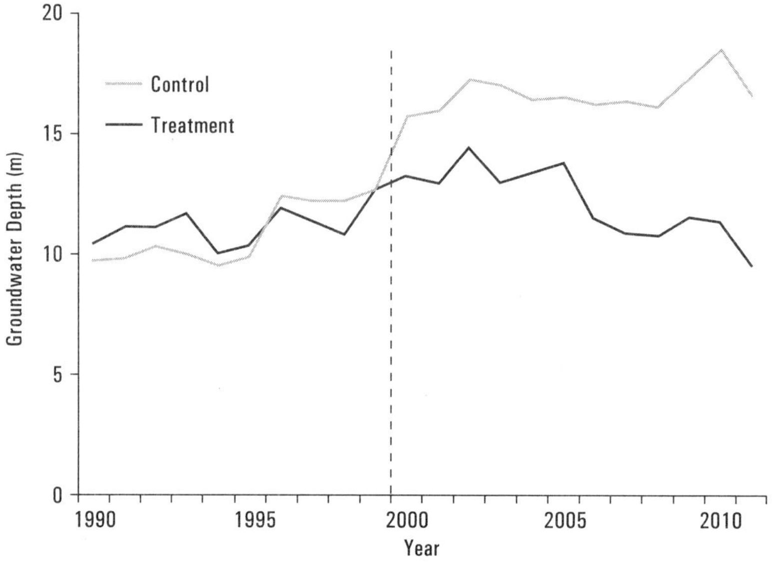

Source: Based on author's calculations.

$$Y_{drt} = \theta_0 + \theta_1\, T_t + \theta_2\, \tau_{dr} + \theta_3\, Post * \tau_{dr} + \theta_4\, X_{drt} + \theta_5\, R_r + \varepsilon_{ist} \qquad (2)$$

where Y_{drt} is the groundwater level in district d in region r at time t, T_t are the year fixed effects, τ_{dr} is the treatment indicator which takes the value 1 if the district is in a treated region, and X_{drt} is a vector of time varying district specific controls. Post is an indicator variable that switches to 1 after 1999. The coefficient θ_3 is the parameter of interest. ε_{ist} is the error term. Robust standard errors are clustered at the level of districts. Year specific common shocks to all districts are absorbed by the time fixed effects. Time invariant district specific omitted variables that affect the likelihood of treatment are controlled for by including the treatment indicator. Region specific time invariant unobservables are absorbed by the region fixed effects R_r in certain specifications. It is important to note that the areas where the subsidy was initiated first were the ones where such decentralized initiatives were successful with the help of NGOs and donor funding. Hence, the estimated coefficient cannot be interpreted as causal. Although pretrends in groundwater level are controlled for, there can be other potential time varying factors that influenced early initiation of the program and are unobserved. An example could be a gradual change in people's attitude toward groundwater conservation or awareness about implications of water depletion.

4.3.2. DELAYED PADDY TRANSPLANTING In the estimation procedure, I employ a difference-in-difference methodology comparing the paddy growing areas in Punjab to the bordering Haryana. Since both states adopted measures to ensure delayed transplanting of paddy at different time, I use the variation in the timing of introduction of the policy to evaluate its impact on groundwater levels. As mentioned before, in Punjab, the de-facto change in date of transplanting happened in 2006 and in Haryana, the mandate was passed in 2009. The rice growing districts were identified using the area under various crops. The districts where the ratio of area under rice to the total cultivated area exceeded the sample median in 2003 for all districts in Haryana and Punjab are considered the high rice growing districts. Since the policy delayed transplanting rice, the policy should have affected the water use in rice growing districts, and hence impact water tables in these districts. Figure 10 maps the high rice production districts (treatment) and low rice production districts (control) in Punjab and Haryana.[6] I compare the high rice growing districts with low rice growing districts before and after the policy change.

The empirical specification is given by:

$$Y_{its} = \beta_0 + \beta_1 \, T_t + \beta_2 \, R_{is} + \beta_3 \, Post * R_{is} + \beta_4 \, X_{its} + \beta_5 \, S_s * R_{is} + \beta_6 \, R_{is} * T_t + \varepsilon_{its} \qquad (3)$$

where Y_{its} is the groundwater level in district i at time t. T_t are the year fixed effects, R_{is} is an indicator variable which takes value 1 if the district is rice growing district and 0 otherwise, and X_{its} is a vector of time varying district specific controls. *Post* is an indicator variable that switches to 1 after the paddy transplanting was delayed and is equal to 0 before that. The coefficient β_3 is the parameter of interest. The regressions include full sets of interaction between state and rice growing districts, and rice growing districts and year indicators. ε_{its} is the error term. Robust standard errors are clustered at the level of districts. I also report Conley (1999) errors to account for spatial correlation in groundwater levels of neighboring districts.[7] Year specific

---

6. High rice production districts are Gurdaspur, Amritsar, Firozpur, Faridkot, Moga, Kapurthala, Jalandhar, Nawanshahr, Ludhiana, Sangrur, Fatehgarh Sahib, Patiala, Kaithal, Kurukshetra, Ambala, Yamunanagar, Karnal, and Panipat. The low rice production districts are Hoshiarpur, Rupnagar, Muktsar, Bathinda, Mansa, Panchkula, Sirsa, Fatehabad, Hisar, Jind, Sonipat, Rohtak, Bhiwani, Jhajjar, Mahendragarh, Rewari, Gurgaon, and Faridabad.

7. The aquifers could be interconnected. The lateral velocity of groundwater is very low. In the short run, cross district externalities are not likely to arise. Conley's standard errors correct for such externalities.

FIGURE 10. Rice Paddy Treatment and Control Districts

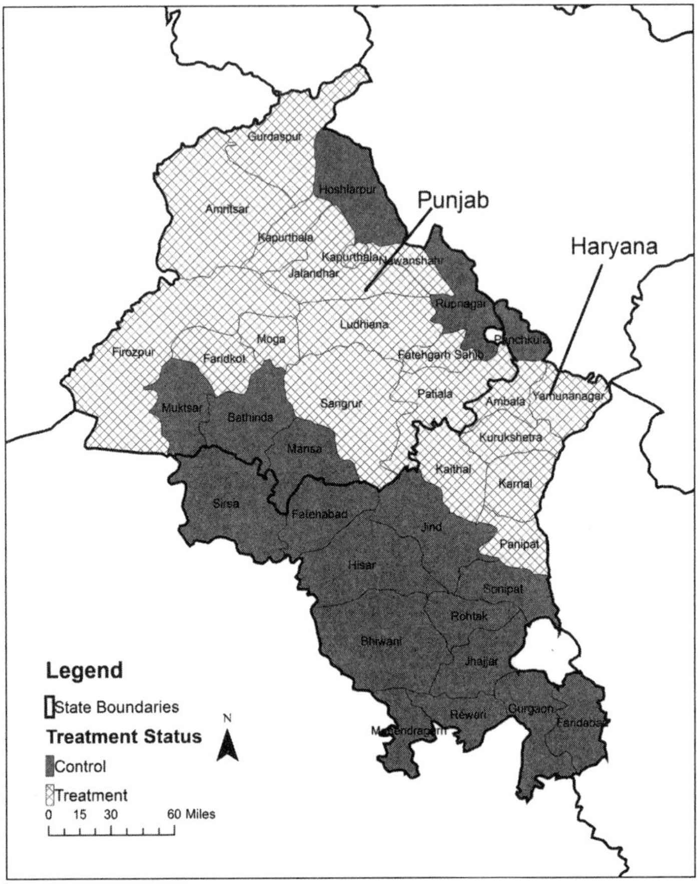

Source: Based on author's calculations.

common shocks to all districts are absorbed by the time fixed effects. Time invariant rice growing district specific omitted variables are controlled for by including the rice growing indicator. The specifications allow for high rice growing districts in the two states to be different by including state times rice growing fixed effects. Differences in high rice growing and low rice growing districts over years are also accounted for by including high rice growing districts times year fixed effects. The vector Y_{its} includes average annual rainfall in the district and demographic controls including percentage of females, percentage of working population, percentage of literate population, percentage of population with some college, and total population.[8] The interaction term *Post* * R_{is} yields the difference-in-difference estimator. In robustness checks, I also allow for state specific trends that non-parametrically account for time varying state specific factors that may have influenced timing of treatment.

4.3.3. RESULTS Tables 2 and 3 report the results for the impact of rainwater harvesting mandates on groundwater levels. Table 2 reports the effect on groundwater levels for four different months—January, May, August, and November. Each specification includes treatment and year fixed effects. I do not find evidence of beneficial effects of rainwater harvesting mandates on groundwater levels at least in the short run. The coefficients on the interaction term are statistically insignificant.[9] In Table 3, this analysis is repeated for annual groundwater levels. Each specification controls for state and year fixed effects. In column (ii), annual average district precipitation is added to the empirical specification and in column (iii), demographic controls interacted with year indicators are added in addition to the precipitation. Although, the interaction term is marginally significant at 10 percent in the columns (i) and (ii), this is not robust to including demographic controls in column (iii). These results do not bear out any evidence of a beneficial effect of rainwater harvesting mandates on water tables in the short run.

Table 4 reports the results for the impact of the Sardar Patel Participatory Water Conservation Project on annual groundwater levels. The subsidy program had an ameliorative effect on groundwater levels. Column (i) reports

TABLE 2. **The Impact of Rainwater Harvesting Mandates on Seasonal Groundwater Levels**

	(i) January	(ii) May	(iii) August	(iv) November
Post * Treatment	0.84*	0.86*	0.51	0.35
	(0.44)	(0.37)	(0.42)	(0.24)
Observations	2,206	2,153	2,060	2,118
R-squared	0.435	0.433	0.405	0.433

Source: Based on author's calculations.
Notes: Robust standard errors are clustered at the state level.
*** p < 0.01, ** p < 0.05, * p < 0.1
Sample is restricted to states which implemented Rainwater Harvesting legislation by 2010. Sample includes observations from 2000 to 2010. Each specification includes year and treatment fixed effects.

8. These variables are available for the year 2001 from the Census of India. These are interacted with year indicators to control for trends in these variables starting at the 2001 initial values.

9. The number of observations change across specifications because of missing data in some of the district year cells.

TABLE 3.   The Impact of Rainwater Harvesting Mandates on Annual
Groundwater Levels

	(i)	(ii)	(iii)
Post * Treatment	0.62*	0.83*	0.64
	(0.29)	(0.41)	(0.36)
Observations	2,230	2,204	2,196
R-squared	0.431	0.456	0.497
District Precipitation	No	Yes	Yes
Demographic Controls	No	No	Yes

Source: Based on author's calculations.
Notes: Robust standard errors are clustered at state level.
*** $p < 0.01$, ** $p < 0.05$, * $p < 0.1$
Sample is restricted to states which implemented Rainwater Harvesting legislation by 2010. Sample
includes observations from 2000 to 2010. Each specification includes year and treatment fixed effects.
Precipitation is district average monthly precipitation in mm. Demographic controls include 2001 district
demographics interacted with year dummies and include percent female, percent literate, percent working,
percent with some college, and total population.

the baseline specification. The coefficient is negative but statistically insignificant. In column (ii), I add region fixed effects. Columns (iii) and (iv) control for annual precipitation levels with and without region fixed effects. The effect continues to be statistically insignificant. In columns (v) and (vi), demographic controls are added interacted with year indicators are added in addition to the precipitation. Both specifications—with and without region fixed effects—yield a negative and highly statistically significant effect of the program. The point estimate of 9.3 is 0.82 of a standard deviation and very large in magnitude. The subsidy program had a huge effect on the annual groundwater level in treated areas. However, these results should be interpreted with caution as the areas that received the early treatment were the areas where decentralized rainwater harvesting was very effective prior to the subsidy program. The government focused the subsidy in regions where NGOs and other donor-funded projects were successful. Hence, I cannot rule out selection bias. As mentioned before, previous experience with such projects may have gradually changed the attitudes toward conservation which is unobserved. Controlling demographic characteristics in column (v) of Table 4 relative to column (iv) changes the results substantially. This strongly suggests that program was targeted selectively in certain types of areas. Figure 9 shows that there are no differential trends in groundwater level prior to the program. Hence, it is likely that the results emerge as a result of this program alone. On the other hand, it is possible that such programs may not be successful in randomly chosen areas, where people do not have prior experience with such projects. More research is required to address selection and establish the causal impact of such subsidy programs.

TABLE 4.   The Impact of Sardar Patel Water Conservation Subsidy Program on Annual Groundwater Level

	(i)	(ii)	(iii)	(iv)	(v)	(vi)
Treatment ×	−4.744	−4.744	−3.742	−4.593	−9.318***	−9.314***
Post-1999	(2.918)	(2.932)	(2.661)	(2.974)	(1.540)	(1.593)
	[2.847]	[2.847]	[2.586]	[2.882]	[1.309]	[1.347]
Observations	550	550	550	550	550	550
R-squared	0.056	0.597	0.249	0.598	0.762	0.810
Year FE	YES	YES	YES	YES	YES	YES
Treatment FE	YES	YES	YES	YES	YES	YES
Region FE	NO	YES	NO	YES	NO	YES
Precipitation (mm)	NO	NO	YES	YES	YES	YES
Census Controls	NO	NO	NO	NO	YES	YES

Source: Based on author's calculations.

Notes: Robust standard errors clustered at district level are in parenthesis and Conley (1999) standard errors correcting for spatial correlation are in brackets.

*** $p<0.01$, ** $p<0.05$, * $p<0.1$

Sample restricted to districts in Gujarat and includes observations from 1990 to 2011. All regressions include a Treatment dummy for districts which received early check dam construction from the Sardar Patel Participatory Water Conservation Program. These include the Saurashtra region, Kachchh, Ahmedabad, and Sabar Kantha. Regions in Gujarat include Kachchh, North Gujarat, Central Gujarat, Saurashtra, East Gujarat, and South Gujarat. Precipitation is district average monthly precipitation in mm. Census controls include 2001 district demographics interacted with year dummies and include percent female, percent literate, percent working, percent with some college, and total population.

Tables 5 and 6 report the results of the impact of delayed paddy transplantation on groundwater levels. The outcome variable is depth to groundwater in meters below ground level (mbgl). Paddy transplantation occurs in June. Table 5 reports the effect of the policy on post-transplanting groundwater level in August and Table 6 reports the results for annual depth to groundwater. Column (i) in Table 5 shows the coefficient of the interaction term from a specification which includes year fixed effects, state × rice fixed effects, and rice × year fixed effects. In column (ii), precipitation is added to the regression specification. Column (iii) controls for trends in demographic variables, and column (iv) includes state specific time trends in addition to the above mentioned controls. In all specifications, the policy increases depth to groundwater. The coefficient is marginally significant at 10 percent significance level is the most conservative specification in column (iv). The August groundwater levels declined in response to the policy. The depth to groundwater level in high rice growing districts post the policy change was 1.17 meters deeper than the low rice growing districts. Similar specifications are repeated for the annual depth to groundwater in Table 6. In each specification, the coefficient on the interaction term is positive and highly statistically significant. In the last column, we observe a decline in depth of 1.60 mbgl and it is significant at 1 percent level. This effect is 0.28 of

TABLE 5. The Impact of Delay in Paddy Transplantation on Groundwater Levels Post-transplanting (Groundwater Level Measured in August)

	(i)	(ii)	(iii)	(iv)
Post * High Rice Producing	1.30**	1.28**	1.13	1.17*
Districts	(0.53)	(0.53)	(0.70)	(0.64)
	[0.51]	[0.51]	[0.62]	[0.57]
Observations	324	321	321	321
R-squared	0.100	0.101	0.252	0.254
State × Rice FE	Yes	Yes	Yes	Yes
Year × Rice FE	Yes	Yes	Yes	Yes
District Precipitation	No	Yes	Yes	Yes
Census Controls	No	No	Yes	Yes
State Specific Time Trend	No	No	No	Yes

Source: Based on author's calculations.
Notes: Robust standard errors clustered at district level are in parentheses. Conley (1999) standard errors correcting for spatial correlation are in brackets.
*** $p < 0.01$, ** $p < 0.05$, * $p < 0.1$
Sample is restricted to districts in Punjab and Haryana. Each regression controls for year fixed effects. Sample includes observations from 2003 to 2011. Districts with rice area as a fraction of total cultivated area above the median in Punjab and Haryana (.30) are classified as rice-producing.
Punjab began limiting paddy water supply in 2006 (two years before its legislation) by way of rationing electricity, and Haryana passed legislation in 2009. Precipitation is district average monthly precipitation in mm.
Census controls include 2001 district demographics interacted with year dummies and include percent female, percent literate, percent working, percent with some college, and total population.

TABLE 6. The Impact of Delay in Paddy Transplantation on Annual Groundwater Levels

	(i)	(ii)	(iii)	(iv)
Post * High Rice Producing	1.25***	1.13**	1.58***	1.60***
Districts	(0.45)	(0.46)	(0.54)	(0.53)
	[0.44]	[0.45]	[0.48]	[0.47]
Observations	324	321	321	321
R-squared	0.090	0.097	0.248	0.249
State × Rice FE	Yes	Yes	Yes	Yes
Year × Rice FE	Yes	Yes	Yes	Yes
District Precipitation	No	Yes	Yes	Yes
Census Controls	No	No	Yes	Yes
State Specific Time Trend	No	No	No	Yes

Notes: Robust standard errors clustered at district level are in parentheses. Conley (1999) standard errors correcting for spatial correlation are in brackets.
*** $p < 0.01$, ** $p < 0.05$, * $p < 0.1$
Sample is restricted to districts in Punjab and Haryana. Each regression controls for year fixed effects. Sample includes observations from 2003 to 2011. Districts with rice area as a fraction of total cultivated area above the median in Punjab and Haryana (0.30) are classified as rice-producing.
Punjab began limiting paddy water supply in 2006 (two years before its legislation) by way of rationing electricity, and Haryana passed legislation in 2009. Precipitation is district average monthly precipitation in mm.
Census controls include 2001 district demographics interacted with year dummies and include percent female, percent literate, percent working, percent with some college, and total population.

a standard deviation and is economically moderate. The findings indicate that the annual groundwater level situation worsened in rice growing areas after the policy change.[10] It is possible that the farmers responded to the policy by increasing the number of irrigations applied or using more water per irrigation after the mid-June transplanting.[11]

What Do We Learn from the Experience with These Policies?

The rainwater harvesting mandates were unsuccessful in reversing the depletion rates whereas the decentralized experience in Gujarat has been more positive. From this comparison, it appears that technical or engineering limitations or short duration that has elapsed since the program commencement are not the principal explanations for success or failure of these policies. The effective policies will need to be decentralized in nature. Engagement of the stakeholders is an important ingredient for these policies to work. Bottom-up rather than top-down policy tools are more successful. None of these policies are pricing mechanisms. In Sekhri (2011b), I show that public wells provision can reduce the rate of depletion. If an optimal price is charged it can also reverse depletion. But this can work only where cost of groundwater extraction is high, or in other words in areas where water tables are deep. In Sekhri and Foster (2008), we find evidence that bilateral trade arrangements between farmers who sell and buy groundwater also decelerate depletion rates. The benefit of promoting these is that these arrangements do not require top down monitoring. Introduction of pricing mechanisms may be another important lever to reduce overextraction.

Future Directions with Policy Choices

What kind of policies—direct or indirect—can or cannot work? Reducing electricity subsidies can potentially affect groundwater extraction rates (Badiani and Jessoe 2011). West Bengal and Uttarakhand have recently adopted metering of electricity for tube wells. Gujarat, under the flagship Jyotirgram Yojana, has separated agricultural feeders from nonagricultural

10. In contrast to these findings, Singh (2009) estimates a 30 cm water-saving effect of the policy but the estimate is based on simulations using historic data from central Punjab and does not account for selection issues.

11. In the absence of farm-level data on applied number of irrigations and water use, it is not possible to establish the mechanism.

feeders, improved the quality of the power supply and rationed the number of hours of electricity to agriculture to eight hours a day. Important policy lessons can be learnt from the experience of these states.[12] Other possibilities include promoting water-saving infrastructure and agricultural practices. More research is required to understand the effect of policies that promote such practices, and is a very promising area of future research.

References

Agriculture Census Division, Ministry of Agriculture, Government of India. 2006. "Agricultural Census of India Database."

Badiani, Reema and Katrina K. Jessoe. 2011. "Electricity Subsidies for Agriculture: Evaluating the Impact and Persistence of These Subsidies in India." University of California Davis Working Paper.

Conley, T. G. 1999. "GMM Estimation with Cross Sectional Dependence," *Journal of Econometrics*, 92 (1): 1–45.

Foster, A. and S. Sekhri. 2008. "Can Expansion of Markets for Groundwater Decelerate the Depletion of Groundwater Resource in Rural India?" Brown University Working Paper.

Government of Gujarat. 2012a. "Details of Checkdams Completed in Gujarat State as on 31 March 2012."

———. 2012b. "Sardar Patel Participatory Water Conservation Scheme—Water Conservation through Partnership between People and Government—Success Story of Gujarat."

Government of Punjab. 2009. The Punjab Preservation of Sub Soil Water Preservation Act.

Haryana Government. 2009. "The Haryana Preservation of Sub-Soil Water Act." March 18.

India Meteorological Department. 2012. "Last 5-years Districtwise Rainfall."

Kelbert, Anna, Adam Schultz, and Gary Egbert. 2008. "Global Electromagnetic Induction Constraints on Transition-zone Water Content Variations," *Nature*, 460: 1003–006.

Kumar, Bidisha. 2007. "Punjab's Depleting Groundwater Stagnates Agricultural Growth," *Down To Earth*, July 31. Available at http://www.downtoearth.org.in/node/6267

Matsuura, Kenji and Cort J. Willmott. 2009. "Terrestrial Precipitation: 1900–2008 Gridded Monthly Time Series." Vol. Version 2.01. Center for Climactic Research at University of Delaware.

Mehta, Ambrish. 2006. "The Rain Catchers of Saurashtra, Gujarat." Chap. 5 in *The Water Revolution: Practical Solutions to Water Scarcity*, edited by Kendra Okonski. London: International Policy Press.

---

12. Mukherji et al. (2010) provide details of the reforms.

Modi, Vijay, Narula Kapil, Ram Fishman, and Lakis Polycarpou. 2011. "Addressing the Water." Columbia Water Center White Paper.

Moench, M. 2001. "Groundwater and Poverty: Exploring the Links," workshop on intensively exploited aquifers, Royal Academy of Sciences, Madrid.

Moench, M. 2003. "Groundwater and Poverty: Exploring the Connections," in R. Llamas and E. Custodio (eds), *Intensive Use of Groundwater: Challenges and Opportunities*, pp. 441–55. Swets & Zeitlinger B.V., Lisse, The Netherlands.

Mukherji, A. 2008. "Poverty, Groundwater, Electricity and Agrarian Politics: Understanding the Linkages in West Bengal."

Mukherji, Aditi, Tushaar Shah, and Shilp Verma. 2010. "Electricity Reforms and Their Impact on Ground Water Use in States of Gujarat, West Bengal and Uttarakhand, India," in *On the Water Front: Selections from the 2009 World Water Week in Stockholm*, edited by J. Lundqvist. Stockholm: Stockholm International Water Institute.

Narula, K., Modi, V., Fishman, R., and L. Polycarpou. 2011. "Addressing the Water Crisis in Gujarat," Columbia Water Center White Paper.

NASA. 2009. "Satellite-based Estimates of Groundwater Depletion in India," *Nature*, 460: 999–1002.

National Sample Survey Office. 2011. "Key Indicators of Employment and Unemployment in India, 2009–2010."

One India News. 2008. *Power Situation Normal in Punjab as Paddy Sowing Begins.* June 11. Available at http://news.oneindia.in/2008/06/09/power-situation-normal-in-punjab-as-paddy-sowing-begins-1213167693.html.

Pandya, Harshida. 2004. "Check Dams Help Raise Water Table in Jamnagar, Amreli," *Business Standard*, February 25.

Parkash, Chander. 2006. "Power Supply to Improve from May 1," *Tribune India.* April 29.

Punjab Government. 2009. "The Punjab Preservation of Sub Soil Water Preservation Act." April 28.

Punjab Newsline. 2006. *PSEB Copes with High Demand of Power for Paddy.* June 13. Available at: http://punjabnewsline.com/content/view/698/70.

Registrar General and Census Commissioner, India. 2001. "Census of India."

Repeto, R. 1994. "The Second India' Revisited: Population, Poverty and Environmental Stress over Two Decades," Washington, D.C., World Resources Institute.

Sekhri, Sheetal. 2011a. "Missing Water: Agricultural Stress and Adaptation Strategies." Mimeo, University of Virginia.

———. 2011b. "Public Provision and Protection of Natural Resources: Groundwater," *American Economic Journal: Applied Economics*, 3 (4): 29–55.

———. 2012. "Wells, Water and Welfare: Impact of Access to Groundwater on Rural Poverty." Mimeo, University of Virginia.

Sekhri, Sheetal and Andrew Foster. 2008. "Can Expansion of Markets for Groundwater in Rural India?" Brown University Working Paper.

Shah, T., C. Scott, A. Kishore, and A. Sharma. 2007. "Energy-Irrigation Nexus in South Asia: Improving Groundwater Conservation and Power Sector Viability," in

M. Giordana and K.G. Villholth (eds), *The Agricultural Groundwater Revolution: Opportunities and Threat to Development*. UK: CAB International.

Shankar, P.S. Vijay, Himanshu Kulkarni, and Sunderrajan Krishnan. 2011. "India's Groundwater Challenge and the Way Forward," *Economic and Political Weekly*, 46 (2), January 8.

Singh Gill and Puneet Pal. 2006. "Punjab Advances Power Austerity Drive." *Business Standard*. April 11. Available at http://www.business-standard.com/india/news/punjab-advances-power-austerity-drive-date/239859/

Singh, Karam. 2009. "Act to Save Groundwater in Punjab: Its Impact on Water Table, Electricity Subsidy and Environment," *Agricultural Economics Research Review*: 365–86.

Todd, D. 1980. *Groundwater Hydrology*. US: John Wiley & Sons.

Tribune News Service. 2006. "Power Woes Return with Paddy Season," *Tribune India*. June 13.

Webber, S. R. and C. J. Willmott. 1998. "South American Precipitation: 1960–1990 Gridded Monthly Time Series (Version 1.02)." Newark, Delaware: Center for Climatic Research, Department of Geography, University of Delaware.

Comments and Discussion

Tushaar Shah
International Water Management Institute

I made several comments on the original draft of this paper at the July 2012 IPF Conference. Unfortunately, they have gone unanswered in the final version. Therefore, in the following, I restate some of the most important reservations I continue to have on the paper.

When India became independent it inherited the world's largest *surface* irrigation infrastructure. Since then, however, the trends in Indian agriculture have made India the *groundwater* champion of the world, in the sense that surface irrigation systems, tanks, surface reservoirs, and canal systems in which India made huge public investments for 250 years have increasingly became irrelevant in Indian agriculture, and their place has been taken by some 25 million private wells and tube wells mounted with small mechanical pumps that irrigate the bulk of India's crops. There are many factors that have driven this transformation of Indian irrigation. By far the most important has been the compulsion for a small farmer to eke out a living from one acre or one and half acres of farm holding, which makes it imperative for him or her to use that land very intensively, cropping it two or three times a year. Having a private captive source of irrigation is critical to do that, which explains the obsessive preoccupation of Indian farmers with well irrigation and the insatiable demand for wells, pumps and power to irrigate.

I have argued that but for this revolution in groundwater irrigation in India, areas that are today considered to be very dry, like the Telangana region, or the Saurashtra region in Gujarat, which had no public sources of irrigation, would have experienced much greater social instability than is the case today. One major reason why one-third of Indian districts are suffering the Naxalite movement, in which tribal farmers are trying to take on the State, is primarily because there is very little development of irrigation here. So agriculture with diminishing landholdings in these regions has become increasingly unviable.

In contrast, in regions where groundwater development has taken place, although it has not made farmers rich, it has made it possible for them to continue subsisting. That is also part of the reason why many Indian states have pursued policies that appear so irrational. For example, there are four or five Indian states that supply totally free electricity to farmers so that the latter can run their pumps as long as the electricity is available and they can keep drawing the water. The other states do not meter the power that they sell to farmers, so that farmers are basically subject to a pricing regime in which the incremental cost of pumping is virtually zero. That means that as long as the power supply is on, the pumps are on and groundwater keeps being drawn.

These distortions have now led to a very vibrant debate. Water is a field in which economists have been conspicuous by their absence in India but this particular subfield seems to be one in which we have seen their greater participation leading to a lively debate.

The paper that professor Sekhri has presented dwells on three or four very important experiments. For the past 50 years the Indian farmers as well as states have been preoccupied with developing and exploiting groundwater as if it were oil. But unlike oil, groundwater is a renewable resource and it is possible to manage it so that you can use it forever, especially in a subcontinent like ours where there is a very substantial amount of annual rainfall to recharge the depleted aquifers. So we should be able to manage our aquifers like we manage our surface reservoirs. A reservoir gets emptied every year and it gets refilled in the monsoon. We could do pretty much the same with the aquifers if we just understood the management of aquifers properly, but we still have not got into that game. Throughout the past 40 or 50 years, the focus of government policy, as well as the focus of the farmers' efforts, has essentially been on making punctures in the earth, making more boreholes, putting up more pumps and pumping more groundwater. There was no attention paid to managing the resource for sustainable use and the three or four efforts that Professor Sekhri's paper studies are among the first efforts in India to actually bring a sustainability dimension to the groundwater economy of India.

I have a number of questions and suggestions on identification. I also find it hard to reconcile Professor Sekhri's conclusions with a growing literature of local studies, based on different datasets (not studying district level groundwater movements) that seek to understand the impact of groundwater demand management in Punjab and rainwater harvesting in Saurashtra. Personally, I would not expect the rainwater harvesting laws—even when implemented and enforced fully, which they are not currently—to have a significant impact even in urban areas let alone rural areas. So, I do not expect the author's model to produce positive outcomes from the mandates studied.

But additionally, there remains the serious problem of implementation of the laws. Although the Punjab water laws were enacted as early as 2001, the actual enforcement in Punjab started in 2009. In Haryana, the law is not enforced even today. So it is just a paper law that has actually not changed behavior. In Punjab, you might find significant impact on farmer behavior in 2009 and thereafter.

Second, I really wonder whether it is possible to control for electricity pricing and supply. These are powerful drivers of farmer incentives. In Punjab, in the opinion of many, more important than the water law is the progressive whittling down of the power supply to farmers and the increasing need for farmers to use very expensive diesel to supplement electricity. If behavior has changed recently, it is probably this partial shift to expensive diesel that probably accounts for the change. To be convincing, the model needs to control for this important change.

Many of the studies that I have seen of Punjab are based not on farmer level data but block level data that show very significant savings in groundwater as well as in electricity use in Punjab as a result of shifting the transplantation of paddy from middle of May to the middle of June.

When it comes to Gujarat, I think that the impact is much stronger than what the author's study suggests. Perhaps if the author were to use block level data in Gujarat, which is available, it might actually provide a much more textured analysis. Also the groundwater or water harvesting structures in Gujarat are orders of magnitude larger in numbers than the paper suggests. The author has probably captured data on the number of structures constructed by just one department, but there are several other departments that are involved. And many more non-government rain harvesting structures have been constructed by diamond merchants in Surat or NGOs or religious movements like the *Swaminarayan Sampraday* and *Swadhyay Parivar*, which have huge followings of farmers. These structures are probably not included in the data, and this is worth checking.

Finally, Andhra Pradesh is another state where there is a very interesting experiment on demand management that should be looked at. This is an FAO supported project in which a group of NGOs have tried to work with 750 to 800 villages educating farmers, women, and children in taking measurements of groundwater level, assuming that greater knowledge of the understanding of hydrological processes would eventually change their behavior. The results of this experiment should definitely be worth a look.

T. N. Srinivasan
Yale University

Before I go to my Power Points let me begin with some general remarks. First is a point made by Mr Shah that we have been involved in irrigation for 250 years. But out of those 250 years in my reading of the literature, for 190 years, that is, before independence in 1947, the irrigation objective was primarily protective, that is to say to ameliorate the effects of famines and droughts and so the irrigation systems were created mainly to address those issues, and not particularly to raise the productivity of the land. So, in protective irrigation the major dimension was to minimize to the extent feasible of the risk due to drought and famine. Second point is that at that time, there were taxes called cesses on crops like rice, sugarcane, or whatever, which were water-intensive, to prevent farmers from using large share of their land for cultivating water-intensive crops and devote more land to less-water–intensive subsistence crops. Third, from that regime, in the post independence period we shifted to returns from irrigation though productivity increases and the land tax, which used to be the dominant source of government revenue and the crop cesses were allowed to wither away. Finally, as Kirit mentioned in his introduction property rights over water in India was associated with property rights over land thereby generating incentives excessive use of groundwater. I mention all these points because they relate to what Sekhri is doing in the paper. Further and unfortunately there is no mention anywhere of the major element of farming, namely risk (from weather, pests and others) in her analysis. This is unfortunate since farmers are, and have always been, making risk return trade-offs in the use of groundwater as well as other inputs and as the groundwater levels become more and more uncompetitive with respect to pumping what is going to happen is related also to how the farmers decisions are going to be made in this regard.

I distributed an op-ed by a very distinguished expert in water policy whom Mr Shah knows very well. He is Professor Asit Biswas, my colleague LKY School, and in the op-ed he was talking of Delhi's ongoing water crisis and this is a drinking water crisis. I want to focus only on one point he makes. The Delhi Jal Board apparently has no information for making critical decisions on water use. It does not have information as to how many consumers it has, what their per-capita water use is, how much water it loses due to leakages and unauthorized connections and how much staff it has per thousand connection. None of that information that Delhi Water Board has and this is the agency that is managing water in Delhi. This is an example of the nature of water management in many aspects of India's irrigation system as well. So, this has to be kept in mind that with no data there is no way you can analyze a problem empirically even if you had a reasonably good analytical model.

Now let me start with Sekhri's paper. Of course the scarcity of water as a resource and near universal inefficiencies and inequities in its allocation are well known. The latest issue of *Global-is-Asian* at LKY School is devoted to the global dimension of this water scarcity issue. I mentioned Mr Biswas's op-ed but there are also examples within India of 24×7 potable water supply that individual towns have been able to mange. Amaravati is an example of such a town, whose remarkable success Isher Ahluwalia in one of her op-eds in the Indian Express has examined. So, it is possible in India with the right institutions and the right incentives to supply 24×7 drinking water to consumers. This again suggests that the failure to do so is not so India-specific. What is India specific are policies that India and regions of India have (or have not) adopted among those that are in principle feasible to adopt.

The literature on issues of water used for irrigation is huge. The distortions in the allocation of water for irrigation are many and a large share of these distortions have been created by public policy. So clearly public policy reform in this area is urgently needed. The impact of distortions of prices of agricultural output and inputs, such as fuel for pumping groundwater including electricity and fossil fuels, distribution of land, and others on the allocation of water and distribution of income and wealth have been discussed extensively in the literature. Issues of pricing of un-priced water have also been discussed.

Closer to the topic of the present paper is the discussion of the conjunctive use of surface and groundwater in India. So, there is a vast literature and I do not see any reference to any of this literature in the paper. For this reason, I had great difficulty in understanding much of the paper. It is quite likely I have misunderstood it, so my comments should be understood as possibly reflecting my misunderstanding.

Let me start with one example, if estimates of groundwater use of China's geological survey which published two years ago in 2009 are to be believed, China is using 250 billion cubic meters of water, not the 105 that is cited in the paper. In any case, in my view, the estimates for such aggregates as India's use or China's use are subject to possibly large and unknown measurement errors and possibly even biases. The paper estimates that there are 27 million pump users in India. I have no doubt there is a band of error around that 27 million. Sekhri does not mention anything about the locations of monitoring wells which provide the data on water pumped on which her entire analysis depends. I have no idea, and Sekhri provides no information, on where the monitoring wells were located. If you want to estimate the average groundwater level in a particular district and you are using data from monitoring wells to do so, if the wells are not randomly distributed over the district but are concentrated in specific areas, the estimates that you get would be biased. As I said, I do not have any idea where these wells are located. Without some idea of the representativeness of the well locations in each district I found it hard to make sense of the reliability of the Figures 1 to 8 in the paper.

The sharp increase at 8 meter in pumping cost, if I understand it, arises from the simple fact that 8 meters of water is equivalent of 30 inches of mercury in a barometer; so if you make the appropriate adjustments for density of mercury and you get this 8-meter figure and so at that level that the usual pumps do not work and you need to go down to submersible pumps or whatever other technology straightforward and as you have rightly said, the fixed cost and the investment that you have to make—so this non-linearity that arises from this physics of atmospheric pressure there is no mystery. It is well-known although Sekhri does not mention it.

The paper has a very short Section on welfare implications. It is evident that there are many intermediate links between the depth of groundwater and long-term food production and between food production and poverty level. Unless they are modeled, both theoretically and in the form econometric estimating equations, it is hard to assess the very striking results about the impact on poverty and impact on food production. Simply running the poverty against level of groundwater is not an appropriate or convincing way of estimating the effect of groundwater on poverty.

In the section on policy reform, the econometrics is focused on just two policies, one on rainwater harvesting and the other on the delay in the transplanting and the two work, if through the water recharge mechanism of groundwater, either from the rainfall water being pumped back into the ground or alternatively by delaying the flow of water in rivers and thereby increasing the recharge. Now, this is not the entire policy regime that one would want to think about when you want to analyze, not just groundwater issues, but also the general issue of water policy.

Sekhri starts the whole analysis from the estimating equations. On equations 1, 2 and 3, the econometric issues of identification and selection bias take significant amount of space. But they are discussed in a routine and familiar fashion and I have no quarrel with it. The discussion in Table 4 on the other hand suggests that the identification procedure used, namely the delay in the policy imposition, did not work as well as one thought. Sekhri herself has mentioned in her discussion under Table 4.

Sekhri starts with estimating equations and proceeds thereafter to discuss the econometric issues that arise in them. I am afraid this is the conventional procedure in empirical analysis these days, where the analyst starts from some estimating equation from somewhere and spends all his/her time discussing how to identify it or what to do with it but not spend enough time on where the equation came from, that is the relevant economic or physical theory underlying it. For me such a procedure is of dubious analytical value, if it has any value at all.

The average groundwater level in a district is the average of the levels of more than one aquifer in the district. If there is diversity of aquifers, as is very likely, the districts may differ in water pumped out as well as recharged. It is simply being assumed that the average groundwater in a district is a good proxy for the stock of water remaining in the aquifers in that district. It need not be, I will present simple model thinking about it where these issues are brought out.

The results presented, and I don't have the tables with me, are rightly of the interaction variable, a product of the dummy for the timing of introduction of policy and a dummy on whether the district is a treated region or not. While it is certainly the coefficient of interest, the other coefficients such as those of time-varying district-specific controls are of interest as well. These and the controls used are not fully described and the phrase "salutary effects of rainwater harvesting," is not defined anywhere though it is said that there were no significant salutary effects from rainwater harvesting.

Sekhri in her presentation went through the tables and explained the coefficients. I found some of these coefficients puzzling. One of those is relating to Table 4. The orders of magnitude were quite large in regressions in columns (v) and (vi) of Table 4 and may be the units of measurement used for the same variable were different in different regressions. In regressions (i) to (iv) of Table 4, the treatment has no significant effect, but in regressions (v) and (vi) not only the magnitude of the treatment effect is large and almost the same in the two, but also both effects are statistically significant at 1 percent level. Regression (v) includes all controls while (iv) omits only the region fixed effects. The first four regressions omit differing set of controls. The argument that differences in the inclusion or omission of particular controls across regressions explains the particular difference in the magnitude and the statistical significance of the treatment effect is not convincing at all, besides raising possible endogeneity issues.

In my last section, firstly, I am going to focus on a single aquifer. For simplicity think of an aquifer as a rectangular tank of water of average height "H(t)" and an unknown base area "A(t)" in year "t." By definition the area is not changing so the "A(t)" is a constant A. Then the stock of water S (t) is AxH (t) since the aquifer it is a rectangle, so height x area is the volume. Its change between end of period t-1 and t is A [H (t).- H(t-1)]. This is the "delta" change in S(t). Delta S(t) is by definition is the net effect of the volume of water P(t) pumped out during the period and the volume of water that was added, that is the recharge in period, R(t) of aquifers plus any random errors for measurement. So, delta S(t) is R(t)-P(t)+ epsilon(t) or H (t)-H(t-1) This change in groundwater level is what I have written in (3). The constant A does not matter, it is simply a scaling coefficient and so this is the story.

The variable P(t), that is the pumped out water, would include for example on the demand side either area sown for various crops or alternatively expected harvest presence for crops in this region and irrigated by water from the aquifer, availability of non-groundwater sources of irrigation, number of pumpers, pumping cost proxy such as fossil fuel, electricity prices, and groundwater use, and service cost of other sources of irrigation, etc, all of these will be included in the function P(t) as other variables besides t.. Similarly I can list s whole list of variables for R(t) besides t. Now, the point is that it is easy to list variables as I have done but given the limited extent available of time series data and groundwater levels, not too many variables can be quoted. This is where your modeling judgment comes in. What you are going to include, what you are going to keep out and then do later the robustness checks about your modeling assumptions. So my only purpose in listing it out all this is to say that you start from a theory and a model and not from just some equation pulled out from somewhere and think about econometrics of that equation. Thank you.

General Discussion

Indira Rajaraman opened the discussion by noting that groundwater use was not just an agricultural phenomenon. There is a huge mineral water industry, which also draws groundwater.

Abhijit Banerjee said that he was baffled by the author's conclusion that there was no impact. In his reading, the impact was actually negative. Banerjee also noted that he was puzzled by the author's comment that people do not want water markets because water is not to be marketed. Irrigation water is sold all the time, people just buy water from pumps. There is no issue of water markets not existing. They are everywhere. But it is not clear why the market would help. The market makes the problem worse. This is an un-priced resource, why wouldn't anyone sell it more if more people want it and the equilibrium occurs where everyone tries to overdraw because everyone thinks that the water will exhaust by the next year. Banerjee said he saw no reason why market would help here.

Devesh Kapoor said that he thought that by far the most relevant to the problem at hand is the procurement price of rice. This is the wrong crop being grown in the wrong place, period. And everything else is dwarfed by the procurement policy.

Another speaker noted that in India 70 percent of water was used for irrigation and the rest for drinking and industrial use. The paper had not discussed industry use, how it could be managed.

Sheetal Sekhri responded that policy other than those directly targeting water use in agriculture were relevant and would definitely include discouraging paddy growing where it should not be grown. Agricultural scientists have been making this point for more than two decades. But given the power of farmer lobbies, this is not going to happen any time soon.

Regarding the point by Banerjee about a negative effect in Table 3, Sekhri said she was not sure where he was looking since the results did show that the situation was getting worse. On the point about why households would want to sell more water, thus, exacerbating the problem was a very intriguing one. Regarding the point by Indira Rajaraman, Sekhri said that about 91 percent of the groundwater that India extracted was used in irrigation. So, agriculture was the main culprit. It was not really industry even though we might routinely bash the industry. Regarding interconnectedness of aquifers, Sekhri said that the point is well taken but it is undermined by the fact that the lateral velocity of groundwater is very low. The first order concern is really depletion over time in a specific place rather than spatial externalities. For surface water those externalities are much more prominent because surface water flows very quickly. So, recharging something in Saurashtra and Gujarat is not likely to have a perceptible effect on Kutch anytime soon.

Turning to the comments by Tushaar Shah, Sekhri said they were very instructive and she was thankful to him for them. The first point that Shah raised was that rainwater harvesting mandates had no effect and that he did not expect them to have any effects because they were in urban areas. But this did warrant a policy analysis because the policies have been enacted and the States are spending significant amount of state money on monitoring and evaluating these policies. They do have staff that gets paid to evaluate the policies.

The second Shah had raised was about Punjab delaying the implementation of the law relating to paddy till 2009 and it then that having salutary effects. Sekhri noted that she had used 2009 as the implementation date and carried out the same analysis and found the same type of effects. Also, Shah had mentioned that there could not have been a change in paddy transplanting prior to 2009. But the statistics say that paddy transplanting in May 2008 declined from 14 percent to 0.2 percent. So, there does seem to be some action before 2009. Shah also noted that electricity prices should be in the model. Sekhri said she thought this was very important for the analysis but the analysis of how the marginal cost of extracting groundwater would affect groundwater extraction rates was a paper in its own right. Shah also mentioned some existing papers finding positive effects of Punjab policy. Sekhri said she had looked at that literature but was not convinced by the methodologies used there. Shah also mentioned that she (Sekhri) had not investigated the effects of check dams or other types of rainwater harvesting initiatives that were being promoted by NGOs and several other types of donors. She felt that the analysis of these dams was fraught with selection issues. Since she could not estimate anything cleanly there, she refrained from it.

Moving on to the comments by T. N. Srinivasan, Sekhri said that he had made several points about the inclusion of certain variables and exclusion of others in the regression analysis. She said that to the extent that the excluded variables were unrelated to the policy implementation in any particular way, their omission would not impact the analysis. Srinivasan mentioned something about statistical significance jumping from column 3 to 4, 5 to 6 in Table 6. But there were only four columns in Table 6. As we move across columns, neither the point estimate nor the statistical significance in Tables 4 and 6 change very much. Srinivasan had mentioned that the paper was confined to only two policies. This was true since the paper did not aim to survey all the policies. There are not too many carefully done empirical studies evaluating any of the policies relating to groundwater so that the paper represented some progress over the existing literature. The welfare implications section is brief but I think it draws out at least the main implications of depletion.

At the invitation of the chair to say a few words on water markets, Tushaar Shah stated that markets were not something to be created. They have been in operation in every nook and corner of South Asia for nearly 30 or 40 years. If anything, we are now shrinking because of falling groundwater levels and greater difficulty in accessing groundwater and because the number of tube wells and pumps has grown so much that every third or fourth farmer in the region has his own bore well. Water markets are very vibrant in the early stages of groundwater development where in a village you would have 15 or 20 tube wells and pumps and 100 to 200 farmers who wanted to use the groundwater and are willing to pay for irrigation service but now with increasing number of farmers acquiring their own tube wells, the scope for large scale water selling is actually declining.

The Chair, Kirit Parikh, concluded with two short observations. One, there is a Working Group report or an Expert Group report by the Planning Commission on Groundwater Management that he chaired and Tushaar was a member of. The author might find it useful. Two, T. N. Srinivasan had mentioned the Delhi Jal Board. In that context, it might be of some interest to know that in 2006 there was a proposal to have a French firm come and do some auditing and help Delhi Jal Board to provide 24×7 water to its customers. The point is that Delhi's total per-capita water availability is more than what is available in Paris for example but the water is available for only two hours or less than that to customers largely because the system is not properly managed. That was torpedoed by lots of activists who are concerned about this foreigners' firm coming and meddling into our affairs.

SHRUTI SHARMA
NIRVIKAR SINGH
University of California, Santa Cruz

Information Technology and Productivity in Indian Manufacturing*

ABSTRACT   India's manufacturing sector is receiving renewed attention as an underperformer in contributing to the nation's Gross Domestic Product (GDP) and employment growth, with a new National Manufacturing Policy (NMP) stating ambitious goals for increasing the share of manufacturing in GDP. In this context, the role of information technology (IT) as a contributor to manufacturing productivity also needs to be carefully examined. This paper uses five years of panel data for Indian manufacturing plants to examine the relationship of investment in IT to productivity, as measured by gross value added. We find some evidence that plants with higher levels of IT capital stock have higher gross value added, controlling for other inputs. However, this effect is attenuated when plant-level fixed effects are included. One possible interpretation of this result is that unobserved managerial quality is an important factor in the impact of IT capital on productivity. We also explore the impacts of skill composition, the use of imported intermediate inputs, ownership and organizational form on the productivity of IT capital. Furthermore, we examine the demand for IT investment, controlling for possible selectivity biases associated with plants that have positive IT investment. We find some evidence that access to financial capital, electric power from the grid, and skilled workers all matter for the decision to invest in IT capital, but these variables are less important for the level of investment in IT, conditional on it being positive.

Keywords: *Information Technology, Manufacturing, Productivity, Innovation*

JEL Classification: *D22, L60, O14, O33*

* *shruti009@gmail.com; nirvikar@ucsc.edu*   This is a significantly revised version of the paper presented at the India Policy Forum, 2012. We are grateful to Jennifer Poole, Carlos Dobkin, and Justin Marion for helpful discussions on this research, to Shubhashis Gangopadhyay and B. N. Goldar for very helpful comments as discussants at the IPF, and Barry Bosworth for a large number of very specific and helpful comments and suggestions. Alireza Kharazi provided excellent research assistance. We also received many helpful comments from the audience at IPF. Remaining errors and omissions are our responsibility.

189

1. Introduction

India's manufacturing sector has played an unusual role in the national growth experience, compared to many other developing countries. In 1950–51, the first year for which the current data series is available, manufacturing was about 9 percent of GDP. By 1979–80, this ratio came very close to 15 percent, but thereafter has barely increased. The highest share of manufacturing for any year was 16.6 percent in 1996–97, and subsequently, the figure has hovered on either side of 16 percent, even in the years when India grew at well over 9 percent per annum.[1] In this context, the new National Manufacturing Policy's (NMP 2012) avowed goal of increasing manufacturing's share to 25 percent by 2022 is ambitious indeed.

The NMP benchmarks India's failure to grow manufacturing's share significantly against the experience of other Asian countries. In South Korea, for example, the share of manufacturing grew from 13.6 percent in 1960 (not much greater than that of India at the time) to 29.6 percent by 1990 (Panagariya 2008, Table 6.2). The pattern in China, however, has been less clear-cut, with manufacturing's share of GDP being estimated at 29 percent in 1965, rising to as high as 40 percent, and then coming down toward 30 percent as the national accounts were recalibrated.[2]

One of the motivations for focusing on manufacturing growth is, of course, its potential to generate employment for the unskilled or semi-skilled. Again, South Korea provides a striking example, having increased the manufacturing sector's share of employment from 1.5 percent in 1960 to 26.9 percent in 1990 (Panagariya 2008, Table 6.2). Again, the numbers for China are less striking: the share of industry (a broader classification than manufacturing) in total employment increased from 18 percent in 1980 to 27 percent in 2008. By contrast, the percentage shares for India have gone from 16 in 1994 to 22 in 2010 (World Bank data). Figures from the Economic Survey of India (2012, Table 9.11) are 11 percent for the share of manufacturing in total employment for India in 1999–2000, 12.2 percent in 2004–05, and 11.4 percent in 2009–10, well below the level for Korea.

India's NMP document quantifies the employment creation challenge, and makes it a central policy issue for the manufacturing sector:

---

1. These percentages are calculated by the authors from National Accounts data from Reserve Bank of India (RBI) (2012).
2. The Chinese figures are from the World Bank's World Development Indicators (http://databank.worldbank.org/ddp/home.do).

Over the next decade, India has to create gainful employment opportunities for a large section of its population, with varying degrees of skills and qualifications. This will entail creation of 220 million jobs by 2025 in order to reap the demographic dividend. The manufacturing sector would have to be the bulwark of this employment creation initiative. Every job created in manufacturing has a multiplier effect of creating two to three additional jobs in related activities. (NMP 2012)

Panagariya (2008), writing several years earlier, reaches a similar conclusion to the NMP:

In contrast to other countries that have successfully transitioned from the primarily rural and agricultural structure to the modern one, rapid growth in India has not been accompanied by a commensurate increase in well-paid formal sector jobs.[3] In large part, this has been due to a stagnant share of industry and manufacturing, especially unskilled-labor-intensive manufacturing, in the GDP. This pattern of growth has meant that the movement of the workforce out of agriculture and into the organized sector has been slow. Modernization of the economy requires the expansion of employment opportunities in the organized sector. (Panagariya 2008, p. 309)

Of course, neither the NMP nor Panagariya is guilty of simple manufacturing fetishism. Clearly, the services sector in India has been successful in generating growth in value added as well as in employment. This includes software and information technology (IT) enabled services, as well as a wide range of other services. The implicit argument, however, is that the services sector alone cannot provide the sustained growth in output or employment that will be needed.[4] There are also issues with respect to the nature of the manufacturing sector itself. For example, Kochhar et al. (2006) suggest that India's manufacturing sector was more diversified, more skill-intensive, and less (unskilled) labor-intensive than average, compared to countries at similar levels of development. This skill bias was accentuated in the 1980s and 1990s, according to their empirical analysis.[5]

3. As elucidated by Panagariya, India's labor laws and infrastructure constraints have led to a classification of firms into the formal, or organized, sector (employing 10 workers and using electric power, or 20 workers even if not using power). Most of the gains in employment in India have come in the informal sector, including rural industry and services.

4. A detailed discussion of services is beyond the scope of the current paper. Singh (2008), for example, provides an analysis of India's service sector in relation to manufacturing and overall growth.

5. Anecdotal evidence suggests that this trend has continued. "Even as high-end engineering boomed, manufacturing jobs dropped slightly between 2004 and 2010, to 50m. Basic industries that soak up labour, such as textiles and leathers, are in relative decline." *The Economist*, August 11, 2012, accessed October 10, 2012, at http://www.economist.com/node/21560263.

In reviewing different countries' development experiences and current policy options, the precise balance between existing and future comparative advantage with respect to labor-intensity and skill-intensity is a matter of debate (e.g., Rodrik 2007; Lin 2011). While the current analysis cannot address these broader issues, the Indian experience has led Arvind Panagariya (2008) to a specific recommendation with respect to development strategy. He argues as follows:

> India must walk on two legs as it transitions to a modern economy: traditional industry, especially unskilled-labor-intensive manufacturing, and modern services such as software and telecommunications. Each leg needs to be strengthened through a set of policy initiatives. (Panagariya 2008, p. 287)

Panagariya's own policy recommendations include somewhat separate discussions for each of his two "legs" of the Indian economy. For labor-intensive industry, he emphasizes labor law reform, bankruptcy reform and privatization, while software and telecommunications require attention to education and urban infrastructure. However, an important potential linkage exists between the two parts of the economy, namely, the use of IT in domestic manufacturing, as a potential avenue to spur productivity and employment growth in that sector. This paper contributes to exploring this linkage.

Accordingly, the rest of the paper is organized as follows. In Section 2, we provide some background on India's manufacturing sector, especially in the context of the use and impact of IT in that sector, but also discussing its broader performance. We review some of the related literature on the impacts of IT investment, including aspects of the macroeconomic evidence, but focusing mainly on studies of firm level data. Section 3 provides an overview of the data used in the paper, which is a panel of five years' plant-level data from India's Annual Survey of Industries (ASI), spanning 2003–07. We discuss some of the features of the data, and provide summary statistics, as well as outlining our empirical methodology.

Section 4 provides the results of our regression analysis of the data. We focus on two behavioral relationships. One such relationship is the factors determining the demand for investment in IT. Another is the factors influencing productivity at the plant-level, as measured by gross value added (GVA). In the latter case, we are particularly interested in the impact of IT capital on GVA. A central finding of our analysis is that, once plant-level fixed effects are accounted for, the estimated impact of IT on GVA is considerably reduced, though it remains statistically and economically significant.[6] We suggest that this finding is consistent with heterogeneity of (unobserved) managerial quality playing a role in the productivity of IT. We find a somewhat similar pattern in the investment demand equation: once plant-level fixed effects are allowed for, the role of existing IT capital stock in determining IT investment demand is negligible, though it remains significant in other estimations. We also find that the decision whether to invest in IT at all is influenced by access to financial capital, outside electricity, and skilled workers.

Our analysis also offers several other innovations. For example, we explore the impact of the skill composition of the labor force on the productivity of IT capital. We also examine the role of imported intermediate inputs in affecting the use and the impacts of IT capital. Another dimension we explore, which has a possible bearing on the role of managerial quality, is the impact of differences in ownership type and organizational form. Thus, the analysis provides a deeper and broader understanding of the role that IT investment has played in the performance of Indian manufacturing plants, by examining how the impact of IT capital on gross value added is affected by these other factors. Section 5 provides a summary conclusion, including some discussion of possible policy implications of our work, especially in the context of the National Manufacturing Policy.

2. Background and Related Literature

2.1. IT and the Economy

We begin this section with an overview of IT in the broader context of economic growth, including macro and cross-country studies as well as micro-level studies from several industrialized economies. In India's case, its software industry has been an important part of the country's growth story, including its contribution to improving the balance of payments and its positive spillovers into information technology-enabled services (ITES), as well as the more subtle impact on attitudes in India (Kapur 2002)—demonstrating that a modern India-based economic activity could be carried out at world class levels. At the same time, the export-oriented nature of the

---

6. The use of panel data at the plant-level distinguishes our analysis from some earlier studies of IT in Indian manufacturing. Our panel data also potentially allows us to explore the possibility of lagged impacts of IT investment, in keeping with what some studies for other countries have found, but in fact these lagged effects are not important. This finding may reflect our use of IT capital, which captures the cumulated effect of past IT investments.

industry's success has led to persistent concerns about whether India's IT industry would remain an enclave, heightening the dualism characteristic of developing economies. This last fear seems to be partly borne out in some of the criticisms brought up in reports based on India's National Manufacturing Surveys, as discussed later in this section, but even more strongly in the idea of a "digital divide."

The concept of a digital divide refers to inequality of access to new digital technologies, and this inequality can be examined across or within countries. In the case of developing countries, both these dimensions of inequality were viewed as potentially troublesome. Addressing concerns about a digital divide within India, private and public efforts to make information technology (IT) available to a broad cross section of the nation's population began in the early days of India's software boom. Several organizations attempted to build networks of rural Internet kiosks, sometimes bundled with telephone service (Singh 2007). These attempts have met with very limited success, far short of the visions that were articulated of tens of thousands of such kiosks. What has spread, of course, is mobile telephony, driven by technological change, access to spectrum, and vigorous competition among several large corporations. Meanwhile, the government has articulated and begun to implement its own vision of rural Internet access, albeit with the usual implementation difficulties associated with public sector delivery of services in India.

Empirical aggregate level studies of the impact of IT on productivity or growth include single country time-series analyses (regression-based as well as through growth accounting) and cross-country regressions. Early evidence for the positive effects of IT on output or growth was hard to come by. In 1987, economist Robert Solow quipped: "You can see the computer age everywhere but in the productivity statistics." A decade later, Robert Gordon, carrying out a sequence of empirical analyses for the US (the global leader in IT adoption), still found little or no empirical evidence of aggregate productivity growth that could be attributed to the use of IT. Later studies for the US, however, found that IT investment was having a discernible positive effect on productivity growth (e.g., Schreyer 2000; Jorgenson 2005).

In the first decade of the new millennium, several cross-country analyses also began to appear. These typically included some measure of progress in ICTs more broadly, including communication technologies along with IT, and findings of positive impacts associated with cross-sectional variation were typical. Several studies extended to considering developing countries, and not just industrialized nations where IT adoption might be more advanced. Lee and Khatri (2003), Pitt and Qiang (2003) and Qiang, Pitt and Ayers (2004) are examples of such studies, while Indijikain and Siegel (2004) have surveyed many additional empirical analyses. Studies such as Kenny (2002, 2003) pointed out the importance of a skilled workforce in increasing the returns to investment in IT.

Cross-country and aggregate single-country studies may not give much insight into the microeconomic factors that govern IT use and impacts, but several firm-level studies have also been carried out, almost exclusively for industrialized country firms. Baldwin and Sabourin (2002) showed that Canadian manufacturing firms that used either one or more ICT technologies had a higher level of labor productivity than the firms that did not. Gretton et al. (2003) examined Australian firms, and found positive links between ICT use and productivity growth in all the industrial sectors that were analyzed. Maliranta and Rouvinen (2004) found strong evidence for productivity-enhancing effects of ICT in Finnish firms. Clayton et al. (2004) examined the economic impacts in the UK of electronic commerce specifically, and found a positive effect on firms' productivity associated with the use of computer networks for trading. Similar positive results for the impact of IT have been found for firms in the service sector than in manufacturing, including Hempell (2004) for Germany and the Netherlands, Doms, Jarmin, and Klimek (2004) for the US, and Arvanitis (2004) for Switzerland. For the US, Brynjolfsson and Hitt (2003) also find positive impacts of IT investments, with the gains increasing substantially over time.

Firm-level studies for the US have also examined the role of workplace organization in determining the effects of investments in IT. For example, Black and Lynch (2004) find that changes in workplace organization explain a large part of the changes in productivity in the US over the period 1993–96, and these in turn influence the impacts of IT use. In particular, they find a significant and positive relationship between the proportion of non-managers using computers and overall productivity. Similarly, Bresnahan, Brynjolffson, and Hitt (2002) examine how a combination of three related innovations: information technology adoption, complementary workplace reorganization, and new products and services resulted in a significant skill-biased technical change which had an important impact on the demand for labor in the US. They find complementarities among all three of these innovations in factor demand and productivity, leading to increases in demand for other inputs and in productivity.

More recently, Bloom, Sadun, and van Reenen (2012) also use a micro panel data set to connect results at the micro and macro level. They use the variation in management practices between US multinationals operating in Europe and other European firms to elucidate the interaction between management and the use of IT. They find that US multinationals obtained higher productivity from IT than non-US multinationals, particularly in the sectors that were responsible for the post-1995 US productivity acceleration. Incorporating data from an extensive management practices survey, they find that the US IT-related productivity advantage is primarily due to its tougher "people management" practices. These results are therefore quite consistent with earlier work on organizational change, stressing flexibility, however, rather than specific types of worker composition.

2.2. Manufacturing and IT in India

Chandra and Sastry (2002) summarize the findings of the 2001 National Manufacturing Survey. The focus is on the organized manufacturing sector, representing less than 1 percent of the country's firms at the time, but employing 19 percent of its industrial workers and contributing almost 75 percent of gross value added. They are quite critical of Indian manufacturing management, arguing that

> [M]anufacturing strategy of most firms is still not addressing certain fundamental issues of competition: need to change product mix rapidly, need to introduce new products based on indigenous R&D, need to use process innovation and quality improvement process to reduce cost of operations and consequently price of product. One wonders if the industry has a good control of the causal factors that define competitiveness in a low margin environment. (Chandra and Sastry 2002, p. 10)

The study notes the lack of spending on research and development (R&D), and the relatively small numbers of employees with advanced degrees, in the sample firms. The authors also note that Indian manufacturing firms give low priority to investments related to information technology, such as computer-aided manufacturing (CAM), computer-aided design (CAD), computer integrated manufacturing (CIM), and computer-aided engineering (CAE). It is also suggested that domestic IT firms do not have the right products for Indian manufacturing firms in these applications.

Indian manufacturing is also found to have supply chain weaknesses, closely related to the inability to share information throughout the supply chain. The survey finds that only 13 percent of firms use a computer-based decision system for supply chain management, though the percentages are higher for enterprise resource planning (43) and shop floor scheduling (37). Only 23 percent of firms in this sample use the web for placing orders with suppliers, and 11 percent sell online to customers. The overall picture is one of very limited use of IT across the board, but especially in network applications.

The 2007 National Manufacturing Survey, the next one following on the 2002 survey, is analyzed in Chandra (2009). The date of the survey corresponds to the end of our own sample period. Supply chain management remains a key weakness in the later survey, and investments in R&D remain low, despite perceptible benefits to innovation. Investment and usage of IT on the shop floor remain low, at about 45 percent for this later sample, which is not much higher than the 2002 figure. The conclusion of the author echoes the theme of his 2002 analysis.

> Once basic IT investment is done, only then will Indian firms be able to implement and take advantage of automation on shop floors. IT firms in India have failed to develop a viable and low cost IT solution for Indian Manufacturing. Firms other than the large ones are struggling on this count. (Chandra 2009, p. iv)

Several other features of Indian manufacturing (at least the sample for the NMS) emerge from the Chandra report. Indian firms surveyed indicate a focus on quality, and trying to achieve that through process improvement. Large scale and low cost are not major goals of the surveyed managers. These characteristics are consistent with formal empirical work and anecdotal evidence. The 2009 report finds some significant increases in IT use in particular areas of manufacturing, but overall IT adoption remains limited among the sample firms. The report also argues that management weaknesses contribute to lack of innovation, as well as inefficiencies in plant location and supply chains.

Chandra (2009) also summarizes regional differences in IT use among the NMS sample firms. IT use is highest in the South, and lowest in the East, but also in Uttar Pradesh (in the North). Interestingly, IT use tends to be concentrated among managers, and to some extent supervisors, with less IT use by operators on the shop floor. To some extent, the pattern of IT use (or non-use) is symptomatic of under-investment in both physical and human capital, reflecting high financial costs as well as an unfriendly policy environment. At the same time, Indian manufacturing firms are able to make strong profits in this period, despite their inefficiencies.

The most recent detailed policy-oriented document, aside from the NMP itself, is a joint study by the National Manufacturing Competitiveness Council (NMCC) and the National Association of Software and Services Companies (NASSCOM). The study and report (NMCC–NASSCOM 2010) were conducted by a consulting firm, but the academic advisors include people like Pankaj Chandra, suggesting some intellectual continuity. The NMCC–NASSCOM report is specifically focused on promoting IT adoption in Indian manufacturing.[7]

The NMCC–NASSCOM report makes several familiar points, but with newer survey data to back them up. It begins by noting the relatively low penetration of IT in Indian manufacturing, especially among smaller firms, as well as its relatively low productivity in terms of value added per capita. As in the earlier reports discussed above, the link between IT use and productivity is not quantitatively established, but the case is made conceptually, by describing the numerous potential benefits of IT across a range of applications, and several brief case studies are presented in the report.

The fine-grained discussion of the range of IT applications distinguishes the NMCC–NASSCOM report. For example, the report brings out the fact that finance and accounting applications run far ahead of core manufacturing process uses of IT. It also systematically considers eight different manufacturing sectors, providing insights into variation across them in terms of IT use. For example, sectors such as automobiles and automobile components are ahead of sectors such as textiles in IT adoption. Some of this variation is obviously a reflection of differences in the sophistication of products and complexity of production processes, but factors such as size, foreign investment and export orientation also play a role.

The report discusses the barriers to IT adoption in the context of the survey data. In many cases, even when IT is adopted, it is restricted to basic or noncore operations, limiting its impact. However, the hurdles to any adoption at all are many: lack of infrastructure such as reliable power, high costs, unsuitability of off-the-shelf IT solutions, lack of awareness among businesses of IT options, lack of enabling business and policy environments, and especially lack of internal capabilities to make and implement informed decisions. In the context of the last point, the report's conclusion is striking.

> ICT adoption levels in manufacturing firms were primarily influenced by their management team. More than three-fourth of the companies especially in the micro and small firms category are strongly influenced by the owner/management team for their ICT investments. (NMCC–NASSCOM 2010, p. 11)

---

7. For brevity and consistency, we use the acronym IT: the NMCC–NASSCOM report uses the term ICT, for "information and communication technology." We treat the two terms as equivalent, since modern digital communications (including voice and video) are essentially based on IT.

Overcoming this particular internal barrier to IT adoption will not be easy, according to the report's findings. External influences such as IT consultants and vendors, government agencies, and even peer group companies were found to be limited in impact. This observation suggests that the strictures placed by Chandra (2009) on the domestic IT industry's failure to promote IT adoption may be too harsh. The NMCC–NASSCOM report does note the importance of clients in influencing IT adoption, suggesting that supply chain network effects may be an important avenue for overcoming barriers. Recall that both Chandra and Sastry (2002) and Chandra (2009) emphasized weaknesses in supply chain management among Indian manufacturing firms.

As the NMCC–NASSCOM report emphasizes, increasing IT adoption in Indian manufacturing will require a systemic approach, with broad participation from many parts of the business ecosystem. The report emphasizes the potential role that can be played by national and local industry associations in developing best-practice business process reengineering guidelines to cope with the organizational changes that are often needed to benefit from IT investments. Human capital development to overcome lack of appropriate skills can be addressed through improving the quality of government provided training programs, and tax incentives for firms to spend on this training. Anomalies in the tax code, broader deficiencies in the legal framework, poor telecoms infrastructure and lack of access to finance all receive attention as barriers to IT adoption that can be overcome through policy attention. The report also discusses possibilities for raising requirements for electronic communications in certain contexts, and the possibility of creating a more efficient national market for IT products and services, through information dissemination, creation of electronic market platforms, and award programs. Many of the issues raised reflect the status of IT as a novelty for Indian manufacturing firms, especially the smallest ones.

2.3. Empirical Analyses of IT in Indian Manufacturing

In between the two poles of India's software exporters and its village computer kiosks, the role of IT in the vast middle of India's economy has remained relatively unexplored in formal empirical analyses. A major exception was the work of Gangopadhyay, Singh and Singh (GSS 2008), using the Annual Survey of Industries (ASI) data, which examined the determinants and impacts of IT use among India's manufacturing units. The GSS study found that IT use was possibly constrained by factors such as the availability of electricity and of short term finance. On the other hand, there was evidence that plants that used IT were more profitable and more productive than those that did not. One of the shortcomings of the GSS analysis was that the non-availability of panel data prevented a clear identification of the chain of causality. For example, IT-using plants could be doing better because of better management, which could be the cause of IT investment as well as of superior performance. One goal of the current paper is to deal with this issue by using panel data. A panel analysis, for example, potentially controls for managerial fixed effects.

GSS (2008) also estimate a full set of demand equations for unskilled and skilled labor (proxied by wage and salaried workers, respectively, as is standard in working with ASI data), and find that IT use increases the demand for both types of workers. We are able to build on the GSS study, but using panel data allows us to control better for unobservable factors. Furthermore, we focus on IT investment demand and the productivity impacts of IT capital, but we are able to explore lagged effects, the effects of changes in labor force composition, and the role of imported intermediate inputs.

One of the issues unresolved in GSS was the role of managerial quality. In this context, two other analyses of management practices are relevant. Bloom and van Reenen (2010) found that Indian firms with strong management practices are comparable to the best US firms on this dimension. However, there is a thick tail of badly run (by their measure of management practices) Indian firms, which often neglect basic tasks such as collecting and analyzing data, setting clear performance targets, and linking pay to performance. Bloom et al. (2012) perform a controlled experiment with a sample of Indian textile firms, and indeed find that the treatment firms improved productivity by 17 percent over the control group. This provides very direct evidence that "management matters" for at least a subset of Indian firms. While we cannot provide such a direct test, our results are certainly suggestive of a similar phenomenon in a much larger sample of Indian manufacturing plants.

Joseph and Abraham (2007) also use ASI data. Their analysis covers the four year period 1998–2002. They estimate regressions for labor productivity and growth in labor productivity, as well as a production function. The estimations are conducted using data at the 3-digit industry level, giving 52 annual observations for each regression. The labor productivity regressions (OLS, random effects and fixed effects) all indicate that IT investment intensity positively affects labor productivity, as do capital intensity, skill intensity and plant size. Regressions for the growth in labor productivity give similar results for the impact of IT investment (still specified in level terms).[8] The production function estimated by Joseph and Abraham appears to use data averaged over the four years of their sample. Output is measured as gross value added, and in addition to labor and capital, the specification includes the ratios of cumulated IT and non-IT investments to total capital as additional variables. Only the IT-capital ratio is found to be significant and positive. Furthermore, growth accounting calculations of Total Factor Productivity (TFP) also suggest a positive relationship (albeit nonlinear) between IT investment and TFP growth.

The most recent study of the impacts of IT on productivity of Indian firms is that of Kite (2012). Kite uses the PROWESS database from the Centre for Monitoring the Indian Economy (CMIE). This data covers large and medium sized firms listed on India's stock exchanges, as well as public sector enterprises. Services firms (including financial services) are included, as well as manufacturing firms. The analysis covers four years, 2005–08, with most firms in the sample reporting data for more than one of the years.

Kite focuses on expenditure on IT outsourcing, proxied by a reported measure of "expenditure on software and other professional services," but also has measures of in-house software and hardware use. She estimates production functions using gross output rather than value added, so intermediate inputs are included as an explanatory variable. Her basic result is that all the three IT variables have positive and significant impacts on output. She also argues that excluding expenditure on IT outsourcing overstates the output elasticity of in-house IT expenditures. The results are shown to be robust to a variety of changes in the sample, specification and estimation method.

Kite goes on to estimate a stochastic frontier production function model to explore how IT outsourcing affects technical efficiency and productivity, as well as going on to derive an estimated aggregate impact of IT outsourcing on India's total growth. This latter figure is calculated to be 1.3 percentage points of growth per year, or 14 percent of the total GDP growth over the sample period. Kite notes that this figure is quite similar to estimates for the US and other developed countries in the 1990s. At various points in the paper, we contrast our data and results with those of Kite, but here we highlight once again an important issue that has only been formally dealt with by GSS (2008), despite its importance in policy-oriented discussions

---

8. Joseph and Abraham also mention two studies based on limited surveys of Indian manufacturing firms, which also find positive impacts of IT investment: Lal (2001) and Basant et al. (2007). Kite (2012) references a firm-level study by Commander et al. (2011), which is related to the earlier study of Basant et al. (2007).

of IT use in Indian manufacturing, namely, the reasons why IT use is not greater, despite its potential contribution to productivity.

3. Data and Methodology

3.1. Data Overview

We use data from India's Annual Survey of Industries (ASI). This data covers manufacturing plants (also commonly referred to as units or factories) across a range of industries, and with national coverage.[9] Until recently, plant identifiers were not available for the data, making it impossible to construct a true panel. Given this restriction, GSS (2008) worked with a cross section of data, or in some cases with pooled data, but without being able to allow for plant fixed effects. More recently, Sharma (2012) constructed a synthetic panel, creating cohorts of firms for each year. While the cohort approach has some significant advantages, for the purposes of the current analysis, it is useful to work with the plant-level data, and we are able to benefit from the recent availability of plant identifiers to construct such a panel.

The ASI data is affected by missing values, and possible reporting errors, so it can be a challenge to use. In this case, we have benefited from the earlier work of Sharma (2012) in cleaning the data. Nevertheless, the number of usable observations is considerably smaller than the total sample size of 15,000 to 50,000 units that are surveyed annually (the number having increased over recent years, after having decreased in the 1990s). The main factor restricting our sample, however, is the presence of plants in every year of the panel. To avoid losing too many observations in the cross section, we restrict the panel to cover the last five years of our data set, going from 2003 to 2007. This gives us about 8,000 plants in our sample. The shorter time period has some advantages, in the sense that these years cover a relatively uniform growth period of the Indian economy, and it is later than the GSS data, allowing us to distinguish our results more clearly. Missing observations and zero values further reduce the estimated sample size. In our regressions, the number of plants is about 2,500 per year. When the dependent variable has missing observations, we also address the possible biases that can arise from selection effects.

The original data are in current values, and while year fixed effects go some way to capturing changes in price levels, they do not deal with

9. GSS (2008) provide a detailed discussion of the ASI data, including the sampling frame, stratification, and other aspects of the sampling methodology.

differences in rates of inflation for different categories of goods. In order to ensure that differential changes in prices are not affecting the relationship between our variables, we deflate each variable according to industry-wise wholesale price indices for each year, using data from the Economic Survey of India, 2012. We do not have a separate deflator for IT capital but use the index for machinery and machine tools.[10] It is also worth remarking at this stage on the choice of ASI data versus the PROWESS data set, which is more commonly used.[11] The latter data set is typically in better shape, having been constructed and validated by CMIE, which is a private firm, and therefore it is more popular with researchers. PROWESS panel data has also been available for some time. The data set is at the firm level, however, and many of the variables in the ASI data are not in PROWESS. In particular, for our purposes, it is useful that the ASI data includes figures for different types of labor, which are not available in the PROWESS data. The latter is also restricted to listed firms and public enterprises, so it gives a much narrower cross-section of Indian manufacturing firms than the ASI data. On the other hand, PROWESS includes service sector firms, which are not in the ASI data. In sum, each data set has its merits, but the ASI data is better suited for our purposes, and relatively under-analyzed.

Given the complexities of the data set, we next provide various summary statistics and graphs to give an initial overview of the properties of the data. Accordingly, Table 1 reports summary statistics for the main variables used in our analysis. Of particular interest is the variable that measures combined hardware and software assets—we refer to this as the IT capital of the plant.[12] Annual IT investment is also reported in the ASI data, and has the same combination of hardware and software included. It should be noted that because of missing observations, the number of observations differs across variables. As long as there is not a systematic pattern of missing observations, reporting the means for different variables with different numbers of observations still provides useful information.

---

10. Some authors have used software price deflators from other countries, when separate data on hardware and software is available. One possibility might be that hardware prices have fallen relative to other goods. In our case, discussions in surveys of IT use in Indian manufacturing (e.g., NMCC–NASSCOM 2010) suggest that the cost of IT capital has not come down so rapidly. If we are underestimating the real amount of IT capital by deflating later years' amounts too much, then our results will be biased upwards.

11. In addition to Kite (2012), see, for example, Alfaro and Chari (2009).

12. Here it must be also be acknowledged that the PROWESS data used by Kite has separate figures for hardware and software.

TABLE 1. Summary Statistics

Variable	Whole data		ITK > 0		ITK = 0		For sample used in the regression	
	Obs	Mean	Obs	Mean	Obs	Mean	Obs	Mean
Gross Valued Added (INR)	23841	3560450	14016	5589169	9825	666349.7	12856	5881595
Plant and Machinery (INR)	38120	2870858	19367	5043062	18753	627532.4	12856	5541915
Transport Equipment (INR)	33277	46163.29	18491	73202.21	14786	12349.09	12856	79706.75
Stock of ITK (INR)	26169	48802.43	19427	65738.96	6742	0	12856	74213.04
Skilled Workers	33687	78.57841	18586	112.3726	15101	36.98523	12856	120.6595
Production Workers	37941	294.339	19231	359.7769	18710	227.079	12856	385.0094
Total Employment	38502	360.2158	19359	466.9185	19143	252.309	12856	505.7222
Skill Composition	33681	0.2318955	18582	0.259475	15099	0.197954	12856	0.258986
Short-term loans (INR)	24550	758357	14602	880092.3	9948	203327.1	10117	1094322
Profits (INR)	31411	1425284	18088	1656997	13323	298384.9	12856	2249648
Electricity Used (External, KWH)	21279	6271616	12503	9599056	8776	1531076	7641	9061525
Electricity Used (Own, KWH)	37366	4480455	19070	7414924	18296	1421846	12615	7920286

Source: Authors' calculations from ASI survey data, 2003–07.
Note: Data used is from Annual Survey of Industries for years 2003–07.

In addition to statistics for the entire sample, we also report the corresponding numbers for each of two subsamples. The first category is plants that report positive levels of IT capital, as measured by the value of hardware and software stock. The second category is all other plants, which either report zero levels of IT capital stock, or have missing values. The latter could be genuine missing values, or they could be cases where the stock is zero. To deal with this problem, we will also consider a two-stage selection correction procedure in the regression analysis, as described later in this section.

The main message of Table 1 is that there is a distinct difference between plants that have positive stocks of IT capital and other plants, across every dimension of comparison. Plants that have positive stocks of IT have higher productivity, as measured by gross value added, higher profits, more workers of each type, and higher levels of equipment and machinery.[13] In the case of some variables, the differences are at the level of one order of magnitude, though they are less pronounced for the labor variables. These patterns were originally pointed out in GSS (2008), and of course there is nothing that can be inferred from these summary statistics with respect to causality. One point worth noting, that was not featured in GSS, is the higher levels of skill composition of the workforce in IT-using plants. Here skill composition is simply the ratio of salaried workers (a proxy for skilled workers) to the total workforce. The other category of workers is production workers, who are identified in this analysis with unskilled workers.

Finally, the last set of data in Table 1 is for the plants that are in our regression analysis. In creating a balanced panel of plants with positive IT capital, we lose a few observations, and the plants are on average slightly larger than those for which IT capital is positive. The comparison across the different sets of data in Table 1 suggests that the restriction of our data set for the regression analysis does not involve an obviously biased subsample.

Table 2 provides summary statistics by region, defined as North, South, East and West. The West region stands out in terms of larger plants, with higher investment, and particularly with higher stocks of IT capital, as well as higher profits and employment. The North region is next in these characteristics, followed by the South and then the East, though the latter two are not so far apart in many respects, in terms of average characteristics of

---

13. Barry Bosworth has pointed out to us that profits are a very high share of gross value added. We have examined the data carefully, including the calculations of GSS (2008), and find this to be a consistent property of the data, probably reflecting definitional idiosyncrasies. For our regressions, we focus only on GVA. GSS found very similar results when GVA is replaced by profits.

TABLE 2. Summary Statistics by Region

Variable	NORTH		EAST		WEST		SOUTH	
	Obs	Mean	Obs	Mean	Obs	Mean	Obs	Mean
Investment in IT (INR)	7541	7880.60	5488	5335.99	5508	10771.54	7632	5903.50
IT Capital Stock (INR)	7541	47175.73	5488	37254.14	5508	74847.73	7632	39917.00
Short Term Loans (INR)	6979	695371.9	5020	417785.4	4694	1149655	6784	804419.6
Profits (INR)	8609	1241761	7430	910802	5567	3059907	8467	988599.2
Gross Value Added (INR)	6789	1667300	5903	3029796	4443	6576671	6706	3945772
Plant and Machinery (INR)	10093	2392712	10270	3036944	6567	4373495	11190	2267855
Transport Equipment (INR)	9381	44885.58	8241	47450.92	6132	62491.88	9523	35793.44
Employment of Production Workers	9960	245.16	10061	259.43	6629	314.45	11291	357.02
Employment of Skilled Workers	8794	82.39	8355	67.37	6232	112.59	10306	63.85
Skill Composition	8792	0.263	8354	0.220	6231	0.262	10304	0.197
Total Employment	10063	315.68	10305	309.84	6699	417.18	11435	411.43

Source: Authors' calculations from ASI survey data, 2003–07.
Note: Data used is from Annual Survey of Industries for years 2003–07.

the plants. The West and North regions are distinct from the other two in terms of having higher skill compositions of the labor force.

The next set of summary statistics is in Table 3, which presents data for just three variables, but with a breakdown by industry. The three variables used for illustrating the substantial differences across industries in the sample are investment in IT capital, gross value added and skill composition of the labor force. There is considerable variation across industries in the last of these variables, and it appears that there is some positive association of skill composition with the relative level of investment in IT capital (after adjusting for size, as measured by gross value added).

It is also useful to get a sense of the variation in the data over time. We illustrate this through some line graphs for selected variables. Figure 1 displays the time pattern over the five years for stock of IT capital, stock of plant and machinery, and gross value added, all measured in Indian Rupees. For the second and third variables, we display the pattern for all plants, as well as for each category of plant divided by whether they report positive IT capital stock or not. The stock of IT capital increases over the five-year period.[14] The real value of the stock of plant and machinery for plants without IT capital does not increase, while there is a small increase in this stock for plants with IT. On the other hand, the average for all plants increases more rapidly, suggesting that the proportion of plants with IT capital is going up over the five-year period. In the case of gross value added, the increase in GVA for plants with IT capital is quite dramatic, and much greater than for plants without IT capital. Whatever the causality, there is a striking difference between the performance of the two categories of plants.[15]

We also illustrate the trends for selected variables, after scaling to correct for size and growth effects. Thus, in Figure 2, we display the trends associated with the stock of IT capital and GVA as ratios to the stock of plant and machinery. The stock of IT capital as a ratio to the stock of plant and machinery is relatively constant.[16] In the case of the ratio of GVA to the stock of plant and machinery, the difference in trends across the two types of plants (with and without IT capital) found in Figure 1 is preserved, even after normalizing by the growth in the stock of plant and machinery.

---

14. We also examined the behavior of IT investment over time. This annual rate also increases in real terms.

15. Interestingly, there are no perceptible trends in employment levels or skill composition for either type of plant in this data set.

16. We did find that the share of annual IT investment to the stock of plant and machinery did increase from 2004 onward.

TABLE 3. Summary Statistics by Industry

	Gross value added (INR)		Investment in ITK (INR)		Skill composition	
	Obs	Mean	Obs	Mean	Obs	Mean
Manufacture of Food and Beverages	5582	729783.1	5182	2377.39	7830	0.217421
Manufacture of Tobacco Products	531	1756950	536	4125.813	887	0.122224
Manufacture of Textiles	2957	1059625	3133	4429.889	4152	0.16006
Manufacture of Wearing Apparel	497	487892.7	691	3751.073	868	0.170738
Tanning and Dressing of Leather Manufactures	404	589026.3	477	3722.112	546	0.183199
Manufacture of Wood and Wooden Products	0	0	303	1635.266	460	0.292009
Manufacture of Paper and Paper Products	0	0	575	7992.88	703	0.2306
Publishing and Printing	558	-220203	675	20280.92	729	0.377984
Manufacture of Chemicals and Chemical Products	2844	5199434	3029	12153.55	3672	0.267725
Manufacture of Rubber and Plastic Products	716	1985985	844	5017.176	952	0.230513
Manufacture of Other Non-metallic Mineral Products	1885	1860147	1636	7323.875	2676	0.20283
Manufacture of Basic Metals	1473	5352452	1631	10904.93	1862	0.225596
Manufacture of Fabricated Metal Products	801	388880	902	2992.697	968	0.236739
Manufacture of Machinery and Equipment	1492	1203041	1611	10250.69	1684	0.312336
Manufacture of Electrical Machinery and Apparatus NEC	858	1877375	939	8435.887	1020	0.280435
Manufacture of Radio, Television and Communication Equipment	372	1467062	457	7046.228	503	0.338064
Manufacture of Medical, Precision and Optical Instruments	518	562697.1	592	4988.25	587	0.335726
Manufactures of Motor Vehicles, Trailers, and Semi-trailers	659	3501614	756	19641.23	833	0.232911
Manufacture of Other Transport Equipment	629	2029383	702	10086.86	755	0.252078
Manufacture of Furniture	555	335705.3	514	1282.662	567	0.255691

Source: Authors' calculations from ASI survey data, 2003–07.
Note: Data used is from Annual Survey of Industries (henceforth, ASI) for years 2003–07.

FIGURE 1. **Trends of Selected Variables**

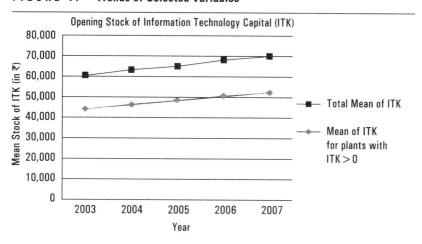

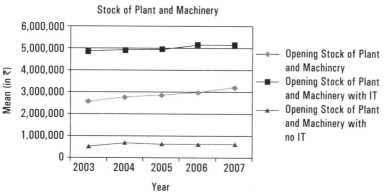

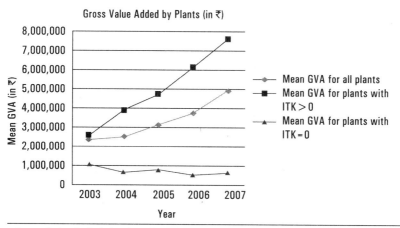

Source: Authors' calculations from ASI survey data, 2003–07.

FIGURE 2. Trends in Ratios of Selected Variables to Stock of Plant and Machinery

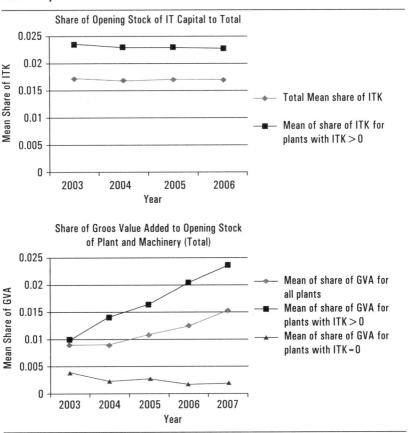

Source: Authors' calculations from ASI survey data, 2003–07.

Finally, in this overview of the data, we also calculated some correlation coefficients. Using deflated data, the correlation between GVA and the stock of IT capital in the data is 0.400, while the correlation between GVA and annual investment in IT capital is lower, but still clearly positive, at 0.214. Skill composition also shows a positive correlation with the IT measures, having correlations of 0.142 with the IT capital stock and 0.112 with investment in IT. We would expect these correlations to be lower, since skill composition does not increase with the scale of the firm, but the positive correlation with IT measures is consistent with the kinds of evidence on the role of human capital in complementing IT that was presented in the previous section.

3.2. Empirical Methodology

The data display several clear patterns, all pointing to a positive association between the use of IT in Indian manufacturing plants and various characteristics of inputs and performance. The patterns are similar to those found in GSS (2008). What is not clear from this kind of data description, of course, is the nature of causal relationships—are the relationships observed in the scatter plots, or in the systematic differences between plants that report using IT and those that do not, due to the use of IT, or are both IT use and performance due to other factors, such as managerial skill, labor force composition or underlying technologies?

We examine this issue using standard regression techniques. In particular, we estimate production functions for our panel data, which allows us to include plant-level fixed effects. We can also use lagged variables as instruments to deal with endogeneity of the input variables. The dependent variable in these regressions is gross value added (GVA). We estimate equations in log linear form, which corresponds to a Cobb-Douglas production function in the absence of any other controls. Since there is missing data on the dependent variable, as well as cases where the value of the variable is negative, we also consider the possibility of selection bias in our estimates, by using two-step Heckman correction procedures.

An important concern in this analysis is that time-varying unobservable characteristics of plants may be affecting the relationship between the stock of IT capital and the gross value added. These will not be controlled by plant fixed effects. In order to overcome this issue, we use instruments that are orthogonal to the error term (and therefore, also plant fixed effects) within a Generalized Method of Moments (GMM) framework. Along the lines of Blundell and Bond (1998), the instruments used in this analysis are both the lagged (first and second) values of the dependent variables, and the lagged (first and second) values of their differences.[17] The results from the GMM

---

17. We use the "system" version of GMM as developed by Blundell and Bond (1998), and implemented in the STATA software package. GMM estimators may be subject to their own biases, including problems created by weak instruments, but they provide a useful alternative to the OLS estimates. In any case, in our specifications, we typically use beginning of period stocks or lagged flow variables to deal with simultaneity issues that would arise for OLS.

specification are presented alongside the results from the OLS specification as a robustness check for each model. Year fixed effects that control for changes in policy or any event that occurred in a year and affected all plants uniformly are included in both the GMM and OLS specifications.

In addition to the production function, we also estimate IT investment demand equations. The objective is to understand the factors that influence the decision to invest in IT, as well as those that determine the level of IT investment in cases where it is undertaken. Here also, we deal with two levels of selection—IT investment may be zero, or it may be missing. We allow for the possibility that each of these forms of selection may bias the estimated IT demand equation, and therefore again use the two-step Heckman procedure with two levels of selection.

The algebraic forms of the estimating equations are standard, but we present them here for concreteness. The basic production function has a standard Cobb-Douglas form and is given by

$$\ln(GVA)_{it} = \alpha + \beta_1 \ln(PM)_{it} + \beta_2 \ln(TE)_{it} + \beta_3 \ln(ITK)_{it}$$
$$+ \beta_4 \ln(SL)_{it-1} + \beta_4 \ln(UL)_{it-1} + u_i + v_t + \varepsilon_{it} \qquad (1)$$

where GVA is gross value added, PM is stock of plant and machinery at the beginning of the period, TE is stock of transport equipment at the beginning of the period, ITK is IT capital stock at the beginning of the period, SL is number of skilled employees, and UL is number of unskilled employees. We will also estimate various extensions of this base specification, incorporating regional dummies, measures of ownership and organization, characteristics of importing inputs, interaction terms, and so on.

The IT investment demand equation as estimated can be thought of as a conditional demand function. We do not have input price data, and we regress investment in a given year on the inputs in the production function. We also attempt to control for financial and infrastructure constraints on the demand for IT investment. Finally, we include inverse Mills ratios to correct for possible selectivity biases caused by the fact that the demand equation includes only observations with reported, positive levels of the dependent variable. These selectivity correction terms are derived from the standard two-step Heckman procedure, where the first step involves estimating probit equations for whether IT investment is reported or not, and whether reported IT investment is positive or not. The probit equations are specified similarly to the demand equation, but include external electricity, and exclude internal electricity and IT capital.[18] The investment demand equation is as follows.[19]

$$\ln(ITI)_{it} = \alpha_1 + \gamma_1 \ln(PM)_{it} + \gamma_2 \ln(TE)_{it} + \gamma_3 \ln(ITK)_{it}$$
$$+ \gamma_4 \ln(SL)_{it-1} + \gamma_4 \ln(UL)_{it-1} + \gamma_5 \ln(STL)_{it-1} + \gamma_6 \ln(\pi)_{it-1} \quad (2)$$
$$+ \gamma_7 \ln(EO)_{it} + \lambda_1 IMR_1 + \lambda_2 IMR_2 + u_{1i} + v_{1t} + \varepsilon_{1it}$$

4. Results

4.1. Role of Plant Fixed Effects

The basic production function results are presented in Table 4. The specification is in logs, so a Cobb-Douglas form is being estimated. The dependent variable is gross value added (GVA). The first three variables are capital stocks, measured at the beginning of the period, thus reducing simultaneity problems. The third of these, IT capital, is of particular interest for us. The labor variables are the numbers of salaried and production workers respectively, interpreted as skilled and unskilled employees. To deal with endogeneity, we use lagged values of these two variables.[20] Table 4 presents four specifications. The first column is a base specification with only year fixed effects, estimated by OLS. All the coefficients except that of transport equipment are statistically significant, have the right signs, and have reasonable magnitudes. The sum of the coefficients, which is a measure of returns to scale, is quite close to one for the base specification.

Adding plant-level fixed effects (column 2) increases the magnitude of the transport equipment coefficient, but reduces the magnitude of all the other coefficients.[21] The coefficient of IT capital stock is now much smaller, but is still statistically significant, and its economic significance

18. We estimated several alternative specifications of the probit equations—the importance of profits was robust across specifications.

19. *STL* stands for short-term loans, π for profit and EO for electricity purchased from outside (the grid).

20. Of course, if there is serial correlation in the error terms, using lagged values will not solve problems created by endogeneity. In GSS (2008), since a panel was not available, endogeneity was dealt with by using industry averages for the employment variables.

21. In the previous version of this paper, we also tried a specification with industry fixed effects. The impact on the coefficient magnitudes was somewhere in between the no cross-sectional fixed effects and plant-level fixed effects. Our industry fixed effects estimates were quite close to those of GSS (2008).

TABLE 4. Production Function Estimation

	(1)	(2)	(3)	(4)
	OLS with year FE	OLS with plant and year FE	First differences with year FE	GMM IV with year FE
Plant and Machinery	0.387***	0.234***	0.225***	0.573***
	(0.0189)	(0.0536)	(0.0524)	(0.113)
Transport Equipment	0.0310***	0.0517***	0.0425**	0.172***
	(0.0113)	(0.0179)	(0.0179)	(0.0541)
ITK	0.215***	0.0418**	0.0377*	0.175**
	(0.0180)	(0.0199)	(0.0219)	(0.0721)
Lag (Production Workers)	0.172***	0.117***	−0.00660	0.343***
	(0.0207)	(0.0347)	(0.0321)	(0.0753)
Lag (Skilled Workers)	0.225***	0.0919***	0.0500	0.120*
	(0.0220)	(0.0334)	(0.0322)	(0.0680)
Constant	3.853***	8.088***		−0.172
	(0.161)	(0.719)		(1.897)
N	11194	11194	7277	11194
adj. R^2		0.047	0.017	

Source: Authors' calculations from ASI survey data, 2003–07.
Note: Standard errors in parentheses (* $p < 0.10$, ** $p < 0.05$, *** $p < 0.01$)
All variables reported are in logs. Data used is from ASI for years 2003–07.

is not negligible. The magnitude of the IT capital stock coefficient is now quite similar to that in Kite (2012).[22] The third column reports estimates for first differences, which are quite similar to the full fixed effects estimates.

The fourth column reports estimates using the Blundell and Bond (1998) GMM estimator for panel data. Several of the coefficients are now quite high, and the sum of the coefficients is great than one. The coefficient of IT capital is in between the higher OLS estimate and the lower fixed effects estimate. The important point is the economic and statistical significance of this coefficient across the different estimation methods. In subsequent specifications, we focus on the OLS with plant fixed effects and GMM estimates.

We also estimated the production function with lags on the beginning of period stocks, including IT capital. We did not find any results to suggest that the impact of IT capital occurs with a lag. Hence, the results presented here for Indian manufacturing plants are somewhat different than the results of Bresnahan et al. (2002) for US data—they found substantial lags in the effects of IT on productivity. One possible source of difference is our use of stocks rather than per period investments. It could also be the case that

---

22. B. N. Goldar, in his comments on the conference draft, pointed out that the OLS coefficient without plant fixed effects implies an implausibly high marginal product of IT capital, given the low level of IT capital relative to plant and machinery.

Indian manufacturing plants have more current and immediate opportunities to enhance productivity through IT investment, than was the case for US firms in the 1990s.

One possible interpretation of the difference between the estimates without and with plant fixed effects is that the productivity of IT capital, more than other inputs, is correlated with unobservable managerial ability, which is captured in the plant fixed effects. Of course, it is possible that there are other explanations, such as different omitted inputs. However, our interpretation is consistent with the work of Bloom, Sadun, and van Reenen (2012), comparing the productivity of IT use by American and European managed firms. This interpretation also provides one possible explanation for why the higher productivity of IT-using firms is not easily mimicked by other firms—they do not have access to an input that is, for various reasons, in short supply in India, that is, managerial expertise or quality (Bloom et al. 2012; NMCC–NASSCOM 2012).

4.2. Selectivity

In the regressions reported in Table 4, one possible issue is that observations where GVA is negative or missing are excluded. This could create a selectivity bias. Accordingly, we checked for both sources of bias, using a two-step Heckman procedure. We estimated a probit equation where the dependent variable was 0 if GVA was missing and 1 otherwise, and a second probit regression where, for observations where GVA is not missing, the dependent variable was 0 if GVA was negative and 1 otherwise. We then reestimated the production function with inverse Mills ratios calculated from the two probit regressions. Neither Mills ratio in this last regression was statistically significant. Moreover the coefficients were quite comparable in magnitude to the production function without the selectivity correction. Hence, we reach the conclusion that selectivity of firms based on missing or negative GVA is not an issue, and we proceed in subsequent regressions without selectivity corrections.

4.3. Intermediate Imports and Skill Composition

Work by one of the authors (Sharma 2012) suggests that imports of intermediate goods have been important in affecting the skill composition of the workforce in Indian manufacturing plants. Several of the papers discussed in the literature review of Section 2 find that the composition of the workforce is a significant factor in affecting the productivity of IT investment at the firm level. Accordingly, we explore the impact of the use of intermediate imports and of skill composition on the production function estimates. These results are reported in Table 5. We estimate each specification by OLS as well as GMM. All the OLS regressions in Table 5 include year and plant fixed effects, while the GMM estimates include year fixed effects.

The first two columns of Table 5 add a dummy variable that is 1 for plants that use imported intermediate goods and 0 otherwise to the baseline specification. The coefficient has the expected positive sign in both the OLS and GMM estimates, and it is statistically significant. Plants that use intermediate goods imports are more productive on average, as measured by GVA. In both cases, the coefficient of IT capital remains positive and significant. The third and fourth columns of Table 5 add an interaction term of IT capital with the import dummy. The interaction term coefficient is negative and significant at the 10 percent level in the OLS estimation, but negative and insignificant in the GMM case. Hence, there is weak evidence that IT capital and imported intermediates might be substitutes to some extent.

The fifth and sixth columns of Table 5 reports results when only skill composition is added to the baseline regression. While the original coefficients are relatively stable to this inclusion (though the coefficient of IT capital is no longer significant in the OLS estimation), the new variable is statistically significant, but does not have the expected sign. We might have expected a positive coefficient, consistent with plants that have relatively more skilled workers being more productive. One possibility is that the estimated negative coefficient is capturing some variation, across industries, which is not being captured in the plant fixed effects. However, this remains a subject for further investigation. The seventh and eighth columns add an interaction term of skill composition with the stock of IT capital. This regression yields a result that is somewhat consistent with previous studies of the effect of joint IT and human capital investment. The coefficient of IT capital is now insignificant, while that of skill composition is more strongly negative. However, the interaction term has a positive coefficient, statistically significant at the 5 percent (OLS) or 10 percent (GMM) level, indicating complementarity between IT capital stock and the proportion of skilled workers.[23]

23. We also estimated a specification with both additional variables (though not with the interaction terms), and the coefficients were quite stable across the specifications. In particular, the coefficient of IT capital had a similar magnitude and degree of statistical significance across specifications. We also estimated the production function using skill composition lagged by one year, to examine whether investments in skilled labor take time to have a positive impact. However, in this case, the coefficients of the new variable and interaction terms were not statistically significant.

TABLE 5. Imported Intermediates and Skill Composition

	(1) OLS	(2) GMM	(3) OLS	(4) GMM	(5) OLS	(6) GMM	(7) OLS	(8) GMM
Plant and Machinery	0.244***	0.475***	0.222***	0.480***	0.299***	0.518***	0.303***	0.483***
	(0.05)	(0.0971)	(0.05)	(0.0898)	(0.04)	(0.107)	(0.04)	(0.0997)
Transport Equipment	0.050***	0.153***	0.050***	0.158***	0.045***	0.165***	0.045***	0.160***
	(0.02)	(0.0479)	(0.02)	(0.0477)	(0.02)	(0.0521)	(0.02)	(0.0504)
ITK	0.043**	0.147**	0.063***	0.183**	0.033	0.180**	−0.007	0.0789
	(0.02)	(0.0622)	(0.02)	(0.0744)	(0.02)	(0.0726)	(0.03)	(0.0868)
Production Workers (Lag-1)	0.112***	0.322***	0.112***	0.314***	0.093***	0.256***	0.096***	0.244***
	(0.03)	(0.0688)	(0.03)	(0.0687)	(0.03)	(0.0579)	(0.03)	(0.0574)
Skilled Workers (Lag-1)	0.090***	0.103*	0.089***	0.106*	0.080**	0.191***	0.078**	0.195***
	(0.03)	(0.0622)	(0.03)	(0.0612)	(0.03)	(0.0612)	(0.03)	(0.0603)
M	0.352***	0.493***	0.738***	1.257**				
	(0.04)	(0.0717)	(0.20)	(0.577)				
M*ITK			−0.039*	−0.0788				
			(0.02)	(0.0583)				
Skill Composition					−0.628***	−1.187***	−2.185***	−5.014**
					(0.15)	(0.284)	(0.72)	(2.101)
Skill Composition*ITK							0.163**	0.402*
							(0.07)	(0.209)
Constant	8.110***	1.608	7.963	1.215	7.695***	1.071	8.003***	2.575
	(0.70)	(1.577)	(0.71)	(1.513)	(0.64)	(1.767)	(0.65)	(1.726)
R-sqr	0.062		0.062		0.053		0.054	
N	11194	11194	1194	11194	11065	11065	11065	11065
Year Fixed Effects	Yes	Yes	Yes	Yes	Yes	Yes	Yes	Yes

Source: Authors' calculations from ASI survey data, 2003–07.

Note: Standard errors in parentheses (* $p < 0.10$, ** $p < 0.05$, *** $p < 0.01$). All Variables except M and Skill Composition in Logs. All models include Year FE. Data from ASI (2003–07).

4.4. IT Intensity and Skill Intensity

We also examined the possibility that the impact of IT depends on the IT intensity of the plant in question. Thus, if the ratio of IT capital to other capital is high, the effect on value added might be different than if the ratio is low. Accordingly, we divided the sample into three roughly equal-sized subgroups, based on the degree of IT intensity, labeled low, medium, and high. We estimated the production function including dummies for the medium and high cases (with the low IT intensity dummy being the excluded one), as well as a specification interacting these dummies with the level of IT capital. Note that even the specification without interaction terms admits the possibility that IT intensity matters, while the interaction terms would reinforce or damp down this effect, depending on the signs of the coefficients. These results are presented in Table 6. The first two columns present the OLS and GMM results without the interaction terms. The OLS estimates suggest that there is no significant difference in the impact of IT capital for medium or high versus low IT intensity.[24] Adding in the dummies actually makes the IT capital term statistically insignificant as well.

The GMM results provide a different picture, with significant values for the medium and high IT intensity firms, but the estimated coefficient of plant and machinery in the GMM case is implausibly high. The third and fourth columns of Table 6 add interaction terms between the IT intensity dummies and the level of IT capital. In the OLS case, the results suggest that IT capital matters most for plants with medium IT intensity. The GMM estimates are again quite different in their implications, but the coefficient of plant and machinery is again implausibly high. Overall, it is difficult to reach firm conclusions about the variation of the impact of IT capital with IT intensity, and this issue deserves further investigation.

Table 6 also reports results for different degrees of skill intensity (measured at the plant-level) and the interaction of skill intensity with the level of IT capital. Columns 5 and 6 report results for OLS and GMM without interaction terms. In both estimations, medium and high skill intensity plants actually have lower base levels of productivity. Once interaction terms between skill intensity and IT capital are introduced, the OLS (column 7) and GMM (column 8) results diverge. The OLS estimates suggest that there are complementarities between skill intensity and the level of IT capital, but this possibility does not show up in the GMM estimates. On the other hand, the GMM estimates continue to show a positive and significant base

---

24. In an earlier draft, we also examined industry level IT intensity, and found that it had no significant impact in OLS estimates.

TABLE 6. Plant-wise IT and Skill Intensity

	IT intensity				Skill intensity			
	(1) OLS	(2) GMM	(3) OLS	(4) GMM	(5) OLS	(6) GMM	(7) OLS	(8) GMM
Plant and Machinery	0.241***	1.187***	0.236***	0.914***	0.234***	0.526***	0.238***	0.508***
	(0.0561)	(0.137)	(0.0558)	(0.111)	(0.0546)	(0.100)	(0.0551)	(0.0912)
Transport Equipment	0.0518***	0.274***	0.0527***	0.184***	0.0525***	0.158***	0.0527***	0.149***
	(0.0179)	(0.0733)	(0.0178)	(0.0534)	(0.0179)	(0.0503)	(0.0178)	(0.0483)
ITK	0.0295	0.0664	0.0163	0.157*	0.0429**	0.168**	0.00148	0.159**
	(0.0233)	(0.0852)	(0.0242)	(0.0873)	(0.0201)	(0.0701)	(0.0286)	(0.0807)
Skilled Workers (Lag-1)	0.0927***	0.247**	0.0920***	0.155**	0.0956***	0.142**	0.0954***	0.130**
	(0.0334)	(0.0997)	(0.0334)	(0.0754)	(0.0334)	(0.0601)	(0.0334)	(0.0589)
Production Workers (Lag-1)	0.117***	0.212**	0.116***	0.180**	0.111***	0.329***	0.112***	0.314***
	(0.0346)	(0.105)	(0.0347)	(0.0835)	(0.0344)	(0.0640)	(0.0343)	(0.0618)
Medium IT/Skill Intensity	0.0719	0.544***	−0.446*	2.170**	−0.160***	−0.128*	−0.511**	0.00406
	(0.0495)	(0.206)	(0.251)	(1.020)	(0.0383)	(0.0748)	(0.217)	(0.574)
High IT/Skill Intensity	0.0563	0.986***	−0.178	3.600**	−0.215***	−0.210**	−0.808***	−0.0987
	(0.0634)	(0.296)	(0.313)	(1.487)	(0.0461)	(0.0956)	(0.251)	(0.718)
Medium IT/Skill Intensity* (ITK)			0.0546**	−0.232**			0.0383*	−0.0145
			(0.0249)	(0.106)			(0.0221)	(0.0607)
High IT/Skill Intensity* (ITK)			0.0248	−0.344**			0.0631**	−0.0135
			(0.0301)	(0.146)			(0.0253)	(0.0743)
Constant	8.070***	−8.892***	8.243***	−4.046**	8.241***	0.797	8.540***	1.354
	(0.730)	(2.052)	(0.752)	(1.732)	(0.726)	(1.636)	(0.732)	(1.487)
N	11194	11194	11194	11194	11194	11194	11194	11194
adj. R²	0.047		0.048		0.051		0.051	

Source: Authors' calculations from ASI survey data, 2003–07.
Note: Standard errors in parentheses (* $p < 0.10$, ** $p < 0.05$, *** $p < 0.01$). All variables except Intensity Measures are in Logs. Data from ASI for 2003–07.

coefficient for IT capital, but this is not the case for the OLS regression. Thus, the evidence for the hypothesis that a high enough skill intensity of labor is required for IT capital to be productive remains mixed.

4.5. Region Effects

Next we consider the possibility that there are differences across regions in the impacts of IT capital on gross value added. Surveys of Indian manufacturing (e.g., Chandra 2009) often note that there are substantial regional variations in the characteristics of manufacturing firms and industries across different regions of India. GSS (2008) note the differences in patterns of IT use across regions, as we have done in Table 2. Results for estimations with regional dummies and with interaction terms between the regional dummies and the coefficient of IT capital are presented in Table 7, for OLS and GMM estimations. We find that, despite the variation across regions in characteristics of plants, including their use of IT, there is no evidence that the impact of IT use varies across the four regions. Columns 1 and 2 present the OLS and GMM results, respectively, when regional dummies are included only in interaction with the ITK variable. Columns 3 and 4 estimate GMM with just regional dummies and then with interaction effects between the regional dummies and the level of IT capital as well.[25] In no case are any of these new terms statistically significant. Thus, despite the substantial differences in plant characteristics across the four regions, these do not seem to translate into differences across regions in the impact of IT capital on gross value added.

4.6. Agglomeration

One important aspect of IT use is its newness as a technology, and the implied possibility that mechanisms of technology diffusion may be important. GSS (2008) consider this possibility in modeling the IT investment decision, by considering state-level and industry-level agglomeration effects. The underlying idea is that IT investment (especially the decision whether to invest or not) will be influenced by the proportion of plants in that industry or state that already use IT. We can extend this logic to the possibility that the productivity of an IT-using plant may depend on the proportions of plants in the same state or the same industry that also use IT. The underlying

---

25. The case of OLS estimation with regional dummies is omitted, because the regional dummies are collinear with the plant fixed effects.

T A B L E 7 .   **Regional Effects**

	(1) OLS	(2) GMM	(3) GMM	(4) GMM
Plant and Machinery	0.234*** (0.0536)	0.470*** (0.181)	1.311*** (0.211)	1.058*** (0.130)
Transport Equipment	0.0515*** (0.0179)	0.260* (0.150)	0.267*** (0.0910)	0.269*** (0.0693)
ITK	0.0403 (0.0346)	0.152 (0.121)	0.320** (0.138)	0.144 (0.210)
Skilled Workers (Lag-1)	0.0915*** (0.0333)	0.255** (0.124)	0.259* (0.143)	0.221** (0.105)
Production Workers (Lag-1)	0.117*** (0.0347)	0.471*** (0.109)	0.131 (0.145)	0.163 (0.106)
East			−2.573 (1.656)	−5.731* (3.193)
West			−1.626 (1.436)	1.553 (2.624)
South			−2.147 (1.966)	−1.968 (3.631)
East*(ITK)	0.0241 (0.0638)	−0.0154 (0.123)		0.641* (0.335)
West*(ITK)	−0.00477 (0.0484)	−0.0882 (0.129)		−0.147 (0.251)
South*(ITK)	−0.00218 (0.0499)	0.0490 (0.115)		0.176 (0.353)
Constant	8.086*** (0.719)	−0.537 (1.387)	−10.56*** (3.161)	−6.892*** (2.660)
N	11194	11194	11194	11194
adj. R^2	0.047			

Source: Authors' calculations from ASI survey data, 2003–07.
Notes: Standard errors in parentheses (* $p < 0.10$, ** $p < 0.05$, *** $p < 0.01$). Year Fixed Effects included in all models. Data used is from ASI for years 2003–07.

mechanism in this case will be a combination of learning by doing and information-sharing among plants in the same state or the same industry.

Accordingly, in Table 8, we present results for state-level and industry-level agglomeration effects in the production function, each considered separately. As in GSS (2008), the degree of agglomeration is measured as the proportion of plants that use IT for the state or for the industry in which a particular plant operates. Columns 1 and 2 of Table 8 present OLS and GMM results for state-level agglomeration effects. There is no evidence of positive agglomeration externalities at this geographic level: indeed, the coefficients are marginally negatively significant. Adding interaction terms in columns 3 and 4 does not change this result, and the interaction terms are insignificant for each estimation method.

T A B L E 8 . **Industry and State Agglomeration Effects**

	State				Industry			
	(1) OLS	(2) GMM	(3) OLS	(4) GMM	(5) OLS	(6) GMM	(7) OLS	(8) GMM
Plant and Machinery	0.234***	0.572***	0.235***	0.673***	0.234***	0.417***	0.233***	0.370***
	(0.0539)	(0.105)	(0.0539)	(0.0975)	(0.0550)	(0.0980)	(0.0552)	(0.0733)
Transport Equipment	0.0524***	0.152***	0.0519***	0.172***	0.0514***	0.0832	0.0511***	0.122***
	(0.0178)	(0.0512)	(0.0178)	(0.0533)	(0.0179)	(0.0533)	(0.0179)	(0.0467)
ITK	0.0422**	0.157**	-0.0851	0.349	0.0418**	0.0838	-0.0995	-0.957**
	(0.0199)	(0.0652)	(0.0834)	(0.223)	(0.0200)	(0.0630)	(0.0804)	(0.380)
Skilled Workers (Lag-1)	0.0916***	0.0874	0.0922***	0.117*	0.0930***	0.0890	0.0917***	0.0610
	(0.0334)	(0.0666)	(0.0334)	(0.0705)	(0.0334)	(0.0770)	(0.0333)	(0.0653)
Production Workers (Lag-1)	0.119***	0.300***	0.118***	0.251***	0.120***	0.202**	0.119***	0.309***
	(0.0346)	(0.0733)	(0.0346)	(0.0764)	(0.0348)	(0.0859)	(0.0347)	(0.0727)
Industry/State Agglomeration Effect	-0.709*	-0.894*	-2.909**	1.083	0.874**	9.794***	-1.772	-20.01***
	(0.427)	(0.531)	(1.470)	(3.421)	(0.408)	(2.687)	(1.575)	(7.221)
Industry/State Agglomeration Effect*ITK			0.232	-0.257			0.280*	2.188***
			(0.142)	(0.369)			(0.156)	(0.746)
Constant	8.453***	1.052	9.646***	-1.960	7.626***	-0.277	8.991***	13.91***
	(0.761)	(1.518)	(1.111)	(2.011)	(0.793)	(1.703)	(1.071)	(3.854)
N	11194	11194	11194	11194	11194	11194	11194	11194
adj. R^2	0.047		0.048		0.048		0.048	

Source: Authors' calculations from ASI survey data, 2003–07.
Notes: Standard errors in parentheses (* $p < 0.10$, ** $p < 0.05$, *** $p < 0.01$). All variables except Industry and State Agglomeration Effects in Logs. Year Fixed Effects included in all models. Data is from ASI for years 2003–07.

Columns 5 and 6 of Table 8 replace geographic agglomeration with industry agglomeration effects. For both estimation methods, the coefficient of industry agglomeration is positive and statistically significant, possibly reflecting diffusion and sharing of knowledge with respect to IT adoption and use. When we add interaction terms, in columns 7 and 8, the results are even more striking, with the positive impact of IT capital being wholly reflected in the interaction term of the degree of IT use in that industry and the level of IT capital in that plant. These results are strongly suggestive of the idea that, to achieve better impacts of IT use, policy should focus at the industry level to encourage IT use. This is consistent, of course, with the recommendations of the NMCC–NASSCOM (2010) report.

4.7. Ownership and Organizational Form

While we do not have data on managerial quality, we can indirectly or partially explore differences in management through a consideration of differences in ownership and organizational form. In each case, there are a large number of categories, and we combine some categories for tractability. In the case of ownership, our baseline category is full ownership by the central government. The included categories of ownership are full ownership by a state government, joint central and state government ownership, joint government and private ownership, and wholly private ownership. The results are presented in Table 9. They suggest that central government ownership leads to lower productivity overall, but to more positive impacts of IT use, since the interaction terms are always negative and almost always statistically significant.

We also consider differences in organizational form, which may also capture differences in effective managerial quality. The reason is that managerial effectiveness may reflect a complex of institutional factors for each plant or firm, proxied by the organizational form. The baseline category in this case is private proprietorship, while the included dummy variables represent, respectively, joint family ownership, partnership, limited liability companies (public or private), government enterprises (excluding handlooms), and a miscellaneous category of other organizational forms, including cooperatives and trusts. The results are presented in Table 10. Statistically significant differences in the impact of organizational form and its interaction with IT capital exist for joint family ownership relative to sole proprietorships, but the results are not stable across the OLS and GMM estimations, so our conclusion must be that the evidence is inconclusive in the case of organizational form and the productivity of IT capital.

TABLE 9. Ownership Form

	(1) OLS	(2) GMM	(3) OLS	(4) GMM
Plant and Machinery	0.235***	0.446***	0.234***	0.434***
	(0.0537)	(0.0779)	(0.0536)	(0.0695)
Transport Equipment	0.0522***	0.173***	0.0533***	0.164***
	(0.0179)	(0.0507)	(0.0179)	(0.0441)
ITK	0.0419**	0.272***	0.133***	0.781***
	(0.0199)	(0.0677)	(0.0467)	(0.288)
Production Workers (Lag-1)	0.118***	0.247***	0.119***	0.251***
	(0.0347)	(0.0710)	(0.0347)	(0.0702)
Skilled Workers (Lag-1)	0.0940***	0.00463	0.0955***	-0.0241
	(0.0334)	(0.0599)	(0.0335)	(0.0611)
Wholly State/Local	0.182	0.963***	1.491**	6.373**
Government (2)	(0.171)	(0.338)	(0.757)	(3.217)
Joint State and Central	0.0250	0.818	0.492	4.003
Government (3)	(0.276)	(0.582)	(0.925)	(3.293)
Joint Sector Public + Joint	0.0283	0.872***	1.056**	6.088**
Sector Private (4)	(0.149)	(0.289)	(0.479)	(3.039)
Wholly Private (5)	0.155	1.236***	1.084***	6.457**
	(0.141)	(0.276)	(0.414)	(3.073)
ITK*(2)			-0.135*	-0.595*
			(0.0788)	(0.307)
ITK*(3)			-0.0418	-0.369
			(0.0847)	(0.306)
ITK*(4)			-0.103**	-0.575**
			(0.0485)	(0.286)
ITK*(5)			-0.0931**	-0.578**
			(0.0437)	(0.290)
Constant	8.109***	0.373	6.988***	-3.913
	(0.740)	(1.202)	(0.834)	(3.085)
N	11178	11178	11178	11178
adj. R^2	0.048		0.048	

Source: Authors' calculations from ASI survey data, 2003–07.
Notes: Standard errors in parentheses (* $p < 0.10$, ** $p < 0.05$, *** $p < 0.01$). All variables except Ownership indicators in Logs. Year Fixed Effects are included in all models. Data used is from ASI for 2003–07.

4.8. IT Investment Demand

The final part of our empirical analysis focuses on IT investment. We estimate a demand equation to examine the factors that influence investment in IT capital. Following GSS (2008), we allow for the fact that all plants do not invest in IT. The choice whether to invest is therefore examined using a Heckman selection model. Furthermore, we extend this procedure to the additional issue that some observations are missing—this extension allows us to correct for biases in reporting data about IT investment.

TABLE 10. Organizational Form

	(1) OLS	(2) GMM	(3) OLS	(4) GMM
Plant and Machinery	0.234***	0.549***	0.232***	0.479***
	(0.0536)	(0.0865)	(0.0534)	(0.0715)
Transport Equipment	0.0526***	0.141***	0.0516***	0.125***
	(0.0179)	(0.0475)	(0.0179)	(0.0449)
ITK	0.0427**	0.151**	0.0157	0.472**
	(0.0200)	(0.0602)	(0.126)	(0.238)
Production Workers (Lag-1)	0.116***	0.310***	0.116***	0.316***
	(0.0347)	(0.0711)	(0.0347)	(0.0689)
Skilled Workers (Lag-1)	0.0932***	0.152**	0.0933***	0.135**
	(0.0334)	(0.0642)	(0.0334)	(0.0614)
Joint Family (2)	0.402	0.417	-1.754*	4.509*
	(0.360)	(0.480)	(0.951)	(2.584)
Partnership (3)	-0.337	-0.720*	-0.431	3.172
	(0.249)	(0.391)	(1.155)	(2.206)
Public and Private Limited	-0.375	-0.435	-0.640	2.699
Companies (4)	(0.240)	(0.372)	(1.055)	(1.930)
Governmental Departmental	-0.276	-1.225***	-0.333	0.128
Enterprise +Public	(0.287)	(0.444)	(1.184)	(2.052)
Corporation (5)				
KVCs, Cooperative Societies,	-0.247	-0.912**	0.155	1.215
Handlooms and Others (6)	(0.271)	(0.415)	(1.127)	(1.997)
ITK*(2)			0.300**	-0.583*
			(0.149)	(0.305)
ITK*(3)			0.0164	-0.436
			(0.137)	(0.269)
ITK*(4)			0.0345	-0.354
			(0.124)	(0.239)
ITK*(5)			0.0111	-0.154
			(0.134)	(0.249)
ITK*(6)			-0.0384	-0.245
			(0.130)	(0.246)
Constant	8.434***	1.122	8.671***	-0.557
	(0.755)	(1.209)	(1.267)	(2.004)
N	11185	11185	11185	11185
adj. R^2	0.047		0.048	

Source: Authors' calculations from ASI survey data, 2003–07.
Notes: Standard errors in parentheses (* $p < 0.10$, ** $p < 0.05$, *** $p < 0.01$). All variables except indicators for Organization in Logs. Year Fixed Effects are included in all models. Data used is from ASI for 2003–07.

The first two columns of Table 11 present results for the two probit regressions that are used in correcting for possible selectivity biases. The first probit (column 1) assigns a value of 1 if the IT investment level is reported and 0 if the value is missing. The second probit (column 2) considers the set

TABLE 11. Investment in IT

	(2)	(1)	(3)	(6)
	Probit for missing values	Probit for zero values	Investment demand (OLS with Plant Fixed Effects)	Investment demand (GMM Blundell and Bond)
Short-term loans (lagged)	0.0187	0.0281**	−0.00724	0.0208
	(0.0128)	(0.0139)	(0.0332)	(0.0385)
Profits (lagged)	0.0838***	0.0949***	0.0705	0.240**
	(0.0168)	(0.0186)	(0.0690)	(0.0990)
Plant and Machinery	−0.0904***	−0.0553**	0.128	−0.438***
	(0.0239)	(0.0241)	(0.165)	(0.124)
Transport Equipment	0.0198	0.0686***	0.141	0.185**
	(0.0152)	(0.0163)	(0.0898)	(0.0882)
Electricity used from an	−0.0241**	−0.0173		
external source	(0.0109)	(0.0116)		
Production Workers	−0.268***	−0.0101	0.254	0.0799
(Lagged)	(0.0300)	(0.0313)	(0.158)	(0.237)
Skilled Workers (Lagged)	0.369***	0.180***	−0.224	0.390
	(0.0359)	(0.0358)	(0.191)	(0.322)
ITK			−0.109	0.577***
			(0.114)	(0.111)
Own electricity used			0.0209	0.0599
			(0.0239)	(0.0366)
Inverse Mills Ratio (Zero			5.595	1.738
Investment)			(6.500)	(8.084)
Inverse Mills Ratio (Missing			−9.797	7.479
Investment)			(6.272)	(10.41)
Constant	1.100***	−0.884***	5.630	−3.099
	(0.232)	(0.241)	(4.106)	(5.282)
N	5357	4632	3859	3859
Pseudo R^2	0.06	0.06		
adj. R^2			0.016	

Source: Authors' calculations from ASI survey data, 2003–07.
Notes: Standard errors in parentheses (* $p < 0.10$, ** $p < 0.05$, *** $p < 0.01$). All variables except Inverse Mills Ratios in Logs. Models (3) and (4) include Year Fixed Effects. Data used in from ASI for years 2003–04.

of observations where the IT investment level is reported, and assigns 1 if it is positive and 0 if the level is reported as zero. Several additional variables are included in the probits compared to the production function, including a variable that measures the amount of electricity purchased from the grid. We also include two measures of financial capacity of the unit, namely, the previous year's profit and the extent to which short-term loans are used by the unit, also lagged. In both the probits, the profit variable has the expected positively signed coefficient, which is also statistically significant—one possible interpretation is that access to retained earnings is important for decisions to invest in a new technology. In addition, the number of skilled workers has a significant coefficient with the expected sign. The two probits suggest that the factors influencing whether IT investment is missing in the data or is reported as zero are not that different.

The final two columns of Table 11 presents the IT investment demand equation, with inverse Mills ratios calculated from the two probit regressions being included to correct for selection biases. The first of these columns reports OLS results with year and plant-level fixed effects, while the second column reports GMM results. The specification also includes the amount of electricity used that is generated from a captive power plant (something quite common in India because of the shortage and unreliability of electric power from the grid). The OLS results are quite inconclusive, since none of the estimated coefficients is statistically significant. In the case of the GMM estimates, it seems that the existing stock of IT capital, availability of skilled workers and higher profits all have positive impacts on the level of IT investment for the subset of firms that do invest in IT. In neither estimation are the inverse Mills ratios statistically significant, implying that there is no evidence of selectivity bias in the investment demand equation.

The first column of Table 11, without plant fixed effects, is not inconsistent with the estimates and interpretation in GSS (2008), but the addition of plant fixed effects provides a somewhat different possibility in terms of the underlying causal story, paralleling our earlier discussion in the context of the GVA production function.

5. Conclusions

India's manufacturing sector has not grown as much as one might have expected for a fast-growing developing country like India. The new National Manufacturing Policy sets ambitious goals for rectifying this perceived deficiency. One possible route to achieving higher productivity and faster growth in manufacturing is the use of IT, for boosting efficiency and supporting other forms of innovation (e.g., new products). Case studies have developed the idea that IT can play this kind of role, while noting the limited adoption of IT in Indian manufacturing. However, empirical studies of the impact of IT on Indian manufacturing are rare. This study aims to contribute to our empirical understanding of the impact of IT on Indian manufacturing, as well as barriers to its adoption.

In this paper we have used five years of panel data for Indian manufacturing plants to examine the relationship of investment in information technology to productivity, as measured by gross value added. This provides some new evidence on the impacts of IT in the Indian manufacturing context. We find some evidence that plants with higher gross value added have higher levels of IT capital stock, controlling for other inputs. However, this effect is attenuated when plant-level fixed effects are included. We interpret this result as an indication that unobserved managerial quality is an important factor in the impact of IT capital on productivity. We also explore the impacts of skill composition and use of imported intermediate inputs on the productivity of IT capital, as well as regional differences, and the relevance of organizational forms and types of ownership.

To investigate possible barriers to IT use in manufacturing, we examine the demand for IT investment, controlling for possible selectivity when estimating demand just for plants with positive investment. The evidence is somewhat mixed, but access to financial capital, in the form of retained earnings from past profits, may play an important role in the decision whether to invest in IT in Indian manufacturing plants. We also find there is some evidence for complementarities between the use of skilled labor and the decision to use IT capital in Indian manufacturing plants.

Our results provide further evidence, beyond previous work of GSS (2008) and Kite (2012) that investment in IT has the potential to have positive impacts on the performance of India's manufacturing plants. The results also complement case study and survey evidence that point toward the same conclusion. Our results also suggest that financial constraints may be the main barrier to investment in IT, rather than infrastructure constraints. Adoption by other plants in the same industry also plays an important role in spurring IT investment within a particular industry. Neither geographic clustering nor regional effects appear to matter significantly for the impact of IT capital on productivity, which is encouraging to the extent that it does not point toward any need for decentralized policies. This observation, together with the relatively large impacts of IT capital implied by our estimates, suggest that national policies to spur the use of IT in manufacturing may be beneficial, and that it may be possible to formulate them in a streamlined manner.

Of course, our results cannot be completely conclusive given the nature of the data exercise, and if variations in managerial quality play a role, then encouraging investment in IT in plants that lack appropriate management or other complementary inputs may not be efficient. At least our study indicates that these issues may need to be tackled jointly. This aligns with the case study and survey evidence, and distinguishes our approach and results somewhat from the previous work of GSS (2008) and Kite (2012), which also found positive impacts of IT use on Indian firms' economic performance.

References

Alfaro, Laura and Anusha Chari . 2009. "India Transformed? Insights from the Firm Level 1988–2005," NBER Working Papers 15448, Cambridge, MA: National Bureau of Economic Research, Inc.

Arvanitis, Spyros. 2004. "Information Technology, Workplace Organisation, Human Capital and Firm Productivity: Evidence for the Swiss Economy," in OECD (2004), *The Economic Impact of ICT—Measurement, Evidence and Implications.* OECD, Paris.

Baldwin, John R. and David Sabourin. 2002. "Advanced technology use and firm performance in Canadian manufacturing in the 1990s," *Industrial and Corporate Change,* 11 (4): 761–89.

Basant, Rakesh, Simon Commander, Rupert Harrison, and Naercio Menezes-Filho. 2007. "IT Adoption and Productivity In Developing Countries: New Firm Level Evidence From Brazil And India," IBMEC Working Paper - WPE–23–2007.

Black, Sandra E. and Lisa M. Lynch. 2004. "What's Driving the New Economy? The Benefits of Workplace Innovation," *Economic Journal,* 114 (February): F97–F116.

Bloom, Nicholas, Benn Eifert Aprajit Mahajan, David McKenzie, and John Roberts. 2011. "Does Management Matter?" Policy Research Working Paper 5573, Washington, D.C.: The World Bank (February).

Bloom, Nicholas, Raffaella Sadun, and John Van Reenen. 2012. "Americans Do I.T. Better: US Multinationals and the Productivity Miracle," *American Economic Review,* 102 (1): 167–201.

Bloom, Nicholas and John Van Reenen. 2007. "Measuring and Explaining Management Practices across Firms and Countries," *Quarterly Journal of Economics,* 122 (4): 1341–408.

Bloom, Nicholas and John Van Reenen. 2010. "Why Do Management Practices Differ Across Firms and Countries?" *Journal of Economic Perspectives:* 203–24.

Blundell, Richard and Stephen Bond. 1998. "Initial Conditions and Moment Restrictions in Dynamic Panel Data Models," *Journal of Econometrics,* 87 (1): 115–43

Bresnahan, Timothy F., Erik Brynjolfsson and Lorin M. Hitt. 2002. "Information Technology, Workplace Organisation, and the Demand for Skilled Labor: Firm-Level Evidence," *Quarterly Journal of Economics,* February.

Brynjolfsson, Erik and Lorin M. Hitt. 2003. "Computing Productivity: Firm-Level Evidence," *Review of Economics and Statistics,* 85 (4, November): 793–808.

Chandra, Pankaj. 2009. "Competitiveness of Indian Manufacturing: Findings of the Third National Manufacturing Survey," IIMB Research Report No. RR-2009–01.

Chandra, Pankaj and Trilochan Sastry. 2002. "Competitiveness of Indian Manufacturing: Findings of the 2001 National Manufacturing Survey," Working Paper No. 2002–09–04, Indian Institute of Management, Ahmedabad.

Clayton, Tony, Chiara Criscuolo, Peter Goodridge, and Kathryn Waldron. 2004. "Enterprise E-commerce: Measurement and Impact," in OECD (2004), *The Economic Impact of ICT—Measurement, Evidence and Implications*. OECD, Paris.

Commander, S., R. Harrison and N. Menezes-Filho, 2011. "ICT and Productivity in Developing Countries: New Firm-Level Evidence from Brazil and India," *Review of Economics and Statistics*, 93 (2, May): 528–41.

Doms, Mark, Ron Jarmin, and Shawn Klimek. 2004. "Information Technology Investment and Firm Performance in US Retail Trade," *Economics of Innovation and New Technology*, 13 (7): 595–613.

Gangopadhyay, Shubhashis, Manisha G. Singh, and Nirvikar Singh. 2008. *Waiting to Connect: Indian IT Revolution Bypasses the Domestic Industry*. New Delhi: Lexis-Nexis-Butterworth.

Gretton, Paul, Jyothi Gali, and Dean Parham. 2003. "The Effects of ICTs and Complementary Innovations on Australian Productivity Growth," July.

Hempell, Thomas. 2004. Does Experience Matter? Innovations and the Productivity of Information and Communication Technologies in German Services, Centre for European Economic Research (ZEW), Mannheim first version: July 2002 , Present version: April 2004. Available at ftp://ftp.zew.de/pub/zew-docs/dp/dp0243.pdf

Hempell, Thomas, G. Van Leeuwen, and H. Van Der Wiel. 2004. "ICT, Innovation and Business Performance in Services: Evidence for Germany and the Netherlands," in OECD (2004), *The Economic Impact of ICT—Measurement, Evidence and Implications*. OECD, Paris.

Jorgenson, Dale W. 2005. "Accounting for Growth in the Information Age," Harvard University working paper. Available at http://post.economics.harvard.edu/faculty/jorgenson/papers/acounting_for_growth_050121.pdf

Joseph, K. J. and Vinoj Abraham. 2007. Information Technology and Productivity: Evidence from India's Manufacturing Sector, Working Paper 389, Centre for Development Studies, Trivandrum, Kerala, India.

Indjikian, Rouben and Donald S. Siegel. 2005. "The Impact of Investment in IT on Economic Performance: Implications for Developing Countries," *World Development*, 33 (5): 681–700.

Kapur, Devesh. 2002. "The Causes and Consequences of India's IT Boom," *India Review*, 1 (1): 91–110.

Kenny, Charles. 2002. "Information and Communications Technologies for Direct Poverty Alleviation: Costs and Benefits," *Development Policy Review*, 20 (2): 141–57.

Kenny, Charles. 2003. "The Internet and Economic Growth in Less-developed Countries: A Case of Managing Expectations?" *Oxford Development Studies*, 31 (1).

Kite, Grace. 2012. "The Impact of Information Technology Outsourcing on Productivity and Output: New Evidence from India," *American Economic Journal: Applied Economics* (forthcoming).

Kochhar, Kalpana Utsav Kumar, Raghuram Rajan, Arvind Subramanian, and Ioannis Tokatlidis. 2006. "India's Pattern of Development: What Happened, What Follows?" *Journal of Monetary Economics*, 53 (5): 981–1019.

Lal, K. 2001. "The Determinants of the Adoption of Information Technology: A Case Study of the Indian Garments Industry," in Matti Pohjola (ed.), *Information Technology, Productivity, and Economic Growth: International Evidence and Implications for Economic Development*, pp. 149–74. Oxford: Oxford University Press.

Lee, Houng and Yogesh Khatri. 2003. "Information Technology and Productivity Growth in Asia," IMF Working Paper- Wp/03/15, January 2003.

Lin, Justin Yifu. 2011. "New Structural Economics: A Framework for Rethinking Development," *World Bank Research Observer*, 26 (2): 193–221.

Maliranta, Mika and Petri Rouvinen. 2004. "ICT and Business Productivity: Finnish Micro-Level Evidence," in OECD (2004), *The Economic Impact of ICT—Measurement, Evidence and Implications*. OECD, Paris.

NMP. 2012. National Manufacturing Policy, Ministry of Commerce and Industry Department of Industrial Policy and Promotion. New Delhi: Government of India.

NMCC-NASSCOM. 2010. A Roadmap to Enhance ICT Adoption in the Indian Manufacturing Sector. New Delhi: NASSCOM.

Panagariya, Arvind. 2008. *India: The Emerging Giant.* New York: Oxford University Press.

Pitt, Alexander and Christine Z. Qiang. 2003. "ICT and Economic Growth: A Developing Country Perspective." Mimeo, IMF.

Qiang, Christine Zhen-Wei, Alexander Pitt, and Seth Ayers. 2004. "Contribution of Information and Communication Technologies to Growth," World Bank Working Paper no. 24.

RBI. 2012. *Handbook of Statistics on Indian Economy.* Mumbai: Reserve Bank of India

Rodrik, Dani. 2007. "Industrial Development: Some Stylized Facts and Policy Directions," in *Industrial Development for the 21st Century: Sustainable Development Perspectives*, pp. 7–28. New York: UN-DESA.

Schreyer, Paul. 2000. "The Contribution of Information and Communication Technology to Output Growth: A Study of the G7 Countries," Paris, Organisation for Economic Co-operation and Development, May 23.

Sharma, Shruti. 2012. "Do Firms Skill Upgrade with a Decline in Input Tariffs? A Pseudo-Panel Analysis," UCSC Working Paper in progress (March).

Singh, Nirvikar. 2007. "ICTs and Rural Development in India," UCSC Working Paper.

―――. 2008. "Services-led Industrialization in India: Assessment and Lessons," in David O'Connor and Monica Kjollerstrom (eds), *Industrial Development for the 21st Century: Sustainable Development Perspectives*, pp. 235–291. New York: Macmillan.

Comments and Discussion

Bishwanath Goldar
Institute of Economic Growth

This is an excellent paper on the impact of Information Technology (IT) investment on productivity in Indian manufacturing. The study uses panel data for Indian manufacturing plants for five years, 2003–04 to 2007–08, drawn from the *Annual Survey of Industries* (ASI). Since the analysis is based on the unit level data of the ASI, its coverage is confined to the registered or organized manufacturing sector. This is, however, not a disadvantage, because, for the issue under investigation, it is the registered manufacturing units that should be considered for the analysis.

To assess the impact of IT investment on manufacturing productivity, a Cobb-Douglas production function (or to be more specific, a value added function) has been estimated for the manufacturing plants covered in the study. Skilled and unskilled labor are taken as two types of labor input, along with plant and machinery, transport equipment and IT capital stock, taken separately as three types of capital input. The analysis is enriched by the detailed investigation undertaken on the factors that might determine how much effect IT investment will have on productivity. Several factors have been considered: skill level of workers, use of imported intermediate inputs, location of the plant, agglomeration effects, and influence of the nature of ownership and form of organization.

An attempt has been made in the study to take care of the econometric problem of endogeneity of inputs in the production function. The labor variables, for example, have been taken with one year lag in the model. Also, the regression equations have been estimated by the ordinary least squares (OLS) method as well as by the system version of the generalized method of moments (GMM) technique which would address the problem of endogeneity. It may be mentioned here that many studies on production function estimation based on firm-level panel data (including some for Indian manufacturing) have used the methodologies suggested by Olley-Pakes and Levinsohn-Pertin for addressing the issue of endogeneity. It seems that the methodology adopted in the study for addressing the problem of endogeneity is not as well founded in the theory of producer behavior as the Olley-Pakes and Levinshon-Pertin methodology which as mentioned above have been widely used in empirical studies on production function and productivity. The main finding of the study is that IT investment has a significant positive effect on productivity in Indian manufacturing, which corroborates the findings of similar studies undertaken earlier (Joseph and Abraham 2007; Gangopadhyay, Singh and Singh 2008). This is an important finding since, as Sharma and Singh note, one possible route to achieving higher productivity and faster growth in Indian manufacturing is the use of IT, which will help in boosting efficiency and support other forms of innovation, for example, introduction of new products. The new *National Manufacturing Policy* has set an ambitious goal of raising the share of manufacturing in aggregate GDP to about 25 percent by 2022 from about 16 percent now. The findings of the paper draw attention to the important role that investment in IT capital can play in attaining this goal.

The results of the econometric analysis show that that there are complementarities between skilled labor and IT investment. Thus, the impact of IT investment on output is greater for a firm that has a relatively higher proportion of skilled workers. Also, there is indication from the econometric results that management quality plays a vital role in exploiting the productivity enhancing potential of IT investment. While one may expect regional clustering to increase the impact of IT investment on productivity, the econometric results do not reveal any such impact.

To analyze the factors determining the firms' decision to invest in IT and the level of investment made, appropriate econometric models have been estimated. The results indicate that access to financial capital, electric power from the grid, and skilled workers all matter for the decision to invest in IT capital, but these variables are less important for the level of investment in IT, conditional on it being positive. Yet, the overall conclusion of the study is that financial constraints are the main barrier to investment in IT capital among Indian manufacturing firms.

Attention needs to be drawn to the fact that investment in IT capital stock is not the only way manufacturing firms can make use of and gain from information technology. The study on the effect of IT on productivity in Indian corporate sector firms undertaken by Grace Kite (2012) presents econometric evidence that points to the productivity enhancing effects of IT investment (corroborating the findings of the Sharma–Singh study under discussion) and also reveals that outsourced IT services contribute to productivity. Interestingly, Kite finds that the elasticity of output with respect to outsourced IT is higher than that with respect to in-house IT capital stock. Does this mean that many Indian manufacturing plants are taking advantage of IT without making any substantial in-house investment in IT capital stock? Evidently, a more comprehensive study of the impact of IT on productivity of Indian manufacturing firms needs to consider not only the investments made by firms in IT capital stock but also the use of outsourced IT services. Why some manufacturing firms have opted for in-house IT investment, some others have opted for outsourced IT services, and others are not using IT at all is an important question to investigate.

IT capital stock per plant (hardware plus software) is only a small fraction of the plant and machinery capital stock per plant. In the Western zone of India, for instance, the IT capital stock is about ₹75 thousand (as reported in the paper), whereas the plant and machinery capital stock is about ₹4.4 million. Yet, the elasticity of output with respect to IT capital stock at about 0.2 is not very low in relation to the elasticity of output with respect to plant and machinery capital stock at about 0.4 to 0.6. The implication is that the marginal product of IT capital stock is very high is comparison with the marginal product of plant and machinery capital stock. Probably, the IT capital stock variable is picking up the influence of certain other factors. One possibility, as indicated by the authors of the paper, is that the IT capital stock variable is picking up the effect of management quality. This is the reason why the introduction of plant fixed effects in the model (or estimating the model in first difference) causes the elasticity of output with respect of IT capital stock to come down drastically to about 0.04. But, even with this elasticity, the rate of return to IT investment is high. The fact that the rate of return to IT investment is high in relation to other capital assets implies that a reallocation of investment toward IT capital would increase productivity in manufacturing plants.

One aspect that is not discussed in detail in the paper, but could have been of interest to other researchers using ASI plant level data is the difficulties encountered by the authors in using unit level ASI data for their econometric analysis. The authors mention that they could create a panel dataset of manufacturing plants for the period 2003–04 to 2007–08 covering about 8,000 plants. A slightly larger figure on the number of plants in the panel dataset is reported by Chattopadhyay and others (2012). They have constructed several panel datasets. In the panel constructed for the period 2003–07 to 2007–08, they include about 10,200 plants. This is higher than the number of plants in the panel constructed by Sharma and Singh. But, the difference could be due to (a) difference in coverage and (b) difference in the treatment of joint-return units. While Sharma and Singh confine their analysis to manufacturing, Chattopadhyay and others consider the entire set of ASI industries. Where multiple units have submitted a joint return, this is probably being treated as one firm in the study of Sharma and Singh, but not in the study by Chattopadhyay and others.

Sharma and Singh observe that due to missing observations and zero values, they are compelled to work with a much smaller sample of plants; in their regression analysis, they are able to use data for only about 2,500 plants. This observation gives an impression that there are many missing observations and zero values in unit level ASI data, which is probably incorrect. This aspect should have been discussed in greater detail, and the number of missing observations and zero values for different variables should have been pointed out. To discuss this point further, Table 1 of the paper shows that for the five year period under study, Sharma and Singh could get about 38 thousand observations on the value of plant and machinery, but only about 24 thousand observations on gross value added (GVA). The gap seems to be attributable to the non-operating units. Out of the approximately 24 thousand observations where GVA data are available, IT capital stock is zero in about 10 thousand cases. This seems to be the dominant reasons why the effective sample size falls to about 2500.

Among various two-digit industries, the average IT capital stock is the highest for printing and publishing industry at about ₹20 thousand per factory (Table 3 of the paper). However, gross value added per factory in this industry (five-year average) is found to be negative at about −200 thousand rupees. This is the only industry in which gross value added is negative at the sample mean. For paper and paper products industry, there are about 600 observations on IT capital stock and about 700 observations on employment. By contrast, there are no observations on gross value added. This suggests that all firms of this industry which were included in the panel are non-operating units. These facts and figures signal certain problems being encountered in using the unit level data of ASI for preparing a panel dataset for the purpose of econometric analysis. A more detailed discussion of these problems would have been useful to other researchers.

Shubhashis Gangopadhyay
India Development Foundation

The paper by Singh and Sharma carries forward the analysis done in Gangopadhyay, Singh, and Singh (GSS 2008) and obtains more refined and richer results. This is largely because when the GSS work was done, there was no panel data available while the current paper uses the newly available panel information. The central theme in the current paper is the use and impact of IT in Indian manufacturing and the reasons why they are as they are. The authors use the Indian ASI data for the years 2003–07. This is an important study given that at one end, India has made huge strides in the global IT industry but the penetration of IT in Indian manufacturing has been relatively shallow. And, whatever penetration there is, it is not uniform either across regions or across sectors.

A major positive aspect of this paper is that it analyses plant-level data. IT-led productivity analyses using financial data have two serious differences with plant-level data used in this paper. First, the financial data is at the level of the company and a company's financials are the aggregate of the activities of all its plants and there could be varying levels of IT use in its different plants which the financial data are unable to separate out. Second, the financials of a company's IT expenditure does not distinguish between IT used in the corporate office vis-à-vis that used in the actual production process. This paper has neither of these two problems.

According to my reading, the major findings of the paper are: (*a*) greater IT use leads to greater productivity; (*b*) the use and productivity of IT in Indian manufacturing are dependent on the managerial skills available in a plant; (*c*) financial constraints are better at explaining the lack of IT than other infrastructural constraints; and (*d*) the level of IT use in a plant is dependent on the overall use of IT in the industry.

I have two major comments on the paper. These are more toward the next round of analysis that needs to be undertaken and less in the nature of what the paper's current shortcomings are. First, a more thorough analysis has to be done regarding the policy implications of the findings. For instance, given (*b*) and the fact that the paper uses plant level data, is the managerial issue one of more and better trained MBAs or, the production of more technically skilled managers on the shop floor. Unfortunately, the ASI data cannot make this differentiation but does point to this possibility. This, then, calls for a more focused survey of the skill levels, and skill types, of the managers in the plants that use more IT versus those that do not but are in the same industry and in the same region. In either case, public investment in skill formation becomes important. Related to this is the second point I wish to make. A number of studies point to the fact that different Indian states have different institutional environments within which firms operate and this, rather than managerial capabilities, could be a major factor (e.g., the Besley and Burgess 2004 paper and Bhaumik, Gangopadhyay, and Krishna [2008] in European Journal of Development Research). The authors, themselves, have noted the difference in IT use, both across regions and across industry.

General Discussion

T. N. Srinivasan questioned the use of plant-level data as opposed to data at the level of the corporation as the latter would allow an examination of investment decisions that involving the return to capital, which cannot be observed at the plant level. The authors responded that the purpose of the present paper involved more of a focus on the production process, which required the plant level data. While it would be interesting to combine observations at both the level of the company and the plant, such a data set was not yet available for India. Devesh Kapoor pointed to a data set of the National Manufacturing Competitiveness Council as a potential supplement to the study since it offers more details regarding the purpose and use of new IT capital investments.

Rajnish Mehra pointed to the lack of a measure of intangible capital and worried that might bias the results of the exercise. Ashok Mody thought that any role for IT capital would have to be small because it was not a major input to most manufacturing plants. He would prefer more of a focus on managerial quality as a key determinant of firms' success. However, the authors noted that there were no available measures of the concept, and in the statistical analysis differences in management performance were absorbed by the fixed effects.

Rajendra Pawar noted that there has been a large number of studies looking at the determinants of firms' success or failure and the role of IT in that process. He thought that it was a complicated problem that required substantial disaggregation to get to the decision levels that mattered. However, those studies suggest that the most important factor seemed to be the knowledge and involvement of top management. Second there was a need for a workforce that understood how to use the IT, and the amount of physical IT capital was a distant third.

References

Besley, Timothy and Robin Burgess. 2004. "Can Labor Regulation Hinder Economic Performance? Evidence from India," *The Quarterly Journal of Economics*, 119 (1): 91–134, February.

Bhaumik, S. K., Shubhashis Gangopadhyay, and Shagun Krishnan. 2008. "Policy, Economic Federalism and Product Market Entry: The Indian Experience," *European Journal of Development Research*, 20 (1): 1–30.

Chattopadhyay, Soumendra, G. C. Manna, and Soumya Chakraborty. 2012. "Fluctuations in ASI Data—An Empirical Study from ASI Panel Data," *Journal of Industrial Statistics*, 1 (2): 208–21.

Gangopadhyay, Shubhashis, Manisha G. Singh, and Nirvikar Singh. 2008. *Waiting to Connect: Indian IT Revolution Bypasses the Domestic Industry*. New Delhi: Lexis-Nexis-Butterworth.

Joseph, K. J. and Vinoj Abraham. 2007. Information Technology and Productivity: Evidence from India's Manufacturing Sector, Working Paper 389, Centre for Development Studies, Trivandrum, Kerala, India.